D1286899

The Human Tradition i.. __

CHARLES W. CALHOUN
Series Editor
Department of History, East Carolina University

The nineteenth-century English author Thomas Carlyle once remarked that "the history of the world is but the biography of great men." This approach to the study of the human past had existed for centuries before Carlyle wrote, and it continued to hold sway among many scholars well into the twentieth century. In more recent times, however, historians have recognized and examined the impact of large, seemingly impersonal forces in the evolution of human history—social and economic developments such as industrialization and urbanization as well as political movements such as nationalism, militarism, and socialism. Yet even as modern scholars seek to explain these wider currents, they have come more and more to realize that such phenomena represent the composite result of countless actions and decisions by untold numbers of individual actors. On another occasion, Carlyle said that "history is the essence of innumerable biographies." In this conception of the past, Carlyle came closer to modern notions that see the lives of all kinds of people, high and low, powerful and weak, known and unknown, as part of the mosaic of human history, each contributing in a large or small way to the unfolding of the human tradition.

This latter idea forms the foundation for this series of books on the human tradition in America. Each volume is devoted to a particular period or topic in American history and each consists of minibiographies of persons whose lives shed light on that period or topic. Well-known figures are not altogether absent, but more often the chapters explore a variety of individuals who may be less conspicuous but whose stories, nonetheless, offer us a window on some aspect of the nation's past.

By bringing the study of history down to the level of the individual, these sketches reveal not only the diversity of the American people and the complexity of their interaction but also some of the commonalities of sentiment and experience that Americans have shared in the evolution of their culture. Our hope is that these explorations of the lives of "real people" will give readers a deeper understanding of the human tradition in America.

Volumes in the Human Tradition in America series:

THE HUMAN TRADITION IN
TEXAS

THE HUMAN TRADITION IN
TEXAS

No. 9
Human Tradition in America

Edited by
Ty Cashion
and
Jesús F. de la Teja

A Scholarly Resources Inc. Imprint
Wilmington, Delaware

© 2001 by Scholarly Resources Inc.
All rights reserved
First published 2001
Printed and bound in the United States of America

Scholarly Resources Inc.
104 Greenhill Avenue
Wilmington, DE 19805-1897
www.scholarly.com

Library of Congress Cataloging-in-Publication Data

The human tradition in Texas / edited by Ty Cashion and
  Jesús F. de la Teja.
    p. cm. — (The human tradition in America ; no. 9)
  Includes bibliographical references.
  ISBN 0-8420-2905-2 (alk. paper)—ISBN 0-8420-2906-0 (pbk. :
alk. paper)
    1. Texas—Biography. 2. Texas—History. I. Cashion, Ty, 1956–
II. Teja, Jesús F. de la, 1956–   III. Series.

CT262 .H86 2001
976.4—dc21   00-067033

♾ The paper used in this publication meets the minimum requirements
of the American National Standard for permanence of paper for printed
library materials, Z39.48, 1984.

For our mothers

Joann Marie Kuzell Cashion

and

Julia María Irimia Castellano

About the Editors

TY CASHION is assistant professor of history at Sam Houston State University, where he teaches courses on the American West and Texas. In addition, he is book review editor for the *West Texas Historical Association Yearbook* and a board member of the East Texas Historical Association. He is the author of *A Texas Frontier: The Clear Fork Country and Fort Griffin, 1849–1887* (1996) and *Pigskin Pulpit: A Social History of Texas High-School Football Coaches* (1998). He has also published articles for such journals as the *Southwestern Historical Quarterly* and *Journal of the West*.

JESÚS F. DE LA TEJA is associate professor of history at Southwest Texas State University, where he teaches courses on Texas, Spanish Borderlands, and Colonial Mexican history. In addition he is book review editor of the *Southwestern Historical Quarterly* and managing editor of *Catholic Southwest: A Journal of History and Culture*. He is the author of *San Antonio de Béxar: A Community on New Spain's Northern Frontier* (1995) and editor of *A Revolution Remembered: The Memoirs and Selected Correspondence of Juan N. Seguín* (1991). He has also published numerous book chapters as well as articles in the *Southwestern Historical Quarterly*, *Journal of the Early Republic*, *The Americas*, and *Historia Mexicana*.

Contents

Introduction

Jesús F. de la Teja

With apologies to the Bard, some are born Texan, some achieve "Texan-ness," and others have Texan-ness thrust upon them. With his death at the Alamo, Davy Crockett falls into the latter category, while Sam Houston's embrace of the Lone Star places him in the middle category, and José Antonio Navarro's birth in Spanish-colonial San Antonio drove his devotion to Texas under four governments. While these men gained legendary status during the pivotal independence era, they could not bring modern Texas into being on their own. In countless numbers and countless ways, men and women of all colors, religions, and economic backgrounds not only came to identify with Texas but also helped to forge the very sense of Texan-ness that is unique among the American states.

What is Texan-ness? The women and men whose lives are represented in this volume would have very different answers to that question. At one time, long ago, there was not even a concept of Texas. For countless centuries, people of various culture groups crisscrossed the region, hunted and fished, planted and gathered, were born and died without thinking of themselves as Texans. That long-lost world is only discernable now through the efforts of archaeologists and those who study the very earliest texts of Spanish and French explorers. Alvar Núñez Cabeza de Vaca, who has had Texan-ness thrust upon him, is the earliest window to the world of the area's Indians. He did not visit all the tribes, nor did he remember everything he saw and heard, but he was an astute and sympathetic observer of the human condition. The pre-contact Indians of Texas cannot tell their story, but because of Cabeza de Vaca's writings we have some sense of who they were and how they lived.

The Spanish military and missionary explorers who ventured into central and eastern Texas late in the seventeenth century are responsible for the earliest sense of Texas as a geographic space. After traveling through territory inhabited by people they perceived as nomadic and barbaric, they came across agricultural communities of elegantly dressed and well-ordered Indians. These members of the great Caddo family of tribes, according to the story, represented themselves as friends, "Techas" of the Spaniards. Consequently, the term "Texas" at first applied only to what is now the region east of the Trinity River. In the course of the eighteenth century, the province's complicated name of Reino de los Texas y Nuevas Filipinas gave way to the simpler Texas. Still, for much of the Indian population, Texas remained an alien idea. Only the Spanish residents of the region from the San Antonio River valley settlements of San Antonio and La Bahía (present-day Goliad) to the East Texas forests considered themselves Texans. The Hispanic residents of the El Paso and lower Rio Grande Valley regarded themselves as residents of New Mexico and Nuevo Santander, respectively. Not that a New Mexican could not become a Texan. Witness the case of Francisco Xavier Chaves, whose decades of service to the Spanish Crown and to the Republic of Mexico put him at the center of seminal events in the early history of the region and allowed him to achieve Texan-ness.

The definition broadened as the region came under the sway of a new people—Anglo Americans from the United States. To Robert Hall and the thousands like him who came in the decades before and after his arrival, Texas was whatever Anglo Americans could make of it. They were not only sure that they could tame the "wilderness," but they were also confident in the rightness of the institutions they brought with them: that peculiar brand of American democracy that supported slavery and an almost equally democratic form of Protestantism that was little tolerant of ritual and hierarchy. They also believed that the natural boundary of Texas lay in the bed of the Rio Grande and that neither Mexicans nor Indians could stop their steady westward advance.

The sheer size of Texas meant that it could never be one thing. For the majority of the population, living in the eastern third of the state, life was very much a reflection of the Old South. Louis T. Wigfall represented this way of life to an extreme. Convinced of the uniqueness and justness of the agricultural slavocracy into which he had been born in South Carolina, he brought those attitudes to Texas and found a constituency among similarly thinking Southerners who had made the state their home. But even as Wigfall and the cotton planters and yeoman farmers he represented attempted to mold Texas into a likeness of the Old South, the Mexican border, the Indian frontier, and the German hinterland precluded such a one-dimensional image from becoming re-

ality. And the career of Captain Thomas Williams serves as a good reminder. The son of Unionist parents, he served in the Union's First
Texas Cavalry Volunteers and in the Republican-dominated State Police during reconstruction. His death in a Lampasas gunfight exempli-
fies the reality of Texas's "Wild West" heritage.

Even as Reconstruction came to an end and the Redeemers reas-
serted their view of Texas as the domain of white farmers and stockmen,
the forces of change loosed by the Civil War and its aftermath created
opportunities for freedmen from throughout the former Confederacy.
Although forced to become Texans before the war, African Americans,
like their white neighbors and former masters, chose to become Texans
afterward. Cheap land and tenancy opportunities or the chance to escape the continued bondage of agricultural labor through military service made Texas—both the eastern "Old South" and the "Wild
West"—attractive to former slaves. Despite increasing discrimination
and segregation and the ultimate frustrations of a system designed to dis-
empower them, such African Texans as the mulatto politician John B.
Rayner built their own Texas around churches, schools, colleges, and
businesses.

And there was much Texas yet to be built at the end of the nineteenth century. The last third of the century brought about the taming
of the western frontier, both in human and in physical ways. As the last
of the independent Indian tribes were forced onto reservations in Oklahoma and New Mexico, vast stretches of Panhandle and trans-Pecos
River land opened to the cattle industry and even to agriculture. Technology played a critical role in this dry, seemingly endless expanse. Railroads made the region increasingly accessible, both to the rest of the
state and to the nation. Barbed wire allowed the control of herds of
cattle in a way that would have been impossible earlier, given the expense of fence-building with other materials. Windmills provided the
water necessary to sustain livestock, crops, and communities. The story
of William Henry Bush makes it clear that in considerable measure the
creation of West Texas was as much the product of entrepreneurship as
it was the hard physical labor of the stockmen and farmers who popu-
late Hollywood's Westerns.

Despite the advances, Texas remained a hard country. As the twentieth century began, it was still an overwhelmingly rural place and the
majority of its population poor, undereducated, and isolated. The life
of Hester Calvert is representative not only of many white women but
black and brown ones as well. While cotton made a few people rich and

powerful, tenancy and sharecropping virtually enslaved countless others. Although we tend to associate the worst aspects of agricultural exploitation with minorities, and rightfully so, many whites were trapped in similar circumstances. Calvert was not among the many thousands of Mexican and Tejano laborers—men, women, and children—whose lives revolved around what came to be called the "Big Swing," the steady northward movement of the harvest from the Rio Grande Valley to the Panhandle created by the state's immense size and consequent shifts in the growing season. She was, however, subject to the periodic upheavals and reversals of fortune brought on by the vagaries of the international cotton economy and the weather. Only in her twilight years did she come to know a new and different Texas—one of paved streets, electricity, and running water, a Texas that finally had joined the twentieth century.

Bringing Texas into the twentieth century and expanding its definition beyond cotton and cattle was a long process of negotiation between competing interests. Against the economic might of transcontinental railroads, exploitive corporations, and the national political parties—all of which seemed unresponsive to the needs of the little man—Texas farmers organized. In the Grange and the Farmers' Alliance they planted the seeds of Populism. Even as the Democratic Party in the state moved to co-opt this revolt from below against the status quo, Texas's small middle class came to see the need for reform. By the first decades of the new century, with the development of the oil industry, the consequent growth in industrialization, and the increasing size and importance of cities, the times were ripe for Progressives to shoulder the mantle of reform from the Populists. The career of Governor Thomas Mitchell Campbell illustrates the challenges to modernization faced by Texas as it incorporated itself fully into the life of the nation.

The new age offered new frontiers that Texans embraced with relish. The internal combustion engine, in part the offspring of the seas of oil flowing beneath the state's pastures and cotton fields, brought forth motorized transportation, the advantages of which were immediately grasped by widely scattered Texans. A pioneer spirit, a willingness to undertake technological innovation, and entrepreneurship had marked the people who called themselves Texans in the nineteenth century and, although reoriented, had remained strong characteristics of theirs in the twentieth. It is not surprising that Texas and Texans took leadership roles in the oil, aviation, and entertainment industries. These endeavors required considerable risk-taking combined with favorable natural conditions. Take the case of Ormer Locklear, for example. From motor-cycles to airplanes was not as big a jump as one might think. Neither, for that matter, was the jump from barnstorming to Hollywood stunt flying; both involved considerable daredevil and exhibitionist tendencies. Or, how about Bob Wills? His success rested as much on grasping the possibilities of radio as it did on bringing seemingly dissimilar forms of music into harmony.

There were still many Texans, however, who could not have heard Wills's Texas Playboys on their own radios. The giant leaps in urban and industrial development that the state experienced through the beginning of World War II had left them behind. In fact, to the majority of the population, these people were not "true" Texans at all. In the burgeoning barrios and "colored" wards of Houston, Dallas, El Paso, San Antonio, and in the fields of South Texas, many of the people who helped build the modern state lived in squalor and isolation. Jim Crow laws meant poor and limited educational, health, and employment opportunities for blacks, and these conditions extended to Mexican Texans throughout much of the state. On the one hand, Emma Tenayuca's experimentation with socialism and communism in her struggle for the rights of Tejano laborers in San Antonio cannot surprise us. On the other hand, Carter Wesley's career reminds us that even under the harsh racist conditions of early twentieth-century Texas, talented people of color could rise to financial success and social and political prominence. As in any community, small or large, majority or minority, leadership is a risky business that produces both controversy and devotion.

African and Mexican Texans, of course, were not the only ones who were underrepresented, underserved, and limited in their opportunities and rights. Women, despite the state's commitment to the concept of community property that came from Spanish and Mexican law, were nevertheless considered legal wards of their husbands. Ma Ferguson's election as governor in 1924, only four years after Texas women gained the right to vote, was an anomaly, as she was merely a stand-in for her husband. Entrenched attitudes toward the mental, emotional, and physical capacities of women, despite their critical role in the World War II industrial boom, continued to restrict their participation in public life and limited their economic opportunities. Just as the 1990 election of Ann Richards as governor and Kay Bailey Hutchison's senatorial career marked the full arrival of Texas women as leaders, the story of Hermine Tobolowsky is a sobering reminder of the limits to full Texanhood that persisted until late in the twentieth century.

The expanding inclusiveness of Texas society, so evident in the increasing diversity of its political players, is nowhere more complete than on the athletic field. At every level, in every part of the state, sports is the great equalizer. Physical talent and determination have provided many a small-town athlete with an opportunity for a college education and a shot at big-city fame and fortune. For much of the twentieth century, throughout Texas's myriad rural communities, local high-school squads gave people a sense of unity and occasions for socializing. And no sport did this better than football. In fact, football for a time seemed so central to the Texas identity that even at the high-school level, coaches felt the kind of pressure to win that we associate with professional or major university football. The career of Gary Gaines, with its ups and downs, serves as a fitting conclusion to this volume, for it serves to highlight the competitiveness and resilience of Texans. High-school football in the state may not be what it was in 1960, but neither is Texas as a whole. Most Texans, I believe, would argue that that is as it should be.

The various stories told in this volume, most of which deal with the lives and careers of everyday people, are part of a rich historical tradition. Until recently, however, it was a tradition very much bound by myth and legend and focused on the nineteenth century, according to Walter Buenger and Robert Calvert in their introduction to *Texas through Time: Evolving Interpretations* (1991). The stories of planters and yeomen, cattle barons and cowboys, Rangers and Mexican bandits, frontiersmen and Indians, are the stuff of the Texas identity and mystique. Library shelves are full of the published reminiscences, biographies, reports, and correspondence of these Anglo Texans, and historians did their part to reinforce this vision by focusing on these stories in their writings. The reader interested in a comprehensive discussion of how Texas history has been written to 1990 should consult *Texas through Time*, which contains essays by the leading practitioners of the historian's craft in most fields of study.

Since the publication of *Texas through Time*, a significant number of works in almost all branches of Texas history has appeared to challenge prevalent views or expand our understanding of the state's past. The *Southwestern Historical Quarterly* and several other regional and topical specialized journals publish a broad range of articles and should be consulted by anyone with a serious interest in Texas history. A number of academic and commercial presses combine to offer hundreds of Texas history titles every year, both reprints of classic (and not so classic) texts and new scholarly and popular studies. Here, there is only enough room to point out some of these recent works that augment the Suggested Readings at the end of each chapter.

The world of Cabeza de Vaca, the other Spanish *conquistadores*, and the Indian peoples whom they encountered are the subjects of study by historians, archeologists, and anthropologists. A massive three-volume biography by Rolena Adorno and Patrick Charles Pautz, *Alvar Núñez Cabeza de Vaca: His Account, His Life, and the Expedition of Pánfilo de Narváez* (1999), is only the latest work on the first European to cross Texas. The most recent research on the Coronado expedition can be explored in *The Coronado Expedition to Tierra Nueva: The 1540–1542 Route across the Southwest*, edited by Richard Flint and Shirley Cushing Flint (1997). Coming from the opposite direction into Texas, the De Soto expedition has also received considerable scholarly attention in the last decade, and many of those findings have been summarized in *The De Soto Chronicles: The Expedition of Hernando De Soto to North America in 1539–1543*, edited by Lawrence A. Clayton, Vernon James Knight Jr., and Edward C. Moore (1993). Studies of pre-contact and proto-contact Indians, while often controversial and not always histori-cal (strictly speaking), are important for understanding why the *con-quistadores* behaved as they did. The East Texas agriculturalists encountered by the survivors of the De Soto expedition are investigated by F. Todd Smith in *The Caddo Indians: Tribes at the Convergence of Empires* (1995). Bringing together what little is known and speculating on what is not, Nancy Parrott Hickerson in *The Jumanos: Hunters and Traders of the South Plains* (1994) sheds light on these mysterious people. By relying on considerable archaeological and environmental evidence, Robert A. Ricklis manages to humanize an Indian group with one of the worst reputations in *The Karankawa Indians of Texas: An Ecological Study of Cultural Tradition and Change* (1996).

The Spanish colonial society and early Mexican national period of Francisco Xavier Chaves continues to receive attention from a small but productive group of scholars. Interests range from the more traditional areas of exploration and mission history to newer lines of inquiry in social and ethnic studies. In the former field, a trio of avocational histo-rians leads the pack: Robert Weddle, Jack Jackson, and William Foster. The latter's *Spanish Expeditions into Texas, 1689–1768* (1995) has proven controversial in its challenge of the work of earlier historians and archae-ologists. In 1992, Donald E. Chipman published the first comprehen-sive synthesis of Spanish Texas ever attempted: *Spanish Texas, 1519–1821*. Operating from the perspective of Mexican colonial history, Jesús de la

Teja's community study, *San Antonio de Béxar: A Community on New Spain's Northern Frontier* (1995), reconstructs the first century of Texas's oldest city. The short but critical Mexican national period has also received attention recently. Andrés Tijerina's *Tejanos and Texas under the Mexican Flag, 1821–1836* (1994) highlights how Spanish and Mexican institutions influenced the development of what increasingly became an Anglo-American-dominated Texas. Certainly, Gregg Cantrell's *Stephen F. Austin: Empresario of Texas* (Yale, 1999), with its considerable focus on Austin as businessman, does much to humanize a figure who had been made larger than life by his previous biographer, Eugene C. Barker, in 1926.

Even the core period for the Texas myth—the revolution and Republic eras of which Robert Hall was a part—has come under critical scrutiny. Reacting to the one-sided and often hagiographic histories of the Alamo and San Jacinto commonly available, Stephen L. Hardin produced *Texian Iliad: A Military History of the Texas Revolution* (1994). Balanced in its coverage of both sides of the conflict, it is often as sharply critical of the Anglo Americans as it is of the Mexican side. Hardin's work is complemented by Paul Lack's rigorously analytical *The Texas Revolutionary Experience* (1992), which focuses on the composition and disposition of the men who brought about independence, including the long-neglected but active Tejano population. Even one of the most colorful episodes, and one which has been central to the Texas Republic myth, the Mier expedition, comes under revisionist attention from Sam W. Haynes in *Soldiers of Misfortune: The Somervell and Mier Expeditions* (1990).

Numerous recent works have challenged the perception of Texas as simply part of the Old South that Louis Wigfall espoused and have taken a more critical view of its role in the coming and aftermath of the Civil War. James Marten, in *Texas Divided: Loyalty and Dissent in the Lone Star State, 1856–1874* (1990), discusses the extent and depth of Unionism in Texas. Richard B. McCaslin chronicles one of the darker chapters of the Civil War era in *Tainted Breeze: The Great Hanging at Gainesville, Texas, 1862* (1994). And Thomas T. Smith's *The U.S. Army and the Texas Frontier Economy, 1845–1900* (1999) makes it clear that the federal government, through the aegis of the military, was instrumental in the state's development. Still other works, such as Donald Frazier's *Blood and Treasure: Confederate Empire in the Southwest* (1995) and Ralph Wooster's *Texas and Texans in the Civil War* (1995), reassert the importance of the role that Texas played in the South's war effort.

Reconstruction, a particularly violent period, as witnessed by the career and death of Thomas Williams, has been one of the most controversial topics in Texas history. New studies focusing on the plentiful sources of the Freedmen's Bureau and other federal and state records, such as Barry A. Crouch's *The Freedmen's Bureau and Black Texans* (1992) and William L. Ricther's *Overreached on All Sides: The Freedmen's Bureau Administrators in Texas, 1865–1868* (1991), continue to offer fresh insight. Taking a look at the equally considerable local record, Randolph B. Campbell relies on county courthouse archives to determine how Reconstruction affected everyday Texans in *Grass-Roots Reconstruction in Texas, 1865–1880* (1997). At the personal level, Barry A. Crouch and Donaly Brice view the career of one of the era's unreconstructed villains in *Cullen Montgomery Baker, Reconstruction Desperado* (1997).

When John B. Rayner set foot in Texas shortly after the end of Reconstruction, he was entering a society in the process of rearranging its race relations. The ethnic dimension of this late-nineteenth-century transformation has not been neglected in the historical literature. Patricia Smith Prather and Jane Clements Monday's *From Slave to Statesman: The Legacy of Joshua Houston, Servant to Sam Houston* (1993) serves as a reminder that bondsmen were not only willing but also capable of making a contribution to the state following Emancipation. In *Tejano Legacy: Rancheros and Settlers in South Texas, 1734–1900* (1998), Armando Alonzo takes a revisionist view of land loss and ethnic continuity in a much-neglected part of the state. And the complexities of ethnicity in the region are clearly evident in *Freedom on the Border: The Seminole Maroons in Florida, the Indian Territory, Coahuila and Texas* by Kevin Mulroy (1993).

Flat, seemingly endless, and all but devoid of both Indian inhabitants and buffalo by 1880, the western plains of Texas were ripe for development by men such as William Henry Bush. They needed the labor of tough and self-sacrificing people to carry out the taming of this last part of the Texas frontier. Fortunately for them, these qualities were plentiful in a population already accustomed to forcing a harsh environment to yield its bounty. Ty Cashion, in *A Texas Frontier* (1996), surveys the social and economic movements at the edge of the Great Plains, where the westering experience turned southerners and other immigrant groups into westerners. In the numerous essays of *Black Cowboys of Texas*, edited by Sara R. Massey (2000), and in Andrés Tijerina's *Tejano Empire: Life on the South Texas Ranchos* (1998), we are reminded that the state's livestock industry was much more diverse than is often depicted in the popular media. Other stories—for instance, *Plains Farmer: The Diary of William G. DeLoach, 1914–1964*, edited by Janet M. Neuge-bauer (1991)—show us that cowboys were not the only ones with tales to share about life on the Texas Plains.

The harsh life of the farm that Hester Calvert experienced was much the same throughout Texas and for people of all ethnic backgrounds. Neil Foley describes the negative impact on whites as well as on African and Mexican Texans of an exploitative agricultural system in *The White Scourge: Mexicans, Blacks, and Poor Whites in Texas Cotton Culture* (1997). A recent oral history anthology, *From Can See to Can't: Texas Cotton Farmers on the Southern Prairies*, edited by Thad Sitton and Dan K. Utley (1997), adds a personal touch to the subject, as does Eddie Stimpson Jr.'s *My Remembers: A Black Sharecropper's Recollections of the Depression* (1996), a rare document from a man at the very bottom of the social order.

It was a social order in need of reform, as many educated and pros-perous Texans knew. Thomas Mitchell Campbell certainly represented the kind of progressive thinking that intended to bring Texas into the twentieth century, if mostly for the benefit of Anglos. In many areas of social improvement, as the literature makes it clear, women exercised impressive leadership. Three works—*Creating the New Woman: The Rise of Southern Women's Progressive Culture in Texas, 1893–1918* by Judith N. McArthur (1998), *Women, Culture, and Community: Religion and Reform in Galveston, 1880–1920* by Elizabeth Hayes Turner (1997), and *Women and the Creation of Urban Life: Dallas, Texas, 1843–1920* by Elizabeth York Enstam (1998)—emphasize how women brought about change despite their lack of sanctioned lines of authority.

For Texas's ethnic groups, the Progressive agenda was of little help in ameliorating trying conditions, although the success of men such as Carter Wesley demonstrates the capacity of the individual to rise above the plight of exploited minorities. Not that Mexican Americans and blacks could not construct the necessary social frameworks in which to maintain their individual dignity and strong community bonds. In *Black Unionism in the Industrial South* (2000), Ernest Obadele-Starks explores the black working-class experience in the upper Texas Gulf Coast re-gion at the time when Wesley was an influential leader. Emilio Zamora's *The World of the Mexican Worker in Texas* (1993) stresses the importance of grassroots, self-help organizing among the state's fastest growing mi-nority group during the same era.

The careers of Ormer Locklear and Bob Wills tell us that as the state moved into the twentieth century, it made new contributions to the life of the nation besides putting steak on its tables. As Joseph A. Pratt and Christopher J. Castañeda demonstrate in *Builders: Herman and George R. Brown* (1999), the modernization of Texas could not have taken place without the massive public works projects that built such marvels as dams and the infrastructure of the defense industry. On a more intimate level, musical contributions extended beyond swing to jazz in general, as Dave Oliphant documents in *Texan Jazz* (1996), and to Mexican-American music, as Manuel H. Peña makes evident in *Musica Tejana: The Cultural Economy of Artistic Transformation* (1999). In the world of letters, Texan voices found national and international stages—especially Katherine Anne Porter, who continues to be the subject of considerable attention. A recent study is *Katherine Anne Porter: A Sense of the Times* by Janis P. Stout (1995). No one has written more on how Texas has been portrayed at the movies than Don Graham, whose efforts include a biography on a real-life Texas war hero who went on to fame in Hollywood: *No Name on the Bullet: A Biography of Audie Murphy* (1989). Much remains to be done, however, to tell the story of Texas's contributions to and participation in the American arts scene of the early twentieth century.

Another area of American culture where Texans have also been contributors, for better and worse, is sports. At the college level, a critical eye has been turned on a number of schools, most prominently Southern Methodist University in *A Payroll to Meet: A Story of Greed, Corruption, and Football at SMU* by David Whitford (1989). In *The Junction Boys* (1999) by Jim Dent, the legendary Paul "Bear" Bryant's Texas A&M tenure comes under scrutiny. Neither has "America's team" been spared critical analysis, as the title to Skip Bayless's *God's Coach: The Hymns, Hype, and Hypocrisy of Tom Landry's Cowboys* (1990) makes obvious. Writers have been kinder to the national pastime. In *Baseball on the Border: A Tale of Two Laredos* (1997), Alan M. Klein explores the social significance of the sport on the Texas-Mexico border. But the area of sports history remains largely unexplored. One exception has been the state's outstanding female athlete, Babe Didrickson, who has received considerable biographical attention, including the recent *Babe: The Life and Legend of Babe Didrikson Zaharias* by Susan E. Cayleff (1995).

Neglected until recently, the contributions of Hispanics such as Emma Tenayuca to the social and economic life of Texas are beginning to draw the attention of scholars. Much of the recent work has had a biographical tone. In *LBJ and Mexican Americans: The Paradox of Power* (1997), Julie Leininger Pycior examines an often-neglected aspect of our thirty-sixth president's complex and often contradictory relationship with his home state—Lyndon Johnson's relations with the growing Tejano population. On the other hand, a recent biography of one of the state's most prominent Mexican-American political leaders during the first half of the twentieth century, *Border Boss: Manuel B. Bravo and Zapata County* by J. Gilberto Quezada (1999), demonstrates that not all Tejanos were faceless laborers. In fact, another biography of a well-known Mexican Texan, *Knight without Armor: Carlos Eduardo Castañeda, 1896–1958* by Félix D. Almaráz Jr. (1999), shows that even under the discriminatory and segregationist conditions of the times some Tejanos could rise to prominence and make significant contributions to the state's culture.

African Americans struggled against the same system but under even harsher circumstances, because Mexican Americans at least benefited from being technically considered "white" and being the majority population in a significant portion of South Texas. It was in that part of the state, in fact, where black soldiers rioted in protest of their treatment by both Anglos and Hispanics. The incident is portrayed in *Black Soldiers in Jim Crow Texas, 1899–1917*, by Garna L. Christian (1995.) Even as they faced almost insurmountable obstacles to equal participation in Texas society, the state's black communities could strive for respectability and prosperity, as William H. Wilson explains in *Hamilton Park: A Planned Black Community in Dallas* (1998). In the long run, however, equal access to the benefits of government and public education required a commitment to the civil rights movement and its various causes. Robyn Duff Ladino, in *Desegregating Texas Schools: Eisenhower, Shivers, and the Crisis at Mansfield* (1996), writes about the failed effort in that community that preceded the more famous incident at Little Rock, Arkansas. In *Make Haste Slowly: Moderates, Conservatives, and School Desegregation in Houston* (1999), William Henry Kellar analyzes how Houstonians desegregated the city's school system without the violent confrontations experienced elsewhere. And in Merline Pitre's *In Struggle Against Jim Crow: Lulu B. White and the NAACP, 1900–1957* (1999), the story of desegregation is further complicated by the fact that White faced the additional challenge of being a woman in a man's world.

Writings on women's history in Texas continue to flourish and to redress past neglect, a situation that surely pleased Hermine Tobolowsky.

Biographies now address the careers of women whose endeavors in the past would have been thought of secondary importance. Debbie Mauldin Cottrell traces the life of the state's first female statewide officeholder in *Pioneer Woman Educator: The Progressive Spirit of Annie Webb Blanton* (1993). In *Texas, Her Texas: The Life and Times of Frances Goff* (1997), authors Nancy Beck Young and Lewis L. Gould reveal the life of a devoted public servant who rose to the post of state budget director. Service in state government is the topic of Nancy Baker Jones and Ruthe Winegarten's prosopographical study, *Capitol Women: Texas Female Legislators, 1923–1999* (2000).

This brief survey of Texas's historical landscape over the last decade or so offers the reader an opportunity to pursue additional study in this field. Such writings can be taken as a model for behavior, as inspiration for further struggle or exploration, or simply for personal enjoyment. They might even help fashion your own definition of Texan-ness and assist you in better understanding the Lone Star State.

1

Alvar Núñez Cabeza de Vaca
An Epic Encounter

John Miller Morris

For all the human diversity in which Texans take pride today, the variety of cultures and languages may never again approach the complexity that Alvar Núñez Cabeza de Vaca noted in his sojourn through Texas almost five centuries ago. He and his small party, survivors of an expedition of would-be *conquistadores*, washed ashore on the Texas coast, horseless, hungry, and in tatters. They spent the next several years among various Indian peoples as they tried to make their way back to familiar ground. In the process, Cabeza de Vaca and his companions negotiated with the Indians on their own terms and gained a respect for the native cultures.

Eventually, he and his companions repatriated themselves, and in the process they infected their fellow Spaniards with tales of the mysteries that lay far beyond the northern horizon. Cabeza de Vaca traversed Texas at a time when the Aztecan and Incan conquests were still recent events. The experiences that he related quickened the Spanish pulse and engendered dreams of other wealthy Indian empires.

John Miller Morris teaches cultural geography at the University of Texas at San Antonio and is the author of *El Llano Estacado: Exploration and Imagination on the High Plains of Texas and New Mexico, 1536–1860* (1997).

At the beginning of a new millennium, Texans fund interplanetary exploration, implement new information revolutions, and even contemplate contact with alien civilizations. It is a measure of our curiosity and craving for diversity that we seek to embrace new civilizations beyond ourselves, indeed, beyond our planet. The space-age technologies found at Mission Control in Houston would seem to point only to the future, but, in fact, they are very useful in exploring the past. Ground-sensing radar, global positioning systems, database computers, and related space-age technologies are widely used today by archaeologists, anthropologists, and geographers to explore the Amerindian past, our hidden heritage.

Of particular interest in this process is information on one of the greatest epic contacts in history—the European discovery of Texas. Some

1

of the remains of the first era of Spanish-Amerindian contact are still with us as rare documents, coins, or artifacts in museums. Other evidence of the native Texans at first contact emerges only from generalized and patient study of their remains—middens, dart points, pottery, burial sites, campfires, shelters, and petroglyphs.

At the dawn of the sixteenth century the Southwestern peoples within the borders of modern Texas were a large archipelago-like group of bands and tribes, some related by ties of language and clan, others so unrelated as to resort to sign language. Hundreds of distinctive peoples followed traditional pursuits of game- and plant-gathering cycles among the diverse bioregions of the state. In the arid southern plains and coasts the Coahuilteco tribes roamed. Along the middle Gulf Coast various Karankawa bands ruled. In wet eastern forests the Caddos lived settled lives around complex villages and gardens. In the far west and northwest the mysterious Teyas (later called Jumanos) dominated the plains, mesas, canyons, and springs of the largest rivers. In the far north, on the wide-open High Plains, a new roving people called Querechos—ancestral Apaches—followed wandering bison herds. Texas was a land of great, even dazzling human diversity.

Many scientists contend that this diversity arose from a few distant Siberian progenitors crossing from Eurasia into North America and peopling two continents over some eighty generations. The Indians of Texas, geneticists now believe, were descendants of a rather small group of original paleo-hunters, the American Adam, as it were. Texas has significant Clovis and Folsom sites, suggesting that aboriginal genes and lifeways were remarkably successful as North America thawed from the Ice Age. Over millennia, geographical isolation and unknown migrations produced a complex mosaic of many peoples. All were secretly united by fundamental genetic similarities but distinguished by emergent spatial differences in language, behavior, culture, and adaptation keyed to environmental niches. It was the reverse of the modern E Pluribus Unum—"from many, one." Prehistoric Texas was E Unus Plures—"from one, many." There were hundreds of such tribal groupings in Texas alone.

"Texas" did not exist in the 1520s, of course, but there was the New World. For the Europeans the Orbis Novum was a fabulous realm across the Atlantic Ocean. The rich and exotic variety of life at the mouth of the Orinoco River led Christopher Columbus to believe that he had discovered the Garden of Eden. Accompanying this diversity of animals, birds, and plants, it seemed, were many equally exotic new peoples.

By the 1530s the vast realm of uncharted coastlines, strange continental interiors, and bizarre peoples was subject to imperial conquest and exploitation as well as discovery. After first settling and exploiting the Antilles islands, Spanish conquistadores began to penetrate the continent of North America. At first they came, like Hernán Cortés, to the middle of the New World, establishing the realm of New Spain with its capital at Mexico City. But within a decade ambitious Spaniards and native allies, with their horses and microbes, began to probe farther into "the northern mysteries"—the vast, unknown, but definitely populated continental interior to their north.

These contacts and penetrations were best accomplished by well-organized maritime flotillas and *entradas*, the latter an authorized incursion into a new land. Many were formidable expeditions, typically with a full complement of soldiery, officials, missionaries, horses, supplies, plans, and dreams of wealth. The *entrada* of Pánfilo de Narváez, for example, sailed from Cuba in 1528 with hundreds of competent expeditioners, including many veterans of the conquest of Mexico. Their official destination was Florida, but their unofficial destiny—at least for the only four men who survived—was Texas. The failure of the Narváez *entrada* in Florida was really the beginning of the discovery of Texas and its peoples.

The expedition of Narváez landed in Florida at the "Bay of the Cross" in April 1528. The men plunged into the landscape, but months of marching, turmoil, difficult terrain, increasingly hostile tribes, and a missed rendezvous with supply ships brought the expedition rather quickly to grief. After wandering and fighting for no appreciable gain, by late summer the force was without adequate strength, provisions, and knowledge to realize their goals. Although they were free to march hither and yon, they could not; they were under a siege of hunger. For all their military prowess, advanced technology, and Renaissance sophistication, they did not know how to live as a hunting and gathering society in a new world. Their ignorance would kill all but three Spaniards and *el negro*, a Spanish-speaking black servant originally from Africa.

Living off the land was something entirely obvious to the natives, even if laborious, trying, and incessant. These tribes labored directly and intimately for their food. It was of such importance that it was worth dying for—in war, hunt, battle, or famine. Perhaps the land shaped them and conditioned their culture in the process. By August 1528, however, the entire Narváez *entrada* was collapsing from malnutrition.

The situation required a bold plan. The Spanish killed and ate their horses while building five ingenious large rafts or barges. They set out in September 1528, hoping to float and oar westward from their Florida "Bay of Horses" along the coastlands of the northwest Gulf of Mexico. This course would turn naturally southward to follow the continental land mass, slowly bringing these lost Christians back to the known coastal settlement of San Esteban del Puerto on the Pánuco River. Instead of safety in a Christian outpost, however, the currents and November storms of the Gulf of Mexico delivered the starving men—or those who survived beaching—to a new life among the fantastic indigenous peoples of the Texas Gulf Coast.

The first intimate, recorded, and extended Spanish-Amerindian contact for Texas began on a bitter day in November 1528. Two barges of shivering, despairing, enfeebled, and famished conquistadores, floating westward from Florida, were caught in a squall. Great waves washed them and their debris ashore on a small barrier island, La Isla Malhado —"The Isle of Misfortune"—just south of modern Galveston Island. Two other barges with expedition members suffered similar fates elsewhere; Pánfilo de Narváez's raft was blown out to sea at night and he disappeared.

Cast up on the low coastal dunes of Malhado were some eighty stunned and dazed survivors. They found themselves at the feet of a fierce, strong, handsome, and decidedly different people—the Capoques, a Karankawa branch of the Texas Gulf Coast. The natives of Malhado were impressive physical specimens. Two dialect groups occupied the island—the Capoques and the Han. By gestures and cries the Spaniards conveyed their wants. As was their custom during emotional moments, the gathered Capoques wept openly, loudly, and ritually at the piteous sight of the famished Europeans. They brought edible aquatic tubers and fish to the separate ragged castaways, crying in unison from time to time to show their concern. Ultimately, as winter closed upon the Texas Gulf Coast, the castaways would have to feed themselves or else brave the risks of human sacrifice and the tribulations of assimilation with the Karankawa.

The native women wore skirts of Spanish moss and worked incessantly. Capoque warriors were tall and muscular, usually going naked. They painted themselves with ochre and sported symbolic tattoos. One of the European survivors was the official expedition treasurer, Alvar Núñez Cabeza de Vaca. He described the natives as having "one pierced nipple and some have both pierced. And through the hole they make they wear a reed [cane] up to two and a half spans long [about two feet] and as thick as two fingers. They also have their lower lip pierced and a piece of reed as thin as half a finger placed in it."*

Karankawa warriors were excellent hunters. Carrying large bows fashioned from cedar and strung taut with deer nerves, they roamed the middle Texas coastlands with packs of dogs (some say the word Karankawa means "dog-raisers" or "dog-eaters"). They fished and seined, harvested oysters, plied burnt-log canoes in shallow coastal waters, and moved their family camps frequently. Karankawa bands inhabited and dominated the barrier islands and nearby coastal prairies in a zone stretching from Galveston Bay down to Corpus Christi Bay. Extinct as a people by the mid-nineteenth century, much of our knowledge of them at the juncture of prehistory and history derives from the published narrative of Cabeza de Vaca.

As a basic reflex toward these useless, hungry mouths, the Capoques and Han tolerated, neglected, or impressed most of the Narváez expedition survivors. By the spring of 1529 only some fifteen men were left of the eighty marooned on Malhado the previous fall. Debilitating hunger and winter exposure had killed the majority. Indeed, most of the Spaniards had arrived in Texas too weak to make a sudden transition to hunting and gathering, especially during the winter season when even native survival skills were challenged. Nor did they have large groups of knowledgeable women working tirelessly on their behalf. Elsewhere on the Texas coast one larger band of European survivors sought an overland route southward, but the watery obstacles—large bays, big rivers, and barrier islands that ended with sea vistas—thwarted their best efforts. They perished from exertion, malnutrition, and tribal hostility.

Relations between the Karankawa and the Spaniards actually had worsened over the cold winter of 1528–29. It is possible that a deadly microbe passed from the Spaniards to the Karankawa, because many natives died during an epidemic illness. The departure of an old person caused less distress for them, Cabeza de Vaca noted, but the death of a younger and loved one involved a Karankawa family in many months of mourning. During this time they obtained little or no food for themselves and depended on handouts from relatives. Now, reduced in numbers and preoccupied with sudden deaths, the Karankawa aban-

---

*This and subsequent quotations are from Rolena Adorno and Patrick Charles Pautz, *Alvar Núñez Cabeza de Vaca: His Account, His Life, and the Expedition of Pánfilo de Narváez*, 3 vols. (Lincoln: University of Nebraska Press, 1999).

doned, ignored, abused, or enslaved the pitiful remnants of the Narváez expedition.

Cannibalism

Worse, in some castaway camps that winter, starving expeditioners had cut up the corpses of their companions, jerking the flesh that they then consumed. When the survivors died, as most of them did, they were consumed in turn. The Han and Capoques were horrified and disgusted at this display of cannibalism by these ugly men. Ironically, later European reports on the Karankawa labeled them as cannibals, perhaps in reference to a practice among some Texas tribes of consuming a very small piece of a slain enemy for ritual purposes. In any case, a general misunderstanding arose that made European mariners dread the so-called Cannibal Coast of the Karankawa country. As late as the 1830s, Karankawa families were hunted down and killed on the basis of unfair but lasting reputations as insatiable cannibals.

Those castaways who survived a year of hunger and exposure were few in number. Since survival lay in assimilation to the coastal tribes, they began to live and work under the whims and blows of their hosts. Like their hosts they often went for days at a time without food. In response to these periodic famines, Cabeza de Vaca wrote, Capoque women suckled their children until they were ten or twelve years old. A developing child thus received some nourishment, even when everyone older had eaten nothing for days. A small number of the hardy and most adaptable expeditioners did survive, spared for the moment and made handy to some native camps as designated labor. These few men began a mental and physical journey that took them into the very fabric of the New World.

The expedition's treasurer, Cabeza de Vaca, was among the few. His epic tale is arguably one of the greatest adventures, even for an age renowned for its exploits and glory. His observations on the Indians of Texas, preserved in his detailed *relación* or written account, were first published in 1542 and have remained in print. Cabeza de Vaca's chapters on his sojourn in Texas also provide the most direct evidence to date of the state's human diversity at the time of first contact.

Cabeza de Vaca barely survived his first year of casual mistreatment, ceaseless hunger, and native superstitions about outsiders. But he proved to be malleable, courageous, and intrepid. With no salvation in sight, and under the blows and passing kindnesses of his captors, he entered increasingly into Karankawa mores and lifeways. Most of 1529–30 was spent learning and pleasing his host-captors. He waded naked into cold coastal waters to gather tubers, shredding his hands until they bled. He carried loads of firewood and precious freshwater to campsites that moved every few days. Most of all, he applied himself to living life one day at a time.

Texas was terribly different from Spain in foodstuffs, animals, and plants. Many were strange and marvelous, but there were also the deadly vipers. Torments were ubiquitous—long periods of hunger, sudden cold fronts, sweltering humidity, ceaseless labor, and heavy loads to carry. Mosquitoes could bite a man, Cabeza de Vaca thought, until he looked as though he had leprosy. The mosquitoes were so bad that great quantities of rotting wood were burnt in rings around the camps. The smoldering wet wood generated clouds of smoke that discouraged insects but also stung the eyes and choked the lungs. Clearly, this land was not the Garden of Eden. But the Karankawa endured it. In fact, they wove around it a human tapestry of dance, ceremony, and celebrations punctuated with bouts of loud song and chanting called *areitos*. Cabeza de Vaca was impressed with Capoque parenting skills. "These people love their children more," he noted, "and treat them better than any other people in the world."

There were only a few bright spots for the Narváez treasurer. First, he was not alone. A few more castaways—Andrés Dorantes, his black servant Estevanico (*el negro*), and Alonso del Castillo—were surviving with different bands of natives. As the seasons went by, it was sometimes possible for the Spanish-speaking survivors to pass along hopes or manage a brief encounter. A second bright spot was that with each season after 1530, Cabeza de Vaca earned a greater margin of respect from his adopted hosts and captors. Indeed, his standing among the restless Karankawa increased until he found both a small calling and a large opportunity: he emerged as a tolerated native trader.

To the north and east of the Capoques lay extensive pine woodlands, thick vegetation, large sluggish rivers, and other tribes. In his travels as a trader, Cabeza de Vaca fathomed the Karankawa and Coahuiltecan cultures, but he apparently made few contacts with the different riverine tribes of East Texas. This missing link is a pity, because the dozen or so tribes of deep East Texas, organized into larger confederacies, were sophisticated in cultural ways much more suitable for European appreciation and survival. They were also avid traders; it is likely that Cabeza de Vaca saw and handled some of their creations and barter items.

The Caddos were talented agriculturalists, inheritors of the ancient mound-building Mississippi culture that had once dominated the fertile drainages of the largest river in North America. Caddo gardens produced enough maize, beans, squash, sunflowers, tobacco, and related food surpluses to support a sedentary lifestyle. Their social and cultural development was consequently elaborate, with leaders called *caddi*, temples and houses, and beautiful pottery, baskets, and trade goods. Caddos were distinctive in appearance, covering their faces and bodies with tattooing and then further levels of paint, feathers, and grease. Some bands practiced cranial deformation on their babies, which gave the adults sloping foreheads and tapered heads. Hairstyles were fantastic and colorful. When Caddo men returned from the forestlands with protein-rich deer, their women turned deerskins into soft, pliable clothing that was often beautifully decorated with paint, shells, feathers, and beads.

Similar to their hungry neighbors along the coast, the Caddo peoples wept openly at greetings and departures thought emotional. Various bands grouped themselves into larger affiliations such as the populous Hasinai, Bidai, and Kadohadacho confederacies. The first recorded Spanish encounters with the Caddo confederacies occurred some fifteen years after Cabeza de Vaca's overland journey. Luis de Moscoso's men, continuing the exploratory endeavors of the deceased Hernán de Soto, crossed the Red River into modern Texas in October 1541. These conquistadores found their travels much facilitated by the stored food surpluses of these eastern tribes. But Moscoso's forcible requisitions of native foods and the plundering ways of his weary companions sowed nothing but anger, fear, and distrust among the Caddos of East Texas.

In 1535, Cabeza de Vaca and three other castaways, kept alive by foraging coastal bands, had neither the force of arms nor the masses of trained men to bludgeon their way forward or back to New Spain. These four survivors would have to find an indigenous way to go forward—some means of overland travel that would avoid tribal hatreds and embrace affections. Of necessity the men traveling along this pathway would have to overcome the manifold divisiveness and chronic strife between all manner of warlike bands on the road ahead. There were many *naciones* or peoples that lay between the Spanish-speaking sojourners and their distant homes.

As a trader, Cabeza de Vaca had negotiated effectively with different ethnic groups. He was thus allowed to wander among the nearby coastal bands with a stock of aboriginal trade goods. Once the costumed official treasurer of a powerful royal expedition, he now stayed alive by dressing in native garb and bartering pearls, ochre, flints, and hides among the strange peoples of the New World. In his peregrinations, he visited or learned of many new groups such as the Deaguanes, Quevenes, Mariames, Guaycones, Yeguazes, and Arbados. He walked from place to place with his goods, was welcomed in new camps, and learned much from his contacts.

Near Matagorda Bay in the spring of 1533 he watched a battle between his hosts, the Mariames, and their rivals, the Deaguanes. Usually these battles were furious and skillful but caused relatively few casualties. Warriors kept low to the ground, moved rapidly, and dodged and fired arrows back and forth. While these clashes might lead to fatalities, they rarely led to annihilations; indeed, their function was to test and intimidate, not to slaughter. Wounds were common but usually proved nonlethal. Women traditionally served as diplomats, peacemakers, envoys, and trusted intermediaries between different or combative male groups.

Slinking away from a difficult life with the Capoques, Cabeza de Vaca spent almost a year and one-half (around 1533–34) living as a trader with the Mariames of South Texas. The Mariames were possibly a Coahuilteco band living between the lower reaches of the Nueces and Guadalupe rivers and speaking a different language. Cabeza de Vaca's narrative thus provides a degree of intimacy with these new people never again achieved by an outsider. The Mariames were fond of pecan nuts, mesquite beans, and the fruit of prickly pear cacti, harvesting great quantities in season. In the summer of 1534 the trader fled to another group, the Avavares, and while with them he plotted to rejoin the three other survivors—Castillo, Dorantes, and Estevanico.

After finally making contact with each other and laying plans to escape from their servitude, the four men arranged for a future rendezvous. In the early summer of 1535 they met as agreed at a favored native place, one where dispersed bands converged for the seasonal feasting on ripe prickly pears. The four sojourners successfully united and made all haste to leave their particular groups behind. They soon began a passage southward through a bewildering array of roving ethnic bands and tribal groupings whose principal similarity was that they inhabited the relatively resource-poor but vast coastal plains of southwest Texas and northeast Mexico.

No other Europeans and Africans are known to have had quite the intimacy of contact with Coahuiltecans as Cabeza de Vaca, Castillo, Dorantes, and Estevanico. Cabeza de Vaca's *relación* thus provides a rare glimpse into the lifeways of these lost peoples. Stretching from the Nueces

River of Texas all the way to the Pánuco River of New Spain (today's Mexico), there were numerous, indeed, hundreds, of *naciones*—that is distinctive tribal bands with names, languages, dialects, and cultural identities now lost to the ages. Over the past hundred years, scholars in Mexico and the United States have put together a revised (if still primitive) understanding of these peoples.

Spanish archives and various documents, from Cabeza de Vaca's castaway narrative in 1542 to Damián Massanet's missionary journal of 1690–91, provide a bewildering array of named tribes or bands living in these coastal plains. Indeed, about a thousand names exist for most likely hundreds of actual bands and tribal groups. A language family called Coahuilteco (after the Mexican states of Coahuila and Texas) is believed to have been spoken by many of the peoples. But, in fact, it is impossible now to know which bands spoke Coahuilteco or its many dialects, which bands did not, and which spoke it as a second language. Thus, past researchers tended to examine the profusion of documentary, archival, and field evidence and then to lump together as Coahuiltecans all the bands in the mysterious inland brushlands (what the Spaniards called the *monte*) of the Gulf Coast region.

Further, recent historical scholarship has largely revised accepted opinions on the Texas route followed by Cabeza de Vaca and his three companions. In the 1930s and 1940s many scholars believed that the castaways had left the prickly pear thickets and slowly ascended rivers reaching into the Hill Country. Cleve Hallenbeck's 1940 book took them deep into the Edwards Plateau region, even wintering around Big Spring. Historians such as Donald Chipman are now convinced that the four men wandered south instead, following along the arc of flat coastal plains in South Texas. They eventually reached the broad Rio Grande and crossed it into Tamaulipas, Mexico.

This revised route fits much better with the archaeological record, as it takes the four on a passage sweeping through the lowland Coahuiltecan groups of South Texas and Northeast Mexico. Texans now recognize that Cabeza de Vaca's odyssey is a shared heritage for two modern nations. Thus, the Texas Hill Country is no longer on the route, but the scenic rivers and sierras of the adjacent Mexican states of Tamaulipas, Nuevo León, and finally Coahuila are brilliant replacements. As the four men journeyed southward they encountered many Coahuiltecan groups in South Texas. Some of these coastal groups migrated inland along the Nueces and Guadalupe rivers and streams in summer and returned to their coastal haunts in wintertime. But for all the native efforts, the bands suffered from periodic hunger and practiced no settled agriculture.

Bands distinguished themselves by ritual tattoos and piercings, decorations, clothing, and important dialectical or language differences. Smaller in stature than the Karankawas, for example, Coahuiltecans followed ageless and perennial migratory movements around the landscape. Cabeza de Vaca's report on the Mariames noted their winter retreats to coastal habitats, while in summer they moved deeper inland for the seasonal ripening of vast prickly pear thickets and in search of game and perhaps bison, those shaggy "cattle" he saw and whose hides he traded. All of these bands claimed and defended hunting and gathering territories.

Food was the absolute determinant. Women and children gathered quantities of sotol cacti for their firepits. They filled baskets with nutritious mesquite beans, pulpy prickly pear fruit, and quantities of other plants and herbs. They collected spiders, ant eggs, larvae, salamanders, and deer dung. Everyone hunted rabbits and other small game, and they set fires to flush out snakes and lizards. They seined creeks for fish, speared fish at night by torchlight, and ate waterfowl. In winter these natives ate almost anything edible. In good times, Cabeza de Vaca wrote, their diet often included large amounts of earth and water mixed in with ground mesquite beans. Such repasts greatly distended their stomachs.

The Coahuilteco were a tough and resourceful people. Men managed the movement of game by setting fires, engaged in communal and enclosure hunts, and fought rival bands for the possession of prickly pear thickets, mesquite and piñon groves, creeks, and better hunting grounds. The stamina of the hunters was so great that they often killed a deer simply by running after it, hour upon hour, until the animal gave way to exhaustion. As the Spanish castaways passed from Indian band to band in the summer of 1535, they were often given venison and other favored foods for their services and as blessings.

The forward momentum of the four survivors was now strictly a function of their recasting into powerful shamans for the Coahuilteco tribes. Cabeza de Vaca knew how to command and wield authority. Estevanico's proven abilities in bridging cultures were an asset; he frequently served as group spokesman. The four men were progressed from one tribal band to another on the basis of their astounding reputations as faith healers. Shamanism was common among Amerindians; it shared important similarities to Eurasian shamanistic beliefs and practices.

Perhaps it made sense to the Coahuilteco that European shamans could protect them from mysterious new diseases—that is, diseases and epidemics largely associated with the arrival of Europeans elsewhere. They also came to believe that these four foreigners had the powers to kill if they so chose.

Moreover, the journey of the castaways was soon shaped to fit the Coahuilteco custom of ritual plunder. Each new group receiving the revered shamans was obliged to offer or give up various possessions (indeed, prized possessions might be hidden away beforehand) to the large retinue of different natives accompanying them. The plundered natives, in turn, would join the four shamans and guide them to another camp, whereupon they would seize the other band's property. This exchange appears strange to a modern world so grounded in materialism and consumption, but it apparently regulated the needs and satisfied the desires of tribe after tribe. In times of drought or distress this application of cultural ecology may have enhanced ultimate survival for all concerned.

Advancing into a new camp, Cabeza de Vaca and his companions typically were greeted with reverence by the entire community. All those present desired and awaited a blessing from one of these shamans. This business of blessing every single person became vexatious. Cabeza de Vaca even was reputed to have restored life to a "dead" (doubtless unconscious) man. His reputation and boldness as a healer was only magnified when he operated on a Coahuilteco warrior and surgically removed an embedded arrowhead from his chest. Castillo, Dorantes, and Estevanico all came to practice group faith healing, which greatly pleased the natives and attracted large crowds. The four prayed, breathed on both the healthy and the afflicted, made the sign of the cross, blessed various foods and offerings, and sometimes cauterized wounds. Gifts, shelter, food, and negotiated guidance to the next community repaid their efforts. Thus, their healing practice allowed them to pass from band to band.

After crossing the Rio Grande and advancing some distance into Tamaulipas, the healers paused near the Sierra de Pamoranes and pondered the road ahead. They then made a fateful decision to turn west and northwest instead of due south. This decision has been much debated by scholars. The town of San Esteban del Puerto, the northernmost Spanish settlement on the Gulf Coast, was known to be directly to their south, but the castaways apparently believed firmly that the coastal route was neither safe nor easy. Perhaps most significantly, there were no domesticated foods in this direction. But inquiries by Estevanico and the others revealed that crops, especially precious maize, were grown to their west and northwest. The Christian shamans thus turned "toward the setting sun" and began a series of overland processions that carried them along the flanking chains of the Sierra Madre Oriental. They were headed into the interior of an unknown continent.

The four healers journeyed for many weeks along river valleys, traveling from the modern state of Tamaulipas into Nuevo León and then into Coahuila. Failing to remember all the confusing names of these Coahuilteco groups, Cabeza de Vaca simply called them all "the people of the piñon nuts" from their regular diet of the edible nuts of piñon trees. Coahuilteco bands in this part of modern Mexico shaped the expedition in profound ways. The four sojourners were given sacred gourds. The ritual plunder of each new band by the accompanying natives (who, blessed and happy, returned home laden with goods), continued.

Almong the Coahuilteco of South Texas and Mexico the four healers had emerged as the revered "Children of the Sun." Their processions were often characterized by crowds of supplicants, attendants, porters, well-wishers, and the curious. During their travels in Mexico each Child of the Sun also came to have a changing retinue of followers who accompanied him. This retinue set up a shelter for each shaman, saw to his wants, and provided women for his comfort.

For the four castaways in the summer of 1535, the reality was an odyssey across a hundred impoverished kingdoms in Texas and Mexico, each keyed to topographic features, new dialects, and strange but intriguing cultural practices. Cabeza de Vaca wrote that they passed through so many peoples that it was impossible to remember them all, and his narrative then no longer bothered to name a *nación* after the Cuchendados of South Texas. As the three Spaniards and Estevanico made their way from one ethnographic divide to another, sent along as healers and benefactors, they discovered that their escape had been converted into a triumphal procession. They began to conduct themselves, therefore, as the great men they were now considered to be.

These tribes populated the lowlands, brushlands, rough sierras, and river valleys of the inland country. The natives' chronic small-scale feuds with their neighbors were suspended to honor the Children of the Sun. After passing northwest along the pleasant rivers of Coahuila in the late summer of 1535, the four sojourners eventually arrived at a broad river, the mighty Rio Grande, now encountered at an upstream point. Wading through the swift currents, possibly at a crossing near Boquillas del Carmen, they recrossed it and climbed onto the dry Stockton Plateau of

West Texas. Soon it was time to say farewell to the weeping "people of the piñon nuts."

On the high limestone plateaus of West Texas, campsites clustered around strong aquifer springs and comfortable ecotones. The ritual plunder-exchange system soon functioned here smoothly, despite the fact that the inhabitants of West Texas spoke and dressed very differently from their Coahuilteco neighbors to the south. Cabeza de Vaca called these *naciones* "the people of the cows," denoting that they had crossed a significant ethnographic divide. They were now in a world of buffalo hunters. Bison robes were thus ritually presented and exchanged as gifts. Cabeza de Vaca, charmed by these big-game hunters, wrote that they were "the people with the most well formed bodies we saw and of the greatest vitality and capacity and who best understood us and responded to what we asked them."

"The people of the cows" were seminomadic bands who seasonally followed the buffalo herds to the north. Most of the tribe's hunters were away at this time of year. Cabeza de Vaca's comments on the "people of the cows" were intriguing at the time, but they were soon amplified by the Coronado expedition of 1540–1542. Indeed, Cabeza de Vaca's observations seem applicable to the protohistoric people called the Teya by don Francisco Vásquez de Coronado's best chronicler.

For weeks the four men traveled northwest in an arc, roughly paralleling the northwest curve of the Rio Grande. Their observations provide direct evidence for the contact of Europeans with West Texas tribes. Around La Junta de los Ríos, the confluence of the Río Conchos from Mexico with the Rio Grande, they passed once more into the domains of native peoples familiar with domesticated crops—frijole beans, squash, and some maize despite a drought—and more permanent settlements, even structures that resembled houses.

Stretching north of the castaways' position at La Junta de los Ríos lay a vast rain-shadow region, the southern grasslands of the Great Plains. Within Texas this land embraced the physiography called the Southern High Plains, which in turn blended into the Edwards Plateau. It was a huge, elevated tableland—so remarkably flat that rainfall mostly spurned rivers and streams. On the High Plains the waters curled upon themselves in thousands of *playas*, perfectly round lakes of interior drainage. The ground was cloaked with seas of short grasses and forbs. Herds of buffalo, numbering in the tens of thousands, groomed and fertilized these grasslands. The colorful canyon margins of this realm had both trees and discharge springs from immense aquifers. The rulers were the bison-hunting Teya people, later named in 1541 by the explorers of the Coronado *entrada*.

A mysterious people, the Teya tattooed patterns around their eyes. They were strong, swift, good-looking, and quite sociable to the first Spanish explorers. In his famous narrative of the Coronado expedition, Pedro de Castañeda reported that Coronado's men had heard testimony from an old Teya man, who recalled with some sincerity that he had been a witness to the procession of the Children of the Sun. Thus, the Spaniards of 1541 heard about the four castaways of 1535, both apparently in contact with the same ethnographic province.

The origins, proper name, language, and identity of these handsome, crop-growing bison hunters are still the grist for academic mills, but elements of their culture suggest an offshoot from one of the Puebloan tribes of the upper Rio Grande in present New Mexico. These "people of the cows" followed the herds toward the High Plains in the summer and fall but retreated to sheltering river valleys where they had settlements and cultivated plots of domesticated plants. Despite the mysteries of their name and origins, they are widely believed to have been the ancestors of the historic Jumano tribes living in Texas in the 1600s.

The Jumanos had a talent for better relations with the Spaniards, perhaps to balance their troubled relations with adjacent native enemies. And the Jumanos were not without enemies. To their north a disruptive, highly adaptive, displaced, and warlike culture had arrived within the past few centuries. The earliest Spanish explorers in New Mexico and Texas called them the Querecho in 1541. Querechos lived on the Southern High Plains as well and were slowly beginning to dominate this realm, displacing their Teya or Jumano competitors southward.

The Querechos were less impressed by the Coronado expedition. Avoidance seemed a good strategy to them. Nevertheless, these dispersed and roving camps and bands were developing an important role for the future. The Querechos of the early accounts glide readily into the warlike Apache tribes that controlled the plains shared by Texas and New Mexico for several centuries. Certainly, the language difference was immense between Teya and Querecho. Like other tribes of the plains, they communicated with a universal sign language, an ingenious lingua franca of gestures and hand signals.

The very presence of a universalizing sign language should remind the modern reader that Texas may have had more linguistic and cultural diversity in the past than at present. English-language dominance, much fewer dialects, global exchange networks, and homogenizing national media stand in contrast to Cabeza de Vaca's and Castañeda's accounts of dazzling differences in diversity—divides that can only be bridged by hands instead of words in landscapes of microethnicity.

After living for many autumn days with "the people of the cows," the four Christian shamans continued their course "toward the setting sun." These travels brought them back again to the upper Rio Grande. Near the vicinity of modern El Paso the four healers recrossed the river and continued westward for weeks across the Greater Southwest. Where possible during that fall of 1535 they chose communities familiar with maize and cotton cultivation. These journeys eventually took them onto and along the aboriginal Turquoise Trail, an exchange network running from the Puebloan cities of modern New Mexico to the agricultural villages of the fertile Sonora Valley. In late December 1535 they reached a populous *ranchería* settlement in the Sonora Valley, which they called Corazones after they were presented with the hearts of six hundred deer. Downstream from the Río Yaqui lay the Pacific Ocean. By the beginning of 1536 they had crossed the entire continent.

Advancing southward now, in the verdant Sierra Madre Occidental that rose from the Pacific Coast, Cabeza de Vaca and his companions heard ominous reports in January and February 1536; they also saw evidence of something dreadful happening to the tribes ahead of them. In fact, armed and brutal Spanish slavers were laying waste to many of the intervening tribes. When Cabeza de Vaca finally encountered a party of Spaniards in the winter of 1536, they were astonished at his bizarre appearance and stories. Although the four adventurers were now among a Christian people, these particular Christians were merciless slavers engaged in their shameful business.

The slaving party was clearly inconvenienced by the sudden rescue of four lost Narváez expedition members. They were also displeased at the reverence and respect shown by the adoring natives to these otherwise weathered, lost, and contemptible fugitives. Indeed, the Spaniards were chiefly interested in enslaving the four healers' native retinues. Cabeza de Vaca's protestations and dissuasions against such beastly conduct probably sufficed only until the four were safely escorted away, under guard. They were soon headed back toward intrigued officials in Mexico City, a journey itself lasting many weeks in May, June, and July 1536.

The astounding news that four men, against all odds, had survived from the Narváez expedition galvanized the capital of New Spain. Viceroy Antonio de Mendoza himself interrogated the survivors after they reached Mexico City. They prepared a written Joint Report on the peoples of Texas. Mendoza even acquired the services of Estevanico for a future reconnaissance. Although the four men had seen no empires of gold, there were stories of minerals, some semiprecious stones, robes sewn from the hides of strange cattle, and hearsay of further settlements deep in the continental interior. By 1539 these tales, magnified in the telling, led to an official inquiry into "the northern mysteries."

Fray Marcos de Niza, a priest, and Estevanico retraced a route up the western coast of New Spain beyond the Yaqui River. Estevanico soon forged ahead on his own and reached Corazones in the Sonora Valley. From there he traveled north and entered the modern state of Arizona. After so many adventures, perils, and travels, el negro was killed by angry Zuni Indians near one of their pueblos. Fray Marcos, alarmed by Estevanico's death, supposedly drew near enough to espy a great city— was it one of the golden Seven Cities of Cíbola? It appeared to him to be rich and fabulous. Fray Marcos's optimistic report, together with the misleading tales of wealth that circulated after his return, soon precipitated the large and expensive expedition of don Francisco into the Southwest. In the spring of 1541 the Coronado expedition brought European explorers directly onto the High Plains of Texas, where they encountered the Querechos and sojourned among the Teyas, as noted above.

Life could never be the same again for Cabeza de Vaca. He returned to Spain in triumph in 1537, wrote his magnificent narrative of survival, and in an audience with the king, presented a bison robe and turquoises to Carlos I. He eventually was appointed as governor of distant Spanish interests in Paraguay. There he made the obvious mistake— at least from a Spanish slaver's perspective—of sympathizing with the indigenous peoples. His resistance to the more brutal forms of exploitation applied to natives engendered considerable enmity among Spanish rivals. He was denounced by fellow Christians, condemned in legal actions, and recalled to Spain. Whose captivity was worse—that of the Karankawa or that of Carlos I's judges? Cabeza de Vaca was banished to North Africa for a time, but the charges against him finally were cleared and he returned to Spain.

After so many adventures, Alvar Núñez Cabeza de Vaca died at home in the mid-1550s. The former treasurer was never able to satisfy the greed that infected the conquistadores, nor was the former healer able to stop the epidemics that killed the majority of natives over the next century. But he had known two worlds, Texas and Spain, and he had served two eras, prehistory and history. Indeed, he died with twice the life and times experienced by most mortals.

Cabeza de Vaca's narrative, and the additional writings of the members of the Coronado and De Soto expeditions, give an impression of profound human diversity in Texas at the time of first contact between Europeans and Indians. Hundreds of native groups, some clustering into larger linguistic or ethnographic provinces, both dominated and adapted to the state's bioregions. From piney woods to high plains, from coastal estuaries to limestone plateaus, the natives sought food, shelter, and society. Their dialects, customs, and practices varied enormously.

Today, Texans are subject to the antithetical forces of globalism and retribalization. Globalism embraces the universalizing, assimilationist, and integrationist forces. Media blockbusters, chain stores, transnational corporations, and blended ethnic identities tend to homogenize both customs and culture. One rule of law covers the state; one computer operating system dominates the market. The electronic exchange systems are increasingly global, as is the pollution, and even bilingual minds face monolingual pressures in politics, society, and business. Species extinctions in Texas degrade biotic diversity in every way and are irreversible.

Modern diversity thus emerges less from tribal affiliations keyed to landscape resources than from retribalizing cultures, employment, class, race, gender, education, housing, religion, and age cohorts ("GenX," "Baby Boomers, "Thirty-somethings"). Tattoos and body piercings today signify something other than defended deer-hunting and oyster-gathering territories, but the practice still distinguishes some people from others. Urban gangs with symbolic gestures, clothing, and colors are not entirely unlike the roving, autonomous Coahuilteco bands too numerous to name. Perhaps our exchange systems are scalable, and they have merely shifted ritual plunder from prehistoric gifts between bands to the industrialized trade between nations—otherwise known as the ritual plunder of the entire Earth.

The epic encounters of Cabeza de Vaca with the Indians of Texas remind us today of one important point: however much we now seem to differ—in our skin pigmentation, class, national origins, beliefs, and customs—we are really one big extended family. Perhaps there are more forces bridging the divides than fracturing the unions. For the tribes of old, the ability of the Children of the Sun to negotiate difference was a reason for dancing and *areitos*. For the postmodern stardust children of Texas, the joy of building bridges from one culture to another is equally keen, equally instructive, and equally suitable for celebrations in song and dance.

Suggested Readings

Adorno, Rolena, and Patrick Charles Pautz. *Alvar Núñez Cabeza de Vaca: His Account, His Life, and the Expedition of Pánfilo de Narváez.* 3 vols., Lincoln, NE, 1999.

Bishop, Morris. *The Odyssey of Cabeza de Vaca.* New York, 1933.

Chipman, Donald E. *Spanish Texas, 1519–1821.* Austin, 1992.

Hallenbeck, Cleve. *Alvar Núñez Cabeza de Vaca: The Journey and Route of the First European to Cross the Continent of North America, 1534–1536.* Port Washington, NY, 1940.

Hodge, Frederick W., and Theodore H. Lewis. *Spanish Explorers in the Southern United States, 1528–1543.* 1907; reprint, Austin, 1984.

Howard, David A. *Conquistador in Chains: Cabeza de Vaca and the Indians of the Americas.* Tuscaloosa, 1997.

Newcomb, W. W. *The Indians of Texas: From Prehistoric to Modern Times.* Austin, 1961.

Sauer, Carl Ortwin. *Sixteenth-Century North America: The Land and the People as Seen by Europeans.* Berkeley, 1971.

Stern, Peter. "Alvar Núñez Cabeza de Vaca: Conquistador and Sojourner." In *The Human Tradition in Colonial America*, ed. Ian K. Steele and Nancy L. Rhoden, 1–19. Wilmington, DE, 1999.

Weber, David J. *The Spanish Frontier in North America.* New Haven, 1992.

2

Francisco Xavier Chaves
Soldier-Interpreter

Elizabeth A. H. John

Francisco Xavier Chaves made an admirable success of a life marked by personal misfortune in volatile times. Born into a prominent family of Spanish New Mexico, he was kidnapped by Comanche raiders as a child. After growing to manhood in the Taovayas and Wichita villages on the Red River, he escaped to San Antonio. Welcomed for his knowledge of the languages and cultures of strategically important Indians, he built a distinguished forty-year career as a soldier-interpreter. In that role, Chaves became indispensable not only to Spanish and subsequent Mexican authorities but also to Indians who needed accurate communication with the Spanish-speaking communities whose presence profoundly affected indigenous worlds. Chaves lived during a time when Spain's hold on its northern borderlands weakened. His life reveals the possibilities of the empire's institutions and policies.

Elizabeth John, who has taught at the University of Oklahoma and Sacramento State University, lives in Austin. She is the author of the classic *Storms Brewed in Other Men's Worlds* (1975; 2d ed., 1996), a panoramic view of two and one-half centuries of the Southwest ranging from the 1540s to the 1790s.

Eight-year-old Francisco Xavier Chaves was tending sheep when, in the late 1760s, Comanches snatched him from his family's land near Albuquerque. Adopted by an Indian mother whose own son had died, Francisco lived the nomadic life of a Comanche boy until her death a few years later. Then he was sold to one of the Taovayas, semisedentary villagers who lived by farming as well as by hunting and gathering. Hence, Chaves grew to manhood at the western edge of the Cross Timbers, in present-day Montague County, Texas. The villages of the kindred Taovayas and Wichitas lay on opposite sides of the Red River, sharing a valuable riverine deposit of salt. Eastern Comanches often came to those villages to barter their meat and hides for vegetable produce and salt, and also for European manufactures—particularly metals and textiles—brought by French traders from Louisiana. Sometimes, French or Spanish adventurers lived at those villages despite Spanish laws to the contrary. In that environment, young Chaves not only became fluent in the Wichitan language of the villagers but also maintained competence in Comanche and in his native Spanish.

In the spring of 1784 a big war party of Taovayas and Wichitas rode south to avenge four of their people who had been killed by Lipan Apaches. Unfortunately for that serious tribal purpose, about fifty adventurous youngsters split from the main party to seek excitement—and horses—around San Antonio, taking Chaves with them. By June, their depredations were making life miserable in San Antonio. In mid-July, some even broke into the backyard of the governor's house, stealing two of his own best horses and two that belonged to his servants, trampling his garden, and wrecking all his melons, squashes, and corn. Convinced that Comanches must have committed the outrage, Governor Domingo Cabello began organizing a major expedition to punish them.

Happily, Chaves slipped away from the raiders as they headed homeward. On July 18 he presented himself at the Presidio de Béxar. Twenty-four-years old, little more than five feet tall, with black hair, gray eyes, and an aquiline nose, he was dressed as an Indian. His eyelids were lacerated for the traditional tattoos meant to mark him for life as Taovayas. How startling that he spoke Spanish to the soldiers who greeted him! Taken immediately to the governor, Chaves explained both the recent spree of the Taovayas lads and current conditions among the Indians whom he knew so well. So began his long, creditable service as interpreter and intermediary with Indians of the northern frontier.

Acting on this new information, Governor Cabello sent an emissary to the Taovayas and Wichitas to inform them of his displeasure with their young raiders and to stress the importance of honoring their treaty obligations to the king of Spain. The response was positive. In February 1785 four Taovayas and Wichita leaders accompanied Cabello's emissary back to San Antonio to repair their relations with the Spaniards. With them came three other residents of those two villages: Pedro Vial and Alfonso Rey, both Frenchmen but fluent in Spanish; and a San Antonio native, Antonio Mariano Valdés, who had lived with the Taovayas for eight years. Each man had broken the law by dwelling unauthorized among Indians, but given the emissary's assurance of the governor's pardon and welcome to San Antonio, they gambled on making new lives there.

Most immediately urgent was a council between Governor Cabello and the four delegates on February 14. Accurate interpretation was essential to a successful outcome. That duty belonged to André Courbière, a Frenchman who had learned the Caddo, Tonkawa, and Wichita languages as a trader at Natchitoches. Since coming to San Antonio in 1779, he had held the unique position of soldier-interpreter in the Presidial Company of Béxar. Now, for the first time, Courbière had in Francisco Chaves an able assistant with intimate knowledge of the customs as well as the speech of the Indians represented in the council. Observing quietly were the three newcomers, whom Chaves must have known at the Taovayas village: Vial, Rey, and Valdés. Never before had Governor Cabello enjoyed access to so much knowledge of the interior nations or so many competent checks on accuracy of interpretation. These Taovayas and Wichita spokesmen had an unusually good chance to convey exactly what they wanted to say.

The delegates apologized, explaining that rash youngsters had acted without their leaders' knowledge and had been severely reprimanded for their folly. They had gotten out of hand in the declining months of the late chief Gransot, but a vigorous successor, Guersec, could control the nation. They prayed the governor to confirm Guersec as great chief of both villages and to allow the Taovayas and Wichitas to show what faithful friends they could be. Chaves, Vial, Rey, and Valdés all vouched for their story and for the excellent qualities of Guersec.

Impressed, Cabello sent the delegates home with a chief's commission for Guersec, stipulating that he require his people to live as vassals of the king of Spain and take them to war only in defense against the king's enemies. It would be his duty to help all other vassals of the king and to join campaigns against the enemies of His Majesty. The four delegates accepted those conditions in the name of Guersec and his people. Vial, Rey, and Valdés affirmed that the people of the two villages truly understood and desired the arrangement. The governor then gave the delegates four horses for their homeward journey and obtained their promise to visit Nacogdoches in June for the annual distribution of gifts to the Indian nations allied with Spain.

The two newly arrived Frenchmen were valuable additions to San Antonio. Vial had brought with him two captives—a 6-year-old Apache girl and an 18-year-old Spanish girl whom he had ransomed from Indians—for which he collected at San Antonio 60 pesos in reimbursement. With that stake, he and Rey rented a little house. There, Vial opened a smithy and proved to be a skilled armorer, locksmith, and silversmith as well as a good blacksmith and an exceptionally alert, intelligent citizen. Rey hung out his shingle as barber, bloodletter, toothpuller, and surgeon. The Presidial Company of Béxar retained him to care for themselves and their families for a small monthly fee, plus the cost of medicines. Unskilled, Valdés hired out as a servant in a local household.

That spring, Governor Cabello was under increasing pressure from his superiors to make peace with the Comanches, which had been a goal of imperial policy for two decades. He consulted Vial about the means of conveying a peace overture into the Comanchería. To the governor's delight, Vial volunteered. Although he spoke their language, Vial did not know the Comanches well enough to venture into their territory alone. However, he believed that his Taovayas friends would support the peace effort by introducing him into the camps of the more moderate eastern Comanche leaders.

Speed was essential. The Taovayas were due to collect their annual gifts at Nacogdoches in June. Vial needed to be there to ask for their help. If they agreed, he would ride with them to their Red River villages, then visit the Comanchería from that base. He chose as his companion young Chaves, whom Vial had known when both of them lived among the Taovayas. More recently, he had seen Chaves demonstrate great competence in interpreting for the governor during the long February talks with the Taovayas and Wichita delegates.

Vial and Chaves left on June 17, 1785, with the necessary horses, equipment, provisions, and two servants, all charged to their personal account. The governor provided generous quantities of the gifts deemed essential to Indian diplomacy. Reaching Nacogdoches in time to win the support of the Taovayas and Wichita delegates, Vial and Chaves rode home with them. They were heartily welcomed at the Red River villages on August 6. Thus, enthused by the prospect of a Comanche peace, the Taovayas and Wichitas spared no effort to arrange for Vial and Chaves a friendly reception in the Comanchería. The principal chiefs of both bands accompanied them westward to the camp designated for their meeting with the eastern Comanche leaders and zealously supported them throughout the successful two-week negotiation process.

On September 11 the assembled Comanches agreed to the peace proposals, designating three chiefs to represent them before the governor. Those three delegates and their wives guided Vial and Chaves back to San Antonio over a rugged westerly route calculated to avoid any encounters with Lipan Apaches. On September 29, Vial and Chaves triumphantly escorted them into San Antonio for a ceremonious welcome by Governor Cabello. San Antonians flocked to welcome the guests, bringing fruit and other gifts to their lodgings.

Another six weeks of vitally important work awaited Vial and Chaves. The peace effort hinged on their effectiveness in informing Cabello as well as on their skill in interpreting for the Comanches, for whom they were on call at all times. While the guests rested, Vial and Chaves spent four days explaining to Cabello their experiences with the Comanches, Taovayas, and Wichitas, trying to give him the best possible basis for negotiation. With Vial and Chaves interpreting, the actual negotiation of peace terms went smoothly and quickly. However, the Comanches stayed nearly three weeks while their exhausted horses recuperated, and thus they continued to need Vial and Chaves as interpreters.

When the Comanches left on October 19, escorted by forty-two soldiers to protect them from skulking Lipans, they asked that Chaves accompany them as interpreter. Once he returned on November 6, it was time to produce the diary required for the official record. Unfortunately, having grown up in captivity, Chaves could neither read nor write. Vial could read and converse sufficiently in Spanish, but his written skills were too rudimentary for an adequate account of their mission. Governor Cabello, therefore, apparently wrote the official diary under their guidance, perhaps helped by Vial's rough notes. By January 1786 the achievement of Vial and Chaves won high praise from the commandant general at Chihuahua.

What rewards did they expect for their superb performance? Chaves wanted to be a soldier-interpreter at Béxar like the highly regarded André Courbière. Cabello wanted to appoint him, but the Presidial Company had no vacancy. Chaves would have to wait nearly two years for an opening. Vial, older, literate, and more ambitious, wanted a more important position, but nothing suitable existed in San Antonio. Frustrated, he volunteered to perform another long-desired feat: to find the most direct feasible route between San Antonio and Santa Fe and to prepare an itinerary for travelers.

In August 1786, nearly a year after their triumphant return from the Comanchería, the commandant general authorized lump-sum compensations for their labors: 300 pesos for Vial and 200 for Chaves. He also authorized Vial's expedition to Santa Fe but did not fund it. Early in October, Vial rode northward to blaze the route to Santa Fe at his own expense. For Chaves, the award of 200 pesos so improved his financial standing that he could marry a San Antonio woman of good family. His bride, Juana Padrón, soon produced the first of their eleven children. Thereafter, family responsibilities loomed large in his life.

After mid-November 1785, San Antonio experienced a surprising stream of visitors—Comanches, Taovayas, and Wichitas—coming to affirm the new accords with Béxar, to trade, and to visit among themselves. Chaves was constantly on call to interpret for them, helped by Vial to the extent that his smithy permitted. For the first four months, Cabello arranged for the visitors to be lodged at the home of Courbière, who had long entertained Indians from northeastern Texas. As was customary in most Indian as well as Spanish cultures, the guests were given all they could eat and drink, but by March 1786 the overwhelming numbers convinced both Cabello and Courbière that no private home could sustain indefinitely such intensive hospitality. To resolve the problem, Courbière donated land next to his own house in the horseshoe bend of the San Antonio River, between the presidio and Mission San Antonio de Valero. There, with materials furnished by the governor, the people of San Antonio constructed a huge, four-room *jacal*, or shack, which first welcomed visiting Indians in July 1786.

While primary responsibility for hospitality at the *jacal* would belong to Courbière, Chaves played a key role as interpreter of the mentalities as well as the speech of Comanches and the Wichitan groups —Taovayas, Wichitas, Tawakonis, and Iscanis. More than ever, Governor Cabello relied on Chaves, paying him as best he could from his own pocket. Apparently, experience at the *jacal* broadened the young interpreter's skills: within two years, Chaves also claimed some competence in the languages of the Tejas, Tonkawas, Cocos, Bidais, Mayeyes, and Akokisas.

Late in the autumn of 1786, Chaves lost his foremost advocate. Aged, ailing Governor Cabello was assigned a less strenuous post in Havana. His ill-qualified successor, Captain Rafael Martínez Pacheco, soon demonstrated alarming incompetence, particularly in Indian affairs, but the new governor had the wit to value the services of Chaves, whom he paid 2 pesos monthly from his own pocket. Martínez Pacheco also allotted him from the presidial warehouse a monthly ration of corn, which helped feed his family, and a few bolts of cloth, which Chaves could barter in the local economy.

Happily, a desertion created a vacancy at the presidio in the spring of 1788. Chaves promptly applied for a position as soldier-interpreter, modeled on that of Courbière. Martínez Pacheco forwarded the petition to regional headquarters in Coahuila, where Commandant Juan de

Ugalde readily approved it. Ugalde had seen Chaves in action at Béxar earlier in the year and understood the value of his services. On July 29, 1788, Chaves enlisted in the Presidial Company of Béxar for a ten-year term as soldier-interpreter, exempt from the routine duties of barracks and horse herd but required to accompany troops on sorties.

Once established in the long-desired position at Béxar, Chaves addressed the question of his ancestry—of some importance to the social standing of his growing family in San Antonio as well as to himself. He needed to go to New Mexico to visit his birthplace near Albuquerque. There he hoped to see his relatives and to obtain legal documentation of his descent. Seven of his Comanche friends, including rising leaders Sojaís and Zoquiné, agreed to accompany him along with their wives. Granted a three-month furlough and the necessary passport, issued on April 7, 1792, Chaves rode southwestward with the regular mail train to Presidio del Río Grande (now Guerrero, Coahuila). Thence, he and the seven Comanche couples rode westward and northward, apparently following the Pecos River toward the pueblo of Pecos, which had become a principal center of Comanche trade.

Early on May 25, a few miles east of Pecos, the group encountered Pedro Vial, who was setting out with two young companions from Santa Fe to blaze a trail to St. Louis. Delighted to see one another, Vial and Chaves led their parties to the bank of the Pecos to camp overnight, reminiscing and exchanging news. Vial, who had chosen to make his career in Santa Fe, had last visited San Antonio three years ago. This reunion would be the last for the old friends.

Chaves rode on to Santa Fe to pay his respects to Governor Fernando de la Concha, whom he had to petition for an affidavit of his descent. That presented no problem: the Chaves family had figured prominently in New Mexico since the earliest Spanish colonization and had long been major landholders in the jurisdiction of Albuquerque. Francisco readily found his father, Ignacio Chaves, at Atrisco, on the west bank of the Rio Grande, where the son was born about 1760. His mother, Gregoria Maese, had died, and Ignacio had remarried. Perhaps Francisco Xavier also saw his two sisters and his brother, Francisco Antonio.

On July 12, 1792, at the pueblo of Isleta, the *alcalde mayor* of Albuquerque presided at the required hearing. Three witnesses testified to the descent of Francisco Xavier Chaves and the circumstances of his capture. On July 18, Governor Concha issued the official documents at Santa Fe. Francisco hurried to Pecos to rejoin his Comanche friends for the long ride home. By October 1792 he was back on duty in San

Antonio, where deteriorating conditions greeted him. In the summer of 1790 the hapless Martínez Pacheco had yielded the governorship to a veteran presidial commander, Manuel Múñoz, who proved entirely too old and ill to manage the province. Neither Governor Martínez Pacheco nor Governor Múñoz ever earned, or merited, the confidence of the Indian allies. San Antonio suffered ever-increasing petty depredations, especially the theft of horses, as Comanche war parties passed en route to and from the Rio Grande in pursuit of Lipan Apaches.

Since their treaty with the Spaniards encouraged relentless war against Apaches, some Comanches stopped at presidios or settlements along the Rio Grande—perhaps to trade, perhaps to visit and rest a while, perhaps to stalk Apaches living nearby, or perhaps to spot tempting horses. Without an interpreter competent in Comanche, who could know? In April 1794, Commandant General Pedro de Nava ordered Chaves to report to the Presidial Company of San Juan Bautista del Río Grande to serve there as interpreter.

Six miserable years ensued. Francisco was desperately worried and unhappy without his family, who remained in San Antonio. At San Juan Bautista, he felt nearly friendless. Not only did he interpret at the presidio, but he also accompanied troops on campaign, either interpreting or fighting as required. His service record shows in 1795 a four-month campaign in which he killed one Indian; in 1796, one campaign; in 1797, one campaign with two battles, in one of which he killed an Indian; in 1798 and 1799, four campaigns. In January 1799 he reenlisted at the Presidio del Río Grande, and in the following year petitioned for transfer back to the Presidio de Béxar. He made two more campaigns from Rio Grande, participating in nine battles and suffering a gunshot wound before another new governor of Texas precipitated his return to Béxar.

Understanding the urgency of accurate communication with Indian visitors—particularly Comanches—who flocked to San Antonio to see him, Governor Juan Bautista de Elguezábal demanded the return of Chaves. By March 16, 1800, Chaves reported for duty at Béxar. There, he enjoyed a decade of work with three successive governors who appreciated the importance and complexity of Indian relations. When Elguezábal died in 1805, his interim successor for three years was Antonio Cordero, then governor of Coahuila, who was famously skilled in dealing with Indians. Under Governor Cordero, San Antonio bustled more than ever with Indian diplomacy and trade. Cordero's replacement in 1808, Governor Manuel María del Salcedo, had little experience of Indian affairs but spared no effort to learn.

Nurturing the Indian alliances—particularly that with the Comanches—was a prime responsibility of those governors of Texas. There was no limit to the time they would spend in conversation with their numerous Comanche visitors, or to the hospitality they provided. Less frequent, but urgently important, were Taovayas or Tawakoni visitors. Given his sole responsibility for interpreting those languages, plus his share of responsibility for visitors lodged at the great *jacal* near the river, Chaves could count on little free time. Moreover, his duty as interpreter sometimes required that he accompany the governor's representatives to Comanche camps.

Supporting his large family on a soldier's pay was a perennial challenge. With the governors' knowledge, Chaves supplemented his income by bartering with Indians. Occasionally, he ransomed captives, a compassionate service sometimes compensated from a public fund. Early in the 1800s, Chaves bought from Comanches an Apache woman and her small daughter, whose plight especially touched him. Baptized as Guadalupe and Trinidad, they became members of his household. Judicial records reflect their experience with the kind Chaves family.

In 1810, San Antonio experienced two grave crises, and the first one soon involved Chaves. Spain's network of Indian alliances frayed as Anglo-American traders based in Louisiana incited Taovayas, Tawakonis, and Comanches to steal horses for the burgeoning market in the United States. Resulting raids menaced not only horses but also other property and the lives of settlers and soldiers in Texas. The foremost eastern Comanche chief, Cordero, strove to repair the alliance, identifying offenders, arranging restitution, and proposing means to prevent future breaches. Never had accurate communication between Comanches and Spaniards been more urgent nor Chaves more constantly in demand, both at San Antonio and farther afield. That crisis eased in October when eastern Comanche leaders rode to San Antonio to explain the breaches and reaffirm their treaty.

Meanwhile, on September 16, deep in New Spain, Father Manuel Hidalgo's cry for independence precipitated a political crisis that soon reverberated in San Antonio. The independence movement evoked sympathy among some San Antonians. However, there is no record of political involvement by Chaves, who owed his livelihood to the establishment and probably had little concept of revolution. Indeed, the 1810 census at Béxar shows a considerable stake in the status quo for Francisco, age 50, and his wife Juana, 40. They had six children at home: two daughters, ages 14 and 15, and four sons, ages 13, 8, 7, and 2. Chaves's listed property included five horses, eight mares, one burro, ten cows, seven bulls, three young oxen and six old oxen, three yearling calves, four yokes, and two carts.

In January 1811 local revolutionaries shipped Governor Salcedo south in irons. Two months later, a junta of local royalists seized control. From January to July, Indian visitors found in San Antonio a puzzling vacuum of authority as well as a dearth of the customary gifts. That was an awkward, potentially dangerous situation for official interpreter-host Chaves. He must have welcomed the restoration of gubernatorial authority in July when Lt. Col. Simón de Herrera became acting governor until Governor Salcedo could resume his post in December.

Unfortunately, just before Salcedo returned, Herrera made a grave error in judgment, which outraged many Comanches. On April 8, 1812, Governor Salcedo rode out with 675 men to talk with the four principal leaders of countless Comanche warriors crying vengeance before the walls of San Antonio. Never had the skill and integrity of interpreter Chaves been more crucial. After much talk, the leaders agreed that their imperfect peace remained preferable to war, and the Comanches dispersed.

Four months later, the oddly assorted Magee-Gutiérrez band of Spanish revolutionaries and Anglo-American filibusters invaded Texas from Louisiana. By April 1813 they destroyed Spanish authority in Texas, occupying San Antonio and executing Governor Salcedo and Commandant Herrera. San Antonians suffered a chaotic four-month occupation, with invaders quartered in many private houses and with no security of lives or property. Chaves claimed losses in that period of twenty-six mares, twelve horses, one burro, three oxen, one cow, two muskets, one pistol, three lances, and one sword, all worth 417 pesos. In August a royalist army recaptured San Antonio, driving the invaders back to Louisiana and imposing a much longer occupation, with extreme measures to root out suspected collaborators with the independence movement. The bodies of those executed hung on the plaza until the following spring.

To eliminate possible subversives among the military, the Presidial Company of Béxar was disbanded, then reorganized. Chaves, never listed as a suspect, petitioned for retirement, pleading his advanced age, ill health, thirty years of service to His Majesty, and the burden of a large family. With his petition denied, Chaves found himself transferred to the Presidial Company of La Bahía in December 1814, but because his duties as interpreter required his presence at San Antonio, he was quickly recalled there as a supernumerary. For the remaining fifteen years of his career, the records list him as a member of La Bahía Company, serving at Béxar.

Never had Indian relations been in greater disarray. When the royalists recaptured San Antonio, some Tejano insurgents sought refuge among Indians: most with Comanches, some with Taovayas and Tawakonis, some with Lipans. Over the next seven years, Indian warriors helped those insurgents wage a deliberate war of attrition—stealing horses, killing cattle, burning pastures, killing or capturing colonists who ventured out to work in their fields, and intercepting mail and supply trains coming from Coahuila. Forty ranches were abandoned as their people sought refuge within the walls of San Antonio. Then, amid ever-worsening famine and terror, in July 1819 a terrible cloudburst over north San Antonio sent the river surging out of its banks in a flood of unprecedented magnitude. Nineteen died. Fifty-five houses, including that of Chaves, were swept away, leaving San Antonio in appalling condition and its residents woefully impoverished.

What role did Chaves play after the disastrous events of 1813 ruptured most Indian relationships with Spanish Texas? San Antonio received relatively few Indian visitors while enduring five successive provisional governors in four years. But Antonio Martínez, who arrived in May 1817, would govern Texas through its last four years under the Spanish crown and its first year of Mexican independence. He soon found Chaves indispensable. In particular in 1818 some Tonkawas resumed cultivation of their treaty relations at Béxar and La Bahía. Having learned Tonkawa during the years when Courbière, now deceased, had routinely interpreted for that nation, Chaves readily assumed responsibility for the frequent Tonkawa visitors. He also dealt with occasional Caddos or Bidais from East Texas and Louisiana, sometimes gleaning useful news from these visitors from that volatile frontier.

Mexico's eleven-year War of Independence ended triumphantly in 1821. On July 17, with his company, Chaves swore allegiance to independent Mexico. Fugitive insurgents could now return home with honor. Some men who had driven the relentless Indian wars against Spanish settlements now used their influence to mediate peace. Tribal delegations flocked to San Antonio. By the end of 1822, all of the tribes in Texas renewed their treaties at San Antonio. Delegates of most tribes accepted the invitation of Agustín Iturbide to ride on to Mexico City to affirm their agreements with his new national government.

Once again, San Antonio was a lively hub of Indian trade and diplomacy, particularly with Comanches. The peace was imperfect—faithfully observed by some but often violated by others. Some old grudges persisted. In 1822 some Comanches objected to Chaves as interpreter, and the Ayuntamiento of Béxar proposed Juan Antonio Urrutia to replace him. Rather than upset Comanches, Governor Martínez reluctantly agreed to hire Urrutia, who could interpret only Comanche and had a dubious reputation. Within two years, Urrutia was fired for malfeasance. Fortunately, the governor had insisted on retaining Chaves for his competence in various Indian languages and for his proven integrity. Clearly, the Tonkawas concurred. In 1822 their principal chief insisted that Chaves accompany him to the Saltillo headquarters of Commandant General Gaspar López, with whom the Tonkawas were to reaffirm their treaty with Mexico. Since the Tonkawa chief would trust no other interpreter, Chaves reluctantly made the trip.

It was a worrisome time for Chaves to be away from home, and he waited impatiently at Saltillo for the commandant general's permission to return to San Antonio. His first wife, Juana Padrón, had died. Chaves, now 62, had married 28-year-old Micaela Fragoso, who is said to have been literate. She produced the first of their five children in 1822. Their household still included the younger children of his first marriage, a considerable responsibility for Micaela in her husband's absence. Francisco sent his wife as much money as he could from Saltillo and particularly urged her not to permit the children to leave school. No one understood better than Francisco Chaves the penalties of illiteracy.

Chaves was back in San Antonio by April, 1823, joining his company in swearing adherence to the Plan de Casa Mata, which boded the end of Iturbide's brief monarchy and the formation of the Republic of Mexico. The new republic would never attain either political or economic stability, but it treated Chaves relatively well. In 1823 he was awarded a monthly supplement of 90 reales in recognition of his long service and increasing physical disability. In 1824 the governor reported that while San Antonio now had others who could interpet the Comanche and Wichita languages, none was as trustworthy as Chaves, who remained active enough to carry out that duty. In 1825 the commandant of La Bahía Company reported that Chaves was serving his duties as interpreter well and lawfully, was robust enough to continue, and wished to do so.

He was now entitled to bonuses recognizing thirty, thirty-five, and forty years of service. In 1828 he was promoted to *alférez*, retroactive to March 21, 1822, with a monthly allowance of 135 reals in recognition of his thirty-five years of service and, simultaneously, to the rank of lieutenant, with a monthly allowance of 260 reals in consideration of forty years of service. Whether the Republic actually mustered the money to pay all those allowances is uncertain, but it clearly meant to honor Chaves. In the summer of 1829 he retired from the Presidial Company of La Bahía as a first lieutenant attached to the Béxar Company, with a monthly stipend of 260 reals.

He enjoyed three years of retirement with Micaela and a wondrous bevy of children and grandchildren. He must have been especially pleased that an older son, Ignacio, was entrusted with fiscal responsibilities for Church and state and served San Antonio in the elective offices of *regidor* and alcalde. Francisco Xavier Chaves died at his home in San Antonio in the summer of 1832.

Suggested Readings

Almaráz, Félix D., Jr. *Tragic Cavalier: Governor Manuel Salcedo of Texas.* Austin, 1971.

Chabot, Frederick C. *With the Makers of San Antonio: Genealogies of the Early Latin, Anglo-American, and German Families, with Occasional Bibliographies.* 1937; reprint, San Antonio, 1970.

De la Teja, Jesús F. *San Antonio de Béxar: A Community on New Spain's Northern Frontier.* Albuquerque, 1995.

John, Elizabeth A. H. "Nurturing the Peace: Spanish and Comanche Cooperation in the Early Nineteenth Century." *New Mexico Historical Review* 59 (1984): 345–69.

———. *Storms Brewed in Other Men's Worlds: The Confrontation of Indians, Spanish, and French in the Southwest, 1540–1795.* 2d ed. Norman, OK, 1996.

———. "Inside the Comanchería, 1785: The Diary of Pedro Vial and Francisco Xavier Chaves," trans. Adan Benevides Jr. *Southwestern Historical Quarterly* 98 (July 1994): 26–56.

Poyo, Gerald E., and Gilberto M. Hinojosa, eds. *Tejano Origins in Eighteenth-Century San Antonio.* Austin, 1991.

3

Robert Hall
Citizen-Soldier of the Texas Republic

Stephen L. Hardin

Robert Hall was one of thousands of Southerners who poured into Texas when the breakaway Mexican state became a Republic. Too late to take part in the revolution, he nevertheless saw enough action as a Ranger to satisfy his sense of Southern honor. Like many hopeful immigrants, Hall found Texas a bountiful land, but its fruits were not there simply for the picking. Here he found a wife, and together they reared several children on farmland that was worked only with considerable sweat and toil. Promise for the future was bright on the Texas frontier, but lingering on the horizon were the omnipresent clouds that threatened Indian raids and a continuation of the war with Mexico.

Indeed, Hall fought in several engagements with Comanches and helped hold the frontier against Mexican soldiers who invaded Texas to keep alive their claims to the lost province. He was attached to Matthew Caldwell's Ranger company as a citizen-soldier during the Battle of Plum Creek and later recorded many of the details of his experience. The folkways and attitudes of overweening pride and a sense of ordained purpose are evident in his portrayal.

Stephen L. Hardin is professor of history at The Victoria College and author of numerous books and articles on Texas history, including *Texian Iliad: A Military History of the Texas Revolution* (1994).

Across the prairie they came, brandishing lances, singing ancient chants. In triumph they rode, flushed with the knowledge that they had conducted the greatest raid in Comanche history. Turf shuddered beneath the hooves of their painted war ponies; each measured gait brought them closer to Plum Creek. These warriors remained unaware, however, that hidden enemies crouched under its banks.

Soldiers of the Texas Republic watched the Comanches approach. Silent and still, they hunkered low as the warriors closed the distance between them. Sweat from nervous hands oiled rifle stocks; trembling thumbs tested, then tested again, edges of Bowie and butcher knives; throats grew arid and black. Men attempted to mock fear with whispered quips, only to emit curious squeaks. Each soldier struggled to control his knotted stomach. One young Texian anticipated the approaching clash with tangled emotions. It would scar his body and his memory, yet he hungered for it. This was not his first battle, nor would it be his last. His name was Robert Hall.

Approaching battle encourages reflection. Those facing death frequently give thought to all the benefits that life has to offer. Certainly, Hall, then only 26 years old, had many reasons to cling to existence. Back in the frontier settlement of Gonzales, Polly, his young bride, awaited his return. Married only three years, the Halls still behaved like newlyweds. Frontier matrimony was frequently a business arrangement: a woman's survival required food and protection, while men spoke of the necessity of an able "helpmate." The Halls, however, were lucky; theirs was a true love match. Robert and Polly devoted their days to the myriad chores required to maintain a Texas spread: tending the corn, chinking the cabin, rounding up wayward stock, killing snakes, mending fences, chopping wood. But nights together more than rewarded the day's toil. With the rampant ardor of the newly married, Robert and Polly summoned the first of their thirteen children. They believed that their Creator had blessed them with strong limbs, a bountiful country, and each other. But now, as he awaited the clash of arms, Hall was no doubt contemplating how easily a Comanche arrow could shatter their future happiness. And as he reviewed the brief span of his life, he recalled the long and meandering trail that had led him to Plum Creek.

Like most citizens of the Republic of Texas, Robert Hall was a true son of the South, and the folkways and outlook of the region marked him as its own. His family hailed from the Rocky River district of South Carolina, where he had been born, one of five children, to James and Rebecca Gassaway Hall. They sprang from the hardy strain that Professor Frank Owsley identified as "plain folk"—while not planter gentry, they were nevertheless self-sustaining, hard working, and clan proud. Most were yeoman farmers who held title to the land they tilled, or else herders who let their cattle and hogs run free in the hardwood forests. Few ever equaled the success of the wealthy planters, or even aspired to it, but some of the more prosperous might manage to own a slave or two without harboring any moral reservations against slavery. It was simply another hard fact of life, well known to plain folk. And young Robert was as plain and folksy as they came.

Money was tight in the Hall household. As a boy, Robert became used to homespun clothes and hand-me-downs. Even as an old man, he recalled his "proudest and happiest day" as the one on which he received his first pair of "jeans pants": "They had been colored with copperas and the buttons were made of pieces of gourd covered with cloth. Although I was barefooted and had on a flax linen shirt, I would not have traded places with the President of the United States when I put on those pants."[1] Fleeing hard times in South Carolina, the family moved in 1828 to Tennessee, where conditions were still rustic and hardscrabble. That frontier state was, nonetheless, the perfect setting for down-to-earth folk with little cash, few pretensions, and an almost limitless capacity for hard work. They threw up a cabin atop the Choctaw Bluffs in Memphis. Later, when greener pastures beckoned, the family shifted to the Rutherford fork of the Obion River in Gibson County.

While lacking in most of the creature comforts, these openhearted people were ever ready to extend hospitality. James and Rebecca taught their children that to refuse a traveler food and lodging for the night was unneighborly, un-Southern, and downright un-Christian. The local preacher reinforced those teachings from the pulpit. Hall allowed as how it was common for the hard-shell Baptist sect to which his family belonged to "turn people out of the church for refusing to keep strangers over night."

The wayfarer could expect the bounty of the family table cheerfully offered in ample portions. Almost every meal included some manner of pork, cornbread, and buttermilk. When the hunter's eye was sure and his hand steady, game supplemented the menu. When times were flush or vegetables were in season, guests might also share in the family's beef, chicken, rice, field peas, sweet potatoes, and greens. While Yankees and Europeans may have been less than impressed with Southern food and backcountry table manners, the prudent learned to keep such opinions to themselves. Plain folk were mule-proud, as stubborn as they came, and would not abide a slight.

One Yankee visitor in Tennessee, for example, rebuked the elderly proprietor of a humble inn for its lack of tea, coffee, or wheat bread. Not satisfied with demeaning her, he further lambasted the locals as "savages." The old lady attempted to maintain her decorum. Not so a Tennessee gentleman, who "colored deep" and inquired with "great spirit": "What country may you call yours, sir?" Affecting a superior mien, the disgruntled Yankee replied that he hailed from the East. There, he continued, people knew how to eat and how to live. "I have not seen a bit of victuals fit to eat since I left," he snarled. "That is a great pity, sir," the Southerner icily observed. "But we, of this country, do not rate ourselves by eating: we rate ourselves by fighting. Would you like to take a shot?"[2]

Robert Hall would have applauded his neighbor's combative conduct. Southerners were touchy about their honor and demanded courtesy. A lawyer recalled that they responded to insults to honor and violations of courtesy with deadly force:

> The major part of criminal cases, except for misdemeanors, were for killing, or assaults with intent to kill. They were usually defended upon points of chivalry. The iron rules of British law were too tyrannical for free Americans, and too cold and unfeeling for the hot blood of the sunny south. They were denounced accordingly, and practically scouted from Mississippi judicature, on the broad ground that they were unsuited to the genius of American institutions and the American character.[3]

The Tennessee of Hall's youth was a violent locale, and he appeared to do everything in his power to keep it that way. Still in his teens, he did a stint as a flatboatman and fell in with a "hard set." On the inland waterways he learned to be quick with his wits and his fists. Hall recalled one "desperado by the name of Phelps," who crowed to anyone within the range of his voice that a "bowie knife was his looking glass, and a pistol shot was soothing to his soul." In the company of such rogues, Hall was party to several life-threatening scrapes.

Others were recreational in nature. On the old southwestern frontier two local toughs might fight it out simply to determine the "he-bull" of the neighborhood. These were no-holds-barred affairs—eye-gouging, ear-pulling, and nose-biting all fell within the bounds of accepted practice. One of the more memorable of these encounters was Hall's set-to with Louis Witherbry, a two-hundred-pounder regarded as "one of the most perfect specimens of physical manhood in the west." A number of Hall's friends were eager to pit him against "the giant," and a horserace provided the venue. Witherbry's brother approached Hall first, cursed him, and knocked him down. With that, Louis stepped in and invited Hall to strip down for a "fair fight." Hall described the encounter:

> The people were all greatly interested in the battle, and they formed a ring and appointed good men to see to fair play. We clinched and fell early in the fight. I instantly saw that I was the strongest man, and I determined never to let him up. He bit me badly on the lip, but I managed to get my arms around his body and I held him so that he could not move. I could not release my arms to strike him, and concluding that all strategy was fair in war, I used

my teeth. The doctors said that I bit nine pieces out of his back. He was yelling all the time like a Comanche in the fire, but I would not let him up until he shouted "'nough." Then the boys made a hero of me. They carried me on their shoulders all over the grounds, and the ladies clapped their hands and hurrahed for the "eighteen year old boy who had whipped the big bully."

Still, not all of his friends were miscreants. Hall savored fond memories of his acquaintance with Congressman Davy Crockett. The noted bear hunter and friend of the common man made a lasting impression on the youthful Hall, who cast his first vote for Crockett at the tender age of eighteen; recall that in his day the legal voting age was still twenty-one. "Of course it was wrong," Hall admitted in his dotage, "but I have never regretted it." The legislator was a true man of the people. "Crockett never missed a gathering of any kind," Hall reminisced. "He was always present at every frolic, log rolling, or house raising." He greatly admired Crockett's down-home manners and told how at a log rolling he witnessed the great man drink "his liquor out of a gourd."

Indeed, it may have been Crockett's example that inspired Hall to come to Texas. Bitter after losing reelection in 1835, the old bear hunter told his constituents that they could "go to hell and I will go to Texas." He left Memphis in November 1835 and visited old Tennessee friends and hunted buffalo in Texas before finally arriving in San Antonio de Béxar in February 1836. Reports of the fighting in Texas began to fire Hall's imagination about the same time that Crockett began his last adventure. But Hall did not travel to Texas with his hero, which was probably just as well. Crockett's visit did not conclude in the manner he would have wished. History does not record whether news of Crockett's death influenced the timing of his decision, but whatever his motivation, Hall joined a group of Kentucky volunteers bound for Texas in the spring of 1836.

Hall's 110-man company was typical of many American volunteer units that flocked to Texas to assist the Texians in their revolt against Mexican centralism. The Alabama Red Rovers, the New Orleans Greys, the Georgia Battalion, and others supplemented the ranks of the local revolutionaries and suffered more than their share of casualties. Indeed, a majority of those who died at the Alamo and the Goliad massacre were not the old contract colonists but recruits from the "old states," many of whom could count their time in Texas by the week. Like the twenty-two-year-old Hall, most of these young men were in search of a noble cause. Chicago resident J. H. Barnard served as surgeon with the rebel garrison at Goliad. As he explained it, he joined the Texians because theirs was a "cause that I had always been taught to consider sacred, viz.: Republican principles and popular institutions." An idealistic concern for the "cause"—and a readiness to die for it—frequently appears in the correspondence of these volunteers. In a letter to his brother, Kentucky volunteer Daniel W. Cloud expressed his dedication in the romantic vernacular common to the mid-1830s: "The cause of Philanthropy, of Humanity, of Liberty and human happiness throughout the world, called loudly on every man who can to aid Texas. . . . If we fail, death in the cause of liberty and humanity is not cause for shuddering."[4] One may only hope that such lofty sentiments comforted Cloud's family when they learned of his death at the Alamo.

Hall's dreams of glorious battle were to go unrealized—for the moment, anyway. By the time his unit arrived, the tiny rebel army had won the battle of San Jacinto, taken General Antonio López de Santa Anna prisoner, and was pursuing the retreating Mexican army beyond the Rio Grande. Hall and his comrades were crestfallen. Their spirits received a boost when in San Augustine they met General Sam Houston. Suffering from the ankle wound he had received at San Jacinto, he still managed to cut quite a figure. "He did all he could to encourage us," Hall recounted. "There is plenty of fine land in Texas," Houston assured the new arrivals, "and I hope to see you all have good homes." Hall and his comrades shared in that hope, but the general and other Texas leaders feared that another Mexican campaign was in the offing. The rebellion might be finished, but Texas still had need of soldiers.

On June 1, 1836, Hall joined the Army of the Republic, but his experience in ranks did not meet his expectations. A volunteer force, it embodied the same egalitarian values that characterized Texas society. General Thomas J. Rusk had the misfortune of commanding—no, that is too strong a word; rather, he had the misfortune of riding at the head of this armed mob. A citizen of the Republic left a colorful description of this headstrong rabble during the summer of 1836:

> Never was an army collected in which the spirit of combat was more supreme. Manhood and personal prowess were the standards of superiority among these men, and they followed their chosen leaders with a fidelity and reckless devotion that had neither stint nor measure. They would have marched unmurmuringly into the open jaws of death, rather than yield a point of pride, or their idea of honor. It was a handful that a soldier might have rejoiced to lead against a host. But they were without discipline, subordination, or effective organization, so that obedience was a mere matter of choice. Released from such necessary restraints, these fiery bands were easily stirred to turbulence and mutiny by the demagogues of the camp.[5]

Altogether they resembled more a pack of beggars than a unit of a regular army. Noah Smithwick, who served in the ranks with Hall, confirmed reports of discord and disorder. "General Rusk, had he been inclined to enforce strict military discipline, knew too well the disposition of the men to attempt it, so we were given, or took, the largest liberty possible to any kind of regulations." Any attempt to restrain these murderous brutes was not only exasperating but also hazardous. The sole officer who attempted to instill order "paid for the folly with his life." As Smithwick related the story, "There came up a violent thunderstorm one night, and when it was over the poor fellow, whose only offense was a little youthful vanity, was found in his tent with his brains blown out."[6]

The duties of a garrison soldier did not provide the thrill and glory for which Hall had traveled to Texas. Stationed at Camp Johnson on the Lavaca River, the Army of the Republic kept watch on the southern approaches that Mexican forces would have to employ during any march from the interior. The soldiers also spent much of their time appropriating the cattle of local Tejanos for the putative purpose of denying the enemy. This beef, of course, also provided a walking commissary for the Texian garrison. Rusk had mustered about two thousand volunteers in and around Camp Johnson. The great number of soldiers, however, contributed to Rusk's quandary. The bankrupt Republic solicited volunteers but could not supply them once they answered the bugler's call.

Hall suffered bitter memories of the tedium of camp food. "We were there nearly four months," he asserted, "and during all that time never saw a piece of bread." The cash-poor government fed its soldiers with one of the few commodities that Texas had in abundance: meat on the hoof. "We lived entirely on beef," Hall protested. Southern boys raised on buttermilk and cornbread found that this high-protein diet grew wearisome in short order. "The best of us," Hall avowed, "would have traded our interest in the fortune of the Lone Star Republic for a good big skillet of cornbread."

Notwithstanding the monotony of the chow and the dearth of activity, Hall insisted that the morale of his comrades remained high—that is, until disease struck the camp. The general lack of order that marked the Texas army extended to its sanitation standards. Ignorance allied to squalor proved a lethal combination. Dysentery, that dreaded blight of nineteenth-century armies, swept through the ranks. Hall recounted that with no proper coffins available, survivors wrapped the victims in blankets to be "laid away in the earth of that camp." He contracted dysentery and would have died if not for the careful attention of his messmate, Jack Bray. In his memoirs, Hall acknowledged his debt to this "old veteran" whose nursing had "saved my life." Following his stint in service, Hall lamented that he lost contact with Bray and "never knew what became of him."

The food, the inactivity, and the dysentery conspired to undercut morale. Hall expressed his discontent in no uncertain terms: "In the fall of 1836 we were all pretty well satisfied that there would be no more fighting. We had been living on beef alone for so long that the patriotism had begun to die out of us." Hall was still frail from his bout with dysentery and "awful sick of the inactivity and hardships of army life." He tried to finagle a medical discharge, but the camp surgeon refused to grant him one until Hall bribed him with a "fine pair of saddle bags." With his wangled discharge securely in hand, civilian Hall turned his back on the boredom and death of Camp Johnson.

At loose ends and with few prospects, Hall knocked about Texas for several months. He traveled to Columbia, the Republic's first capital. There he met several "noted" Texians and even the captive Santa Anna. After resting in Columbia, Hall determined to abandon Texas and go to Mississippi. While riding his Mexican mule through Montgomery County, however, he "fell in love with the country and concluded to settle there." During the summer of 1837, he brought in a "fine crop," but agricultural concerns did not entirely absorb his thoughts.

Hall discovered that "three of the prettiest girls in Texas" lived on a nearby farm and he resolved to claim one of them as his bride. During the Runaway Scrape of 1836, Colonel John King of Gonzales moved his daughters out of that endangered settlement to a more secure area in Montgomery County. A son, William P. King, had not joined them; he had gone with a Gonzales contingent to reinforce the Alamo and shared the fate of the garrison. Resplendent in his Sunday-go-to-meeting clothes, Hall brazenly rode out to the Colonel's Montgomery County residence where he first cast eyes upon Mary Minerva King. It was love at first site. Hall fell victim to "the beauty of Polly King," and the lady responded. In short order, the couple became engaged.

"The course of true love never did run smooth," the Bard affirmed. Colonel King, away while this young stranger was courting his daughter, had led a group of men back to Gonzales to survey the damage incurred during the Runaway Scrape. In March 1836, Houston's retreating forces had burned the town. Marauding Comanches had come in their wake and destroyed whatever the Texians missed. The settlers returned to wrecked cabins, ruined fields, and scattered cattle. Undeterred, King and his party began the task of rebuilding their home. They erected a fort against the Indians and planted a new crop for the future. Only after he had secured the homestead did Colonel King return to Montgomery County for his daughters. Before he arrived, however, John McGuffin, a rival for Polly's affections, met the Colonel en route and slandered Hall to his prospective father-in-law. According to McGuffin, Hall was already married and had abandoned his wife in the United States. The scheme worked to perfection and the wary father received Hall with an appreciable lack of enthusiasm. "I knew something was wrong," Hall recounted, "but, feeling conscious of my integrity and the purity of my motives, I concluded to be patient, and hoped to win the old man's approbation by brave, upright, and honorable conduct."

Hall soon had a chance to prove himself. During the summer of 1837 a Comanche war party raided into Grimes County and killed a Mrs. Taylor and her little girl. Ironically, Indians had slain Mrs. Taylor's husband the previous month. Residents of Montgomery County soon learned of the foray and sounded the call for volunteers to pursue the Indians. Hall answered the summons, but here his version of events fails to correspond with the historical record. According to Hall, the volunteers elected Colonel King to lead the expedition, but old settler and chronicler A. J. Sowell stated that the command fell upon Jerry Washam. The party trailed the Comanches until they found them near the confluence of the Brazos and Navasota Rivers. According to Hall, a "desperate affair" ensued wherein he "fought three Indians single handed, and making two bite the dust, he conquered the last one by breaking his neck with his fist." Sowell, however, insisted that the hostiles "scattered and it was impossible to follow them, so the pursuers commenced their return." Was there a skirmish, or not? Given Hall's penchant for self-aggrandizement, readers would probably be safer placing their bets on Sowell.

Hall maintained that it was his heroic conduct during this expedition that won King's consent. Following the clash (which may or may not have occurred), Hall recounted that the Colonel called him to his side.

"A brave man never lies," King declared. "Tell me the truth. Have you got a family back in the States?"

"Colonel," Hall is supposed to have replied, "I was never married in my life, nor did I ever love another girl but your daughter. If you will give her to me I will do everything in my power to make her a good husband."

"Give me your hand, my brave boy. I believe you will do it."

With her father's blessing, Robert married Polly on June 20, 1837; their union would last forty-five years. "I was the happiest man in the world," he exclaimed. "We were always happy together and never happy out of each other's sight. In our old age we did more courting than we did under the swinging moss on the old plantation when we were young and Polly's voice was full of sweeter notes than the mockingbirds in the trees."

Late in the autumn of 1837, Hall and his new father-in-law moved their families back to the desolate Gonzales. Although the threat of Mexican invasion had passed, Indian raids continued unabated. Comanche war parties swept down from their camps beyond the Balcones Escarpment to harry the isolated western settlements. Towns such as San Antonio, Bastrop, and Gonzales bore the brunt of these incursions. Hall was, nevertheless, eager to make a home for himself and his bride. For these people, fending off Indians was simply one of the chores of frontier life. "We built a little fort," Hall recounted, "and prepared to settle down."

It was touch-and-go that first year, and Robert bore painful memories of their "remarkable hardships." It especially hurt him to see his beloved Polly suffer want. By the time she was reduced to one old patched dress, he could bear it no longer. Ignoring Polly's protest, he determined to ride a hundred miles to buy her a new one. "The Indians were awfully bad that fall," he acknowledged, "but I could not bear to see my wife in rags." He made the trip in "a little more than two days," returning with two dresses, groceries, and "many other little things to please a woman's heart."

Eager to protect home and hearth, Hall joined Matthew "Old Paint" Caldwell's company of Rangers and served as second lieutenant. The Rangers were the only force upon whom frontier folks could rely. The Texas government was bankrupt; it possessed a bantam regular army but could ill afford to uniform, arm, and deploy it. Regulars, furthermore, proved all but useless against Indians. The times required an inexpensive partisan force that mustered in minutes, supplied its own mounts, provided for itself in the field, and required no fancy uniforms; in short: Texas Rangers.

In October 1838, Comanches raided Gonzales and abducted Matilda Lockhart and Mitchell Putnam's four children. Caldwell's Rangers pursued the warriors to their camp, but in the face of overpowering numbers could not rescue the captives. Even as an old man, Hall expressed frustration at being unable to effectively defend the females and youngsters: "It was a matter of great regret with the frontier settlers that we were not strong enough to fight the red devils who held the two young ladies and several children captive."

He was not, however, blinded by hatred. As Hall increased his skill as an Indian fighter, he carefully observed their customs and habits. He cultivated friendly tribes such as the Lipans and Tonkawas, who on several occasions proved to be useful allies against the implacable Comanches. Unlike many of the old Texians, Hall rejected the-only-good-Indian-is-a-dead-Indian bigotry and extolled the honesty, courage, and loyalty of the Lipans, whom he described as "the most faithful of allies and the most terrible of foes."

In August 1840, Gonzales residents received reports that an enormous Comanche raiding party had penetrated the settlements, and Caldwell's Rangers assembled to confront the marauders. Ranger Captain Ben McCulloch informed Caldwell that a column numbering some six hundred braves had attacked Victoria and cut down several citizens in the streets. Afterward, they fell on the tiny port settlement of Linnville where they again killed several men, kidnapped women, and burned the town to ashes. On August 11, Caldwell dispatched Hall and John Baker to scout the countryside to locate the enemy's position. After searching all night, the pair caught sight of the Comanche host and galloped back to Plum Creek to report the enemy's position. There on the banks of that shallow stream, contingents of the regular army, Rangers, and volunteer militia had gathered to cut off the Comanches' line of retreat.

Also present were some unlikely allies. Captain Edward Burleson arrived on the field with his Ranger company and his old friend Chief Placido with twelve of his Tonkawa braves. Placido had proven a trustworthy partner on several occasions. His Tonkawas loathed the Comanches as bitter tribal enemies and were eager to resume their ancestral strife. Unlike their antagonists, the Tonkawas were not horsemen. On the day before, Burleson had sent his brother Jonathan to summon the chief and his warriors. About ten o'clock that evening Placido set out toward Plum Creek, jogging alongside Jonathan's horse. The Tonkawas ran nonstop throughout the night, covering some thirty miles until they reached the rendezvous site the following morning. The Texians watched astounded as the "Tonks" readied for battle with no visible evidence of fatigue. Part of that preparation involved tying white handkerchiefs around their arms to identify themselves as "friendly" Indians in the coming melee.

General Felix Huston of the regular army assumed command of this disparate force. When Hall reported the Comanches' approach, the general dispatched him to take five men and "select a good position to make an attack."[7] Hall concealed his five-man squad, awaited the arrival of the enemy, and relished his memories of Polly. His reverie faded when the approach of between six hundred and one thousand Comanche warriors focused his attention solidly on the present. Even Texians who were there that day could not agree on the exact number of the enemy. Dead Comanches were easier to count than live ones. "They were on the prairie," Hall noted, "and the column looked to be seven miles long." He wondered what the day would bring or if, indeed, he would be alive to contemplate its sunset.

What he saw next demonstrated the destiny that awaited the unwary. "Here I witnessed a horrible sight. A captain and one man rode in among the Indians. The captain escaped, but I saw the Indians kill the private." Not wanting his men to suffer that fate, he ordered them to "keep a safe distance and pick off an Indian as the opportunity presented." He could not help but marvel at the appearance and the courage of the Comanches:

> It was one of the prettiest sights I ever saw in my life. The warriors flourished their white shields, and the young chiefs galloped about the field with the long tails streaming from their hats and hundreds of vari-colored ribbons floating in the air, exhibiting great bravado. Some of them dashed courageously very close to us, and two or three of them lost their lives in this foolhardy display of valor.

General Huston stood his ground as Hall and his men galloped back to the Texian line. Unwisely, the general opted to assume a defensive posture and receive the Comanche attack. If he had been fighting Europeans, that maneuver may have been prudent, given the enemy's numerical advantage. When fighting Indians, however, a bold charge usually won the day. The Comanches swarmed forward to assail the Texian line. While most of Huston's troopers remained dismounted, some thirty Rangers on horseback dashed among the Indians. One witness testified that they performed "personal heroism worthy of all praise."[8] Even so, the Rangers could not provide protection for the grounded militiamen, several of whom were wounded. According to the established tenets of Plains warfare, one man in each squad held the horses of the men in the firing line. These mounts offered splendid targets, and racing warriors brought them down like tethered cattle. This one-sided affair had lasted about thirty minutes when the Ranger captains implored Huston to allow them to mount and countercharge. They explained that while their men remained dismounted, the enemy was free to exploit his superior mobility. Still, Huston stubbornly maintained his defensive position.

Comanche arrows found their marks, but so, too, did the Texian rifles. When a chief wearing a "tremendous headdress" fell to accurate rifle fire, his mourning warriors "set up a peculiar howl." Ranger captains recognized an opportunity in their adversaries' sudden demoralization. Almost apoplectic with rage, Caldwell shouted into Huston's face: "Now, General, is your time to charge them! They are whipped!"[9] Without waiting for orders, the captains ordered their companies to mount and led them in a spirited rush. Astride their mustangs, Rangers could match Comanche mobility and bring their deadlier firepower to bear. In a sprawling melee the official chain of command became less important than the proven leadership of each troop captain.

Giving full vent to their frenzy, Hall and his fellow Rangers charged "howling like wolves." The herd of captured horses, perhaps as many as two thousand head, stampeded and raised dust "so thick that the parties could see each other but a short distance." The Comanches, checked by their mass, could not maneuver. "Our boys charged with a yell," Hall remembered, "and did not fire until they got close to the enemy." Cramped warriors were unable to break free from the throng; Rangers darted along the perimeter. Only then, where they could not miss, did the Rangers open fire. They gunned down as many as fifteen amid the swirling press of warriors and ponies.

It was at this point that Hall felt a thudding blow to his leg. "Just as we rode against them I received a bullet in the thigh," he recorded. The wound was serious, and his blood flowed until "it sloshed out of my boots." Succumbing to loss of blood, he tumbled off his horse and lay in the dust in danger of being trampled. "After a moment I felt better," he recounted, "and made an effort to rejoin the line." Then, disoriented by his wound and the fog of battle, Hall came face to face with an Indian and was about to shoot him when the brave threw up his hands and shouted, "Tonkawa!" Notwithstanding his white handkerchief insignia, this Tonkawa warrior had almost fallen victim to friendly fire. Hall had just fallen into line when a Comanche dashed toward Dr. Alonso Sweitzer. "I fired right into his face and knocked him off his horse," Hall reported, "but did not kill him." He was perturbed that the warrior escaped with his life but took some consolation in appropriating the "fine hat he had stolen" at Linnville.

Caldwell had been right after all: the Comanches would not stand against a determined charge and superior firepower. "The Indians scattered," General Huston reported, "mostly abandoning their horses and taking to the thickets."[10] A running fifteen-mile pursuit ensued as Rangers chased fleeing Indians as far as the present locations of San Marcos and Kyle. Once there, the tribesmen reached the hilly region of the Edwards Plateau and relative safety.

Toward sundown, Ranger detachments returned to the site of the initial engagement near Plum Creek and found the rest of the Texian army sifting through discarded Comanche possessions. These included items of almost every description: bags of silver, bolts of cloth, kegs of liquor, cases of books, full suits of clothing, pouches of tobacco—even a number of live baby alligators that warriors had stashed in saddlebags to convince folks back in the Comanchería that they had raided all the way to the coast. "We hardly knew what to do with all this stuff," Hall reminisced, "and we finally concluded to divide it among ourselves."

The horrific events of August 12, 1840, branded themselves on Hall's memory, but it was during the aftermath of battle that he witnessed a bizarre episode. The Tonkawa contingent had not eaten in almost twenty-four hours and now they prepared a ritual feast. Amid much singing and dancing, they produced the corpse of one of the despised Comanches. Then, as the nauseated Texians watched, they "cut him into slices and broiled him on sticks." A brave offered a "slice of Comanche" to the wounded Hall. "I was very hungry," he later admitted, "but not sufficiently so to become a cannibal."

Suffering the painful effects of his thigh wound, Hall could not travel back to Polly as quickly as he would have liked. He asked his father-in-law, Colonel King, to hurry back to Gonzales. Since Hall was unable to wear his boots, the Colonel was kind enough to carry them home. Her father told Polly that Hall would return in a matter of days, but then she discovered her husband's boots—still full of dried blood. Polly became hysterical. Her father now had to tell her the full truth but insisted that Robert was only "slightly wounded." Despite her father's reassurance, Polly believed the worst. Finally, she caught a glimpse of a bedraggled figure limping toward their cabin. "When she saw me walking home she ran to meet me," Hall related, "and declared that she never intended to let me go to fight Indians any more."

Despite Polly's good intentions, she should have known that her Robert would never remain safe at home if a good fight were to be had. And during the bellicose decade of the Texas Republic, conflicts were always likely. Texians faced threats not only from hostile Indians but also from Mexican soldiers. These concerns were especially vexing for Polly and the other Texas ladies:

> It is a great wonder that the women were willing to stay in a wilderness where they were at any time liable to be murdered by Mexicans or tortured at the stake by merciless Indians. No pen will ever be able to do justice to the courage, patriotism, and devotion of the women who stood by their brothers, fathers, husbands, and sweethearts while they were repelling the Mexicans, destroying the Indians, killing the snakes, and building the roads in the wilderness of Texas.

Although the United States, Great Britain, and France had all recognized Texas independence, Mexicans still claimed their former province. Their agents attempted to incite Texas Indians against the infant Republic, and fears of these efforts resulted in President Mirabeau B. Lamar's rout of Chief Philip Bowles and the Cherokees in 1839. Lamar also suspected Mexican intrigue in the Great Comanche Raid of 1840. In the wake of Plum Creek, apprehension and anger smoldered between the rival republics.

Then in 1842 the Mexican army demonstrated that it could do more than provoke the local Indians. That year witnessed two Mexican forays across the Rio Grande: General Rafael Vásquez's in March and General Adrian Woll's in September. Officials in Mexico City trusted that these incursions would be enough to keep their claims of Texas possession alive and frustrate annexation discussions. As it turned out, however, they were also a clarion call to enraged Texian settlers such as Old Paint Caldwell, John C. "Jack" Hays, and Robert Hall.

When news reached Gonzales that French soldier of fortune Adrian Woll had occupied San Antonio de Béxar with fifteen hundred Mexican troops, some two hundred volunteers mustered at Cibolo Creek above Seguin to repel the invasion. "Capt. Caldwell himself came to my house after me," Hall crowed. "Our commander, Old Paint Caldwell, was equal to a thousand men," he maintained. "No man who ever stood on Texas soil was his equal in battle. As soon as the bullets began to whistle he seemed to grow taller and look grander." Departing Cibolo Creek, Caldwell led his unit to a point about six miles east of Béxar on Salado Creek. On September 18, Caldwell dispatched Hays and a company of Rangers to lure Woll out of the town. Old Paint intended to fight the Mexicans on his ground, not theirs. The French-born general responded to this bold challenge; one observer overheard him brag that he "would go in person and drive the Texian wolves from the bushes." [11] At the head of between four and five hundred cavalrymen, Woll pursued Hays's Rangers toward the timbered site along Salado Creek. There, Caldwell waited to spring his trap.

The crafty Woll, however, refused to be snared. He ordered his vanguard advance to reconnoiter and they engaged their antagonists in a desultory firefight. Caldwell had lost any chance for surprise; there would be no ambush this day. Woll brought up his main force and concentrated his artillery, infantry, and cavalry for several carefully planned assaults on the Texian position. Hall remembered how the "Mexican infantry and artillery advanced and took up a position on a slight elevation." As the Mexican ranks came within range, heavy firing erupted all along the Texian line. Ensconced in thick woods, the Texians felt relatively secure from the effects of enemy fire. To his consternation, however, Hall discovered that the timber provided scant shelter against the effects of concentrated artillery. "The tree I first picked out to protect me," he groused, "was shot entirely off by a cannon shot." That was only one of the day's incidents. He also remembered the actions of one of the Texian riflemen, Parson Carroll. Every time the Methodist preacher's bullet found his mark, he shouted: "God take your soul!" Caldwell dispatched Hall down Salado Creek to watch for enemy attempts to flank the Texians. He took position in a tree and dropped an enemy soldier who was slipping up on one of his comrades.

Woll continued to hurl his *soldados* against murderous fire, but they could not drive the Texians from the dense woods. As Hall told it, "We killed and wounded a great many of the enemy when they made the general advance." It was a classic tactical standoff. The superior range and accuracy of the Texian long rifles made it impossible for Woll's troops to approach close enough to bring their superior numbers to bear; the Texians' numerical inferiority made it impossible for them to abandon their defenses.

Woll perceived the dilemma. He dispatched Tejano loyalist Vicente Córdova on a wide sweep around Caldwell's flank. Hall reported that Córdova's detachment, composed primarily of Cherokee Indians, "advanced upon us along a ravine that intersected the creek." Alerted now to the threat to his flank, Caldwell shifted his forces to meet it. The enemy's cavalry, infantry, and artillery advanced within forty yards of the Texian flank, but "our boys stood firm," Hall boasted. Heavy Texian fire soon checked Córdova's movements. The Mexicans in this assault group charged manfully but suffered many casualties, among them their commander. Texian rifleman "Willis Randall shot and killed Old Cordova," Hall recounted.

As long shadows fell across the field late that afternoon, General Woll broke off the battle and retired into San Antonio. He had suffered about sixty men killed, and an indeterminate number received serious wounds. The Texian losses in the principal engagement were one man killed and nine to twelve wounded. Caldwell's men soon learned, however, that thirty-six of their comrades lay dead on another part of the battlefield.

Nicholas Mosby Dawson had raised a company of fifty-three Fayette County volunteers to resist Woll's foray. Departing La Grange on September 16, they arrived on the outskirts of Béxar on September 18, just in time for the battle. Dawson's men could hear the din and marched to the sound of the guns. They had reached a point about 1.5 miles from Caldwell's position when five hundred irregular Mexican cavalrymen attacked them. Dawson's company took cover in a mesquite thicket and unleashed an intense fusillade. The Mexican cavalry withdrew beyond rifle range but remained on the field. When Woll brought up his artillery, the Texians found themselves in a lamentable dilemma. If they abandoned the mesquite grove, Mexican horsemen would ride them down with lances; if they remained in place, canister shot from the enemy's cannon would rip them to shreds. Dawson had lost about half of his unit to the cannonade when he attempted to surrender. Some of his men refused to quit shooting, however, and the Mexicans gunned him down. By the time the firing stopped, the Mexicans had killed thirty-five Texians, including Dawson. They took fifteen prisoners, five of whom were wounded. Only two of the Fayette County men escaped to tell the tale. Of the fifteen prisoners, only nine survived captivity. Texians would ever remember the episode as Dawson's Massacre.

Back along Salado Creek, Caldwell's men heard firing in the distance but knew nothing of Dawson's predicament. "We heard the rattle of musketry and cannon east of us," Hall remarked. "We could not imagine what was going on. We afterwards learned that Capt. Dawson . . . was trying to cut his way through the Mexican lines. The world knows the story: They were all massacred."

After the battle along Salado Creek, Woll abandoned Béxar and retreated toward the Rio Grande. Hall joined in the pursuit that proved fruitless. As it did on so many occasions, dissension and discord hamstrung Texian efforts. "Our officers constantly differed with each other,"

Hall carped, "and many wanted to play the general; consequently Gen. Woll marched away from us." For once, Hall's appraisal was not exaggerated. Other Texians on the pursuit also expressed frustration and disgust at Caldwell's inability—or unwillingness—to engage the retreating Woll. Mary Maverick of San Antonio recorded the degree of Captain Hays's distress:

> Hays' gallant spirit was wounded by this unaccountable and ignominious scene and his feelings found utterance in tears—yes, tears of shame and rage. The Texan army at last came forward, but it was too late, the enemy had escaped. The Texans were so disgusted and mortified that all discipline was lost and they returned in angry and humiliated squads to San Antonio.[12]

Incidents such as the Vásquez and Woll raids, along with the luckless Mier Expedition that followed, persuaded many Texians that their only hope for a secure future lay in annexation to the United States. President Sam Houston redoubled his efforts to join Texas to the "old states," but numerous hurdles remained. On June 8, 1844, U.S. President John Tyler brought an annexation treaty to a vote on the Senate floor. Massachusetts's senator John Quincy Adams led a New England faction that soundly defeated the measure. Adams and his northeastern allies would go to any lengths to keep another slave state out of the Union.

In the United States, however, a new mood was sweeping the nation. The allure of Manifest Destiny greatly influenced the presidential election of 1844. Democrat James K. Polk was the only candidate who was forthright in his support of expansion and the annexation of Texas. With his victory at the polls, events unfolded quickly. Tyler, the lame duck president, wished to seize the moment and achieve annexation on his watch. Learning from his earlier mistake, he sought admission this time by joint resolution of Congress, not by treaty—a tactic that required a simple majority instead of a two-thirds vote in the Senate. The House endorsed the annexation proposal on January 25, 1845; the Senate followed suit on February 26. Following a long and rancorous process, Tyler affixed his signature to the resolution and dispatched it to Texas. The pro-annexation forces had cleared the path for admission. All that remained was acceptance of the offer.

Meeting in Austin on July 4, Texas delegates overwhelmingly approved Tyler's annexation resolution. On December 29, 1845, President Polk signed the bill of formal admission, but Republic officials were to remain in office until February. On February 19, 1846, Anson Jones, the last president of the Texas Republic, transferred control of the government to Governor James Pinkney Henderson. With that move, President Jones hauled down the Lone Star flag and hauled up the Stars and Stripes. This act heralded the death of a sovereign nation but the birth of a sovereign state.

Most Texians exulted in their new status, but for a few old-timers the dream of Texas nationalism died hard. Mary Maverick spoke for the majority: "Thank God, we are now annexed to the United States, and can hope for home and quiet."[13] But Texas statehood brought with it only more conflict. Hall later fought with General Zachary Taylor in the Mexican War and, while other men his age remained by their hearths, he also fought for the Confederacy. After the Civil War, he raised his children and cattle. In 1880 he buried Polly, his life's partner. Hall spent his declining years living with his children in Cotulla, surrounded by grandchildren and respected by the community. In 1898 he printed his memoirs. On December 19, 1899, at eighty-five years of age, he joined his beloved Polly in death. As he looked back on his life, Robert regarded the years of the Texas Republic as his happiest and viewed statehood as a mistake. He spoke for many old warriors of his generation: "I was opposed to annexation, and voted first, last, and all time for the Lone Star."

Notes

1. Except where noted, all quotations are from "Brazos," *Life of Robert Hall*, intro. by Stephen L. Hardin (1898; reprint, Austin: State House Press, 1992).

2. Grady McWhiney, *Cracker Culture: Celtic Ways in the Old South* (Tuscaloosa: University of Alabama Press, 1988), 95.

3. Joseph G. Baldwin, *The Flush Times of Alabama and Mississippi: A Series of Sketches*, intro. and notes by James H. Justus (1853; reprint, Baton Rouge: Louisiana State University Press, 1987), 58–59.

4. Hobart Huson, ed., *Dr. J. H. Barnard's Journal: A composite of known versions of the Journal of Dr. Joseph H. Barnard, one of the surgeons of Fannin's regiment, covering the period from December, 1835 to June 5, 1836* (Goliad, TX: privately printed, 1949), 1.

5. William Preston Johnson, *The Life of Gen. Albert Sidney Johnson, Embracing His Services in the Armies of the United States, the Republic of Texas, and the Confederate States*, new intro. by T. Michael Parrish (1879; reprint, New York: Da Capo Press, 1997), 70.

6. Noah Smithwick, *Evolution of a State: or, Reminiscences of Old Texas Days* (1900; reprint, Austin: University of Texas Press, 1983), 101–3.

7. John Henry Brown, *Indian Wars and Pioneers of Texas* (1890; reprint, Austin: Statehouse Press, 1988), 81.

8. Ibid., 82.

9. Ibid.

10. Huston report, *Austin City Gazette*, August 19, 1840.

11. Joseph Milton Nance, *Attack and Counter-Attack: The Texas-Mexican Frontier, 1842* (Austin: University of Texas Press, 1964), 361.

12. Mary Maverick, *Memoirs of Mary A. Maverick*, ed. by Rena Maverick Green, intro. by Sandra L. Myres (1921; reprint, Lincoln: University of Nebraska Press, 1989), 83.

13. Ibid., 69–70.

Suggested Readings

Brown, John Henry. *Indian Wars and Pioneers of Texas*. 1890; reprint, Austin, 1988.

McWhiney, Grady. *Cracker Culture: Celtic Ways in the Old South*. Tuscaloosa, AL, 1988.

Nance, Joseph Milton. *Attack and Counter-Attack: The Texas-Mexican Frontier, 1842*. Austin, 1964.

Smithwick, Noah. *Evolution of a State: or, Reminiscences of Old Texas Days*. 1900; reprint, Austin, 1983.

Sowell, A. J. *Early Settlers and Indian Fighters of Southwest Texas*. 1900; reprint, Austin, 1986.

Wilbarger, J. W. *Indian Depredations in Texas*. 1889; reprint, Austin, 1995.

4

Louis T. Wigfall
"Just Plain Mean"

Dallas Cothrum

During the Civil War era, the South produced a breed of politicians called "fire-eaters" for their vitriolic defense of that section's way of life and their advocacy of secession from the Union. Louis T. Wigfall, a South Carolina-born U.S. senator from Texas, asserted himself at the fore of that divisive delegation. Typical of his fellow fire-eaters, Wigfall displayed an impulsive, combative temperament whose political legacy reflected few accomplishments. In its place was a record of obstructing any effort at compromise and progress. As a young man, Wigfall achieved some success as an attorney in his home state and determined to gain public office. But soon a series of fistfights and duels with opponents exhausted his political capital there. Retreating to Texas, he found a more forgiving climate and soon began denouncing Sam Houston's efforts to keep the state tied to the Union. His views struck a chord with Texans, who sent him to Washington. When the war began, Wigfall served briefly as brigadier general before winning a seat in the Confederate congress. Yet, once more, his divisive presence disrupted the workings of government, and the rubble of a vanquished South served as his only monument.

Dallas Cothrum is professor of history at the University of Texas at Tyler and author of the forthcoming Civil War biography, *Jo Shelby: Reluctant Guerrilla.*

When an intense Confederate bombardment on April 12, 1861, caused the American flag flying above Fort Sumter to topple, a powerfully built and brave Southerner seized the opportunity to return triumphantly to his home state of South Carolina. Even as artillery fire from the Confederate battery on Fort Moultrie continued to rage in Charleston Harbor, Louis Trezevant Wigfall, then a U.S. senator from Texas, commandeered a small skiff. Ignoring the pleas of his comrades, he embarked on an unauthorized mission. While three African-American oarsmen and the craft's pilot cautiously picked their way through the mayhem, Wigfall remained undaunted. Even the explosion of a thirty-two-pound ball within a few feet of the skiff failed to avert his attention from accomplishing his mission and making an enduring

name for himself. Upon reaching Fort Sumter, he found an open port-
hole on the town side of the fort and entered the Federal installation.
The confident Rebel, dressed in a blue coat, a red silk sash, and formidable spurs, sported a handkerchief tied to his sword and defiantly asked
an astonished officer to take him to Major Robert Anderson, the fort's
commander. The officer complied. After negotiating the surrender of
the fort, Wigfall returned to the boat, and the crew rowed him back to
Charleston where he received a triumphant welcome.

His journey to Sumter completed a lifelong quest to drive the South
out of the Union and establish a separate Southern nation. The mission
also distinguished him as the most celebrated fire-eater in the Confederacy. Historian U. B. Phillips concluded that fire-eaters differed from
fellow politicians by their consistent and determined advocacy of Southern independence. In defending these extremists, he maintained that
they turned to secession only after persistent antislavery agitation from
Northerners. Further, these leaders asserted that the liberty of citizens
had been abused by the continual usurpation of power by Washington.
As a result, they sought to foment a revolution against politics and return the South to the principles of eighteenth-century limited government. Fire-eaters planned to transform political behavior by ending
corruption and partisanship and returning to the purified form of re-
publicanism originally envisioned by the Founding Fathers.

A less apologetic analysis reveals that their historical significance
rests with their ability to successfully persuade moderates that secession
was the best and only course of action. Fire-eaters capitalized on the
turmoil of the 1850s, the election of Abraham Lincoln in 1860, and the
rise of the Republican Party to influence Southerners to follow their
bombastic exhortations. These individuals promoted states' rights and
the protection of slavery, even at the expense of the individual liberty of
citizens. They argued that slavery benefited society and threatened that
its elimination would break apart the Union. Wigfall, like all fire-
eaters, confidently proclaimed the viability of a Southern republic without offering a detailed plan for how it would operate. Ultimately, the
extremists proved incapable of governing amid the tempest that they
had created. Instead of promoting Confederate nationalism and protecting their state, the fire-eaters, and Wigfall in particular, turned to
criticism and undermined the government's ability to wage war.

These champions of states' rights neglected the interests of their
states in order to create a new nation. Throughout his political career,
Wigfall neglected his obligations to Texas—a serious problem for a pur-

ported states' rights advocate. He concentrated, instead, on removing the entire South from the nation and setting up a new government. In the process of driving Texas from the Union, he made the state into something it was not—a part of the Old South.

A tendency toward recklessness and selfishness marked Wigfall's youth. Born into a leading family in Edgefield, South Carolina, on April 20, 1816, he enjoyed the comforts of an upper-class lifestyle in his earliest years. His father had succeeded as a merchant in Charleston before becoming a planter. His mother, Eliza Trezevant, was descended from one of the state's oldest and most respected families, thus ensuring her son a place of importance in a society ruled by a well-accepted hierarchy. The loss of both parents by age thirteen, however, changed his aristocratic and privileged life. Denied the social standing and considerable influence of his parents, Wigfall was forced to use his own abilities as well as his good name to gain entrance into South Carolina's elite circle of power. Still, the advantages of a substantial inheritance and a devoted guardian provided him with a proper upbringing.

During Wigfall's youth, the U.S. government focused its considerable might against his home state. In 1828 the "tariff of abominations" shattered the harmony between Columbia and Washington. The teenager witnessed South Carolina's defiance of federal power and its outspoken advocacy of states' rights. Southern spokesmen, led by John C. Calhoun, hurled bombastic diatribes against Congress, arguing that the tariff protected Northern industry at the expense of the South. Calhoun argued that the states were supremely sovereign because they had ratified the Constitution. Therefore, state governments could nullify, or void, a federal law that they believed was unjust or injurious to its citizens.

Wigfall and his relatives concurred with the extremist views of Calhoun. His older brother Arthur, the editor of the Edgefield newspaper, unequivocally supported nullification. More important, his cousin James Hamilton served as South Carolina's governor during the crisis. While a compromise tariff ended the standoff in 1833, Wigfall continued to follow Calhoun's philosophy and promoted the doctrine of states' rights. While most Jacksonians were enjoying an unsurpassed flowering of American democracy, innovation, and experimentation, Wigfall reached maturity in South Carolina's tempest of sectional conflict that charted the course of Southern independence.

During his youth, academics failed to captivate Wigfall's attention as much as politics. The South Carolinian briefly attended the University of Virginia, where he distinguished himself only by being expelled after challenging a classmate to a duel. He returned home to complete his degree at South Carolina College and graduated in 1837. His service in the Seminole War developed his interest in the military which, in his estimation, would give him enough expertise to criticize Jefferson Davis's strategies during the Civil War. In 1839, Wigfall went back to Edgefield intending to practice law. The new attorney struggled and found himself with a substantial debt due to his penchant for gambling and liquor. In 1841 his economic circumstances improved when he borrowed money from his bride-to-be, a second cousin, and settled his debts. Following his marriage, Wigfall pledged that "wine and women have lost their charms for me. Ambition shall be my mistress and Law my liquor." While he displayed remarkable ambition, it would be in politics, rather than the law.[1]

Wigfall's erratic behavior thwarted his desire for public office and eventually forced him to leave the state. In 1840 he engaged in a fight with Preston Brooks, a leading South Carolina politician from a rival faction, and then challenged him to a duel. Colleagues interceded, but the two hotheads held an intense animosity for one another. Each man continued to ridicule the other until Brooks's father, in his son's absence, published a vitriolic attack against Wigfall. In typical fashion, Wigfall responded by challenging the man to a duel. Though rebuffed in his effort, Wigfall posted placards around town denouncing him. During the process, he witnessed a Brooks family friend attempting to remove the placard and, taking cool and deliberate aim, mortally wounded the man. Another Brooks supporter at the scene called Wigfall a cold-blooded murderous scoundrel. He, of course, challenged that man to a duel. Neither party was injured in the incident, but the situation remained unresolved until Preston Brooks returned home and demanded satisfaction. The meeting on a Savannah River island resulted in Brooks striking Wigfall in the thigh and then sustaining a serious injury to his hip. The two wounded men allowed a board of honor to settle the conflict. Although the board's decision appeared to favor Wigfall, he remained unsatisfied. "I can stand any thing," he moaned, "but being told that my honor is as good as Preston Brooks'."[2]

The incident proved significant for both parties. Critics called Wigfall bloodthirsty and a savage murderer who used a code of honor to justify his reckless actions. He later confirmed the opinion: "Blood is a very common fluid. It is worth very little. A man is killed, it does not matter much; it is really a matter of small consequence to him, to his family, or to the country." One Carolinian labeled him wholly unprincipled and treacherous to the last degree. In a five-month period, Wigfall had taken part in a fistfight, three near-duels, two duels, and one shooting: one man was dead and two were wounded, including Wigfall. His image had been ruined as well as his political prospects. Already a member of a less powerful faction in state politics, he was deserted by his friends. Brooks, however, fared better despite the fact that the wound required him to use a cane for the remainder of his life. (He later would gain great favor as a champion of Southern nationalism and honor when he used his cane to beat fellow congressman Charles Sumner nearly to death.)[3]

Wigfall moved to Texas in 1846 in an effort to remake himself and shed his reputation for violence, drunkenness, and insolvency. Only his political rivals brought up his questionable past. Texans overlooked his personal shortcomings because many men had moved to the state with tarnished reputations. This dramatic movement from 1836 to the beginning of the Civil War radically changed Texas as the population more than quadrupled to over 600,000 residents. Most of the influx resulted from migration out of Southern states. These individuals brought with them a strong commitment to the values of the Old South, including states' rights and slavery. Not surprisingly, Texas moved away from the heritage of independence that was the legacy of the Republic and fell in line with that of the South.

Wigfall embodied the staunchest beliefs of the Democratic Party, including states' rights, slavery, white supremacy, low tariffs, and secession. Like many recently arrived citizens in Texas, he maintained that Texas was a Southern state little different from South Carolina or Mississippi. In the process, Wigfall moved Texas away from its heritage as a unique region. He was a product of the South and was committed to protecting the region, even at the expense of his new state.

He arrived in Marshall (after briefly residing in Nacogdoches), the county seat for Harrison, and established a law practice with Judge William B. Ochiltree. Harrison had more slaves than any other county and was among the wealthiest in the state, making the area decidedly similar to the Old South. Wigfall fit in perfectly in the town and earned a reputation as an excellent attorney, a talented speaker, and a promising politician. A dark side lurked, however, recalled one observer; he was a desperate man—a tyrant at heart, yet a man of wonderful ability. How strange that such a mind should be combined with such a heart! Despite his peculiarities he represented Harrison County at a convention to organize the Democratic Party in Texas. He emerged as the leader

of the Southern Rights Democrats who decried the abuse of power by
the federal government. The county approved of his actions and elected
him to the lower house of the Texas legislature in 1850.[4]

Quickly, Wigfall distanced himself from other Democrats. Defying
conventional wisdom and practical advice, he launched a withering attack against Sam Houston. Throughout the 1850s he derided the Old
Hero's actions and depicted him as a traitor to his region. He objected
to Houston's stance on both the Compromise of 1850 and the Kansas-
Nebraska Act, charging that Houston was sacrificing the best interests
of the South to his desire to become president. In reality, Houston's
concerns rested with ending the problem of sectionalism and alleviat-
ing Texas's severe economic distress. Houston's actions in the Senate
eliminated the debt incurred during the revolution and Republic periods and settled the boundary for the state. Despite his accomplishments
in the national government, Houston left the Senate in 1857 to return
home and run for governor, hoping to end the spread of sectionalism.

Wigfall greatly aided Hardin Runnels, a newcomer from Mississippi, in the gubernatorial race, demonstrating that he could match
Houston's considerable speaking skills. Since the Old Hero would not
debate him, Wigfall resorted to following him around the state and coun-
tering his arguments. He emphasized that Houston had not protected
the expansion of slavery and preferred Washington to Texas. Such criticism irritated Houston, who called him "a murderer named Wiggletail"
who had wiggled out of trouble in South Carolina. One spectator agreed
as Wigfall was attacked at Linden and noted: "He was as usual [attack-
ing] Sam Houston, when one of the *sovereigns* present remembered that
he had served in Wars with Sam Houston, and would not have him
[Houston] abused—and suiting the action to his words knocked Wigfall
down with a single blow, and jumping on him, gave him a drubbing
before the bystanders could interfere." The witness concluded, "I am
rather a Quaker in feeling and don't like violence—but really I cannot
think it misapplied in this case." While Wigfall's tactics outraged some
people, his efforts helped Runnels win the election. Wigfall also emerged
with a reputation as the leading Democrat in the state. Although Houston would overcome Runnels two years later, extremism had seized
Texas.[5]

In 1859 the state legislature selected Wigfall for the U.S. Senate.
Upon hearing of Wigfall's election, Houston remarked, "Thank God
this country is so great and strong, it can bear even that." His election
signaled that many Texans, shocked by John Brown's raid at Harper's

Ferry, were determined to send to Washington "the most violent partisan in the state," according to Judge O. M. Roberts.[6] On his arrival in the Capital, Wigfall ignored the tradition of freshmen senators not participating in discussion. Instead, he seized every opportunity to demonstrate his commitment to protecting Southern interests. He maintained that the slave trade must be reopened so that Africans could experience the benefits of slavery. Like many proponents of the "positive good" school, Wigfall contended that slaves were well cared for and would benefit from the influence of Christianity. He also argued that interference with private property, including slaves, was morally unjust. His actions led many members of Congress to conclude incorrectly that Texas differed little from the other states of the Old South, although it had fewer slaves than any of the other states in the region and was not as devoted to plantation-style agriculture. Wigfall, however, remained committed to protecting the lifestyle that he had witnessed in South Carolina, even if it did not benefit the Texans.

Contrary to the opinion of many plain folk in Texas and other parts of the South, Wigfall opposed the Homestead Act proposed by Tennessee's Andrew Johnson, claiming that the allotted 160 acres was too small to be agriculturally productive. Wigfall realized that the measure eliminated plantations by aiding the common man. Like most fire-eaters, he represented the interests of the large land and slave owners over those of the common person. He commented that while the legislation would provide land for the landless and a home for the homeless, it would not provide slaves for the slaveless. Wigfall believed that slavery defined the South and created a sound economy, culture, and superior lifestyle, and he protected the institution at all costs. He completed his alienation from Johnson, his Southern colleague, saying, "Now let the Senator from Tennessee put that in his pipe and smoke it."[7] Not surprisingly, such arguments outraged Northerners and demonstrated Wigfall's renegade tendencies and his inability to cooperate.

Like Calhoun had done previously in the Senate, Wigfall proclaimed the supremacy of the states. He maintained that they were thirty-three separate nations that had confederated and could leave the Union at any time. In one speech he threatened: "If this government does not suit us, we will leave it." He further warned that "disunion is imminent if a Republican is elected." Wigfall realized that his rhetoric would have no impact on his Northern colleagues. Instead, he merely hoped to widen the gap between the regions and hasten secession. He complained of Northerners: "You denounce us, degrade us, deride us, tell us we shall

live under a Government that we say is not tasteful to us; you tell us that
we are degraded, that we are not your equals." Wigfall also objected to
attempts to block secession. He explained: "When we say to you, if we
cannot live together in peace, we will separate, you say we shall not; and
then, because I do not choose to make a ninny of myself . . . I am
charged with conspiracy . . . to dissolve the Union." Like his fellow fire-
eaters, Wigfall viewed the task of destroying the Union not as a conspiracy but as a sacred duty. He refused to accept an inferior status and
vowed to secede from the Union: "I would burst it; I would fracture it,
splinter it into more fragments than gunpowder would blow glass."[8]

Wigfall went about his task of breaking apart the Union with great
zeal. Rather than limiting debate to the Senate, he engaged colleagues
in hotels and bars and bullied them. Often these politicians conceded
the point to him, not wishing to risk his famous temper. He returned
again and again to the theme that the South already existed as a separate
and unique region and that it was natural for its citizens to finalize their
differences by leaving the Union. He explained to an English traveler:
"We are a peculiar people, sir!" He continued his dissertation on Southern exceptionalism with the argument that the British came by their
knowledge only from Northern writers and newspapers and had received
inaccurate information regarding the South. He depicted a politically
idyllic region devoid of parties and partisanship. He continued: "We
have no press—we are glad of it. We do not require a press because we
go out and discuss all public questions from the stump with our people."
However, in actuality, the South had widely divergent political philoso-
phies and an active and outspoken press.[9]

Wigfall also staunchly defended the region's lack of manufacturing.
"We are an agricultural people; we are a primitive but civilized people.
We have no cities—we don't want them," he told the traveler. The Texan
confidently espoused what would become the foreign policy for the
Confederacy:

> We have no commercial marine—no navy—we don't want them. Your ships
> carry our produce, and you can protect your own vessels. We want no manu-
> facturers: we desire no trading, no mechanical or manufacturing classes. As
> long as we have our rice, our sugar, our tobacco, and our cotton, we can
> command wealth to purchase all we want from those nations with which we
> are in amity, and lay up our money besides.

Wigfall's optimistic, but naive, analysis of Confederate foreign policy
rested on the assumption that Southern cotton and agricultural products fueled the world economy. King Cotton diplomacy, however, failed

as British textile manufacturers imported a surplus of raw cotton in anticipation of the Civil War as well as found new sources of the crop within their empire. Wigfall's championing of an early nineteenth-century lifestyle based on agriculture ignored the realities of industrialization and typified the lack of pragmatic analysis on the part of the fire-eaters.[10]

Focusing his concerns on disunion and sectionalism left Wigfall no time to work on remedying problems in the state. Unlike Sam Houston, Wigfall expended little effort to solve the problems of Indian attacks on the frontier. His South Carolina background and home in East Texas did not provide him with any knowledge of Indian matters; and, like many people who had not experienced this conflict, Wigfall chose not to consider the topic. In representing Texas, he rarely looked to the West. Instead, he attempted to link the state to the Old South, contenting himself that the frontier period had long since passed. He failed in that endeavor as well.

His efforts to extend the Southern Pacific Railroad into Texas proved unsuccessful and helped to keep the state isolated from the Confederacy throughout the war. The lack of railroads prevented the rapid movement of troops and supplies from Texas to threatened areas in Louisiana, Arkansas, and Missouri. The situation frustrated many Southern leaders who reported that supplies flowed into the state by way of Matamoros, Mexico, but the dearth of railroads thwarted efforts to move those badly needed resources out of the Rio Grande Valley. Residents in western parts of the state bitterly complained that the lack of soldiers and transportation also made protecting the outskirts of civilization impossible. During the Civil War the frontier receded sixty miles or more, yet Wigfall ignored the situation, deeming it insignificant to the war effort. As both a U.S. and Confederate Senator, Wigfall concerned himself only with East Texas and other areas with large concentrations of slaves, ignoring the needs of the majority of Texans and plain folk of the Old South. Unfortunately, during Wigfall's tenure in office, South Carolina added a third representative and the Lone Star State had only one. Ironically, had the fire-eater involved himself in pork barrel politics the Confederacy would have benefited from internal improvements.

By 1860, Wigfall concentrated his attention on undermining any efforts aimed at compromise. During the election, he helped divide the Democratic Party. Wigfall openly disavowed the strongest candidate, Stephen A. Douglas, worrying that his election might thwart secession. Wigfall complained that Douglas had failed to uphold protection of slavery in the territories. He also maintained that Douglas planned to

aid Democrats in the North and West by offering internal improvements, free homesteads, and protective tariffs. As a result, Wigfall helped
convince Texas Democrats to bolt the party and back John C.
Breckinridge for president. The split in the Democratic Party allowed
Abraham Lincoln, a Republican, to win the election. For Wigfall, party
loyalty mattered far less than destroying the Union. Lincoln's election
galvanized Texas to withdraw from the Union, joining South Carolina,
Mississippi, Alabama, Louisiana, Georgia, and Florida (these states
were later supplemented by North Carolina, Tennessee, Virginia, and
Arkansas).

In January 1860, as Texans went to the polls to ratify the legislature's
decision to secede, congressmen led by John J. Crittenden met in a final
attempt to save the Union. The effort attracted leaders from across the
nation and served as the best way to prevent a civil war through a negotiated settlement. Wigfall, however, opposed the Crittenden Compromise despite the fact that it provided for a constitutional amendment to
prevent Congress from interfering with slavery, allotted compensation
to owners for fugitive slaves not recovered, and extended the spread of
slavery to the Pacific. The measure garnered great interest, even among
fire-eaters. Only Wigfall and one other Southern senator rebuffed all
efforts at compromise. Even U.S. Senator Jefferson Davis, later chosen
president of the Confederacy, made substantive efforts to preserve the
Union. Wigfall, however, refused to vote and ensured that the compromise would not pass. His rejection of the proposal demonstrated that
his primary commitment was to destroy the Union rather than to protect slavery or follow the wishes of his constituents. Moreover, he chas-
tised those who entertained efforts toward a peaceful solution. He
maintained that he would not "be led by the nose as tenderly as asses
are . . . and vote for resolutions that mean nothing, in order that Senators may telegraph over the country that all is peace and quiet."[11]

Instead, Wigfall coauthored the Southern Manifesto, claiming that
no hope remained for the Union since no legislation or constitutional
amendments could save it. "We are satisfied the honor, safety, and independence of the southern people require the organization of a southern
Confederacy," the declaration ended. The election of Lincoln and the
secession of Texas brought Wigfall's career as a fire-eater to a successful
conclusion. In following the example of Calhoun, he had tirelessly argued that the South should leave the Union. Finally, he had accomplished his goal: "A man who is distasteful to us has been elected, and
we choose to consider that as a sufficient ground for leaving the Union,

and we intend to leave the Union."[12] Texans agreed and overwhelmingly approved of secession. Politicians of the Lone Star State rewarded Wigfall's efforts and selected him to represent Texas as a delegate at the Confederate Provisional Congress in Montgomery, Alabama. Unbelievably, Wigfall declined, opting to remain in the U.S. Senate. The decision revealed his selfish and obstructionist tendencies.

As the last Texan in Washington he argued and threatened his colleagues despite the heightened tension caused by secession. His main purpose, however, was to aid the South. Wigfall sent letters to Davis to apprise the new leader of the rapidly changing conditions. His actions infuriated the *New York Tribune*, which claimed that he was abusing his franking privilege and promoting treason.

His observations varied markedly in reliability. In one letter he concluded that President James Buchanan's dismissal of Secretary of War John B. Floyd, a moderate from Virginia, meant war. Buchanan removed Floyd due to his Southern sympathies (he later served as a brigadier general in the Confederate Army) and financial irregularities in the War Department. Wigfall, however, preferred to make bold, unsubstantiated statements that might hasten the onset of hostilities. Like many Southerners, he also mistakenly concluded that Lincoln's Inaugural Address amounted to a declaration to invade the South. He failed to listen to the president's promise that "the Government will not assail you," nor did he report Lincoln's vows: "I have no purpose, directly or indirectly, to interfere with the institution of slavery in the States where it exists. I believe I have no lawful right to do so, and no inclination to do so."[13] Wigfall preferred to scare Southerners: an invasion would be directed by Lincoln not only to abolish slavery but also to subjugate the Southern people. On other occasions, Wigfall provided sound information. He accurately reported that Fort Sumter and Fort Pickens, in Florida, should be attacked immediately because reinforcements would be forthcoming.

In addition to antagonizing his colleagues and acting as an intelligence operative, Wigfall found time to aid the Confederate war effort. He helped Texas military leader Ben McCulloch acquire weapons for a cavalry regiment. On March 2, 1861, Wigfall addressed his Senate colleagues for the last time. In his valedictory speech he challenged: "We have dissolved the Union; mend it if you can; cement it with blood."[14] By the end of the month the Texan had left the Capital and stopped briefly in Baltimore to set up recruiting station for the Confederacy before moving on to Virginia to encourage the Old Dominion to join the Southern cause. On April 1 he finally arrived at Charleston, where he took part in the surrender of Fort Sumter and became the hero of the Confederacy's high point. Unknowingly, Wigfall had also reached his personal watershed and would only hurt the cause for which he had so long fought.

Wigfall's decision to take part in the military events of Fort Sumter typified the problems suffered by the Confederacy at the hands of fire-eaters. The Texas politician had no plans for the nation beyond secession. Once a Southern nation had been formed, Wigfall had no clear mission beyond increasing his own fame. He elected not to help in the Montgomery Convention because he would gain little attention for setting up the government. Ironically, Wigfall, who had shown no interest in the specifics of the new nation's governmental procedures, would come to be its most outspoken critic. He knew only what type of government he did not want. Typical of fire-eaters, Wigfall had the ability and knowledge only to start a fight but lacked the political sagacity to win it. Had these leaders built a new country with the same singlemind-edness with which they had torn apart the old one, the Confederacy might have not been so politically divided.

The unsettled nature of the new country allowed Wigfall to serve as both a military leader and a Confederate senator. Typical of many South-erners, he believed that serving in the military was more significant than serving in the new Confederate Congress. As a result, one of the most experienced politicians used his influence to gain command of the 1st Texas Infantry and set about preparing his unit for war when his talents might have been better used in stabilizing the government. Mary Chesnut, a friend of the Wigfalls, noted: "How that redoubtable Wigfall did rush those poor Texans about. He maneuvered and marched them until I was weary for their sakes. Poor fellows! It was a hot afternoon, the thermometer was in the nineties."[15] Wigfall directed his men, later known as Hood's Texas Brigade, in action at Gaines Mill, Second Manas-sas, and Antietam. Colleagues regarded his performance as adequate, although some criticized his drunkenness while on duty. His military service brought him into conflict with Davis. The Texan concluded that he should have been promoted to brigadier general more quickly, al-though he received his commission in November 1861. Shortly after-ward, however, he resigned his position and served in the Confederate Senate throughout the war.

Wigfall's performance earned him a strong reputation with military leaders, including Robert E. Lee. As a result, generals often relied on

Wigfall to implore the Confederate Congress to assist them. Lee pleaded with Wigfall: "I have not heard from you in regard to the new Texas regiments which you promised to raise for the army. I need them very much. I rely on those we have in all tight places, and fear that I have to call upon them too often. They have fought grandly and nobly, and we must have more of them. Please make every possible exertion to get them on for me. You must help me in this matter."[16] Wigfall assisted his military friends when he could but resisted their proposal to increase the army by arming slaves.

Wigfall played a critical role in the political side of the war effort. He dominated the Confederate Congress. His stature did not help his constituents because he neglected his duties. Many Texans harbored bitterness for his lack of leadership. For example, they sought a rail line to connect the state to other regions of the country, but Wigfall made little progress and the area remained isolated. He finally proposed legislation authorizing the construction of a line, but by the time it passed the Congress, New Orleans had fallen to Union troops and Texas was effectively severed from the rest of the South. Davis refused to help and regarded the Lone Star State as little more than an afterthought. Wigfall protested Davis's lack of attention, but his own focus rested with events outside of Texas.

Ironically, the former champion of states' rights advocated a stronger Confederate central government in an effort to control the states. Wigfall devoted his energies to bolstering national power. He lamented the steadfast commitment to states' rights: "It seems to me that the people do not properly realize the fact that their interests are identical with those of the government." He worked in the Congress to undermine the powers of the states. Moreover, he favored entirely Confederate armies under Confederate generals, which angered Texans who insisted on state-directed units so that they might have the autonomy to protect the frontier. Proposing the first conscription act in American history, Wigfall argued that men from ages sixteen to sixty should serve the government. He further authorized the military impressment of private property. On another occasion he introduced a bill authorizing the executive branch to suspend the writ of habeas corpus so that the government could better enforce its conscription laws.

In February 1865 he shocked many Southerners when he led a successful effort in Congress to take control of all railroads, but he failed in his efforts to prevent the Confederacy from dying of states' rights. One Wigfall critic complained: "Your acts . . . were positively cut-throat.

. . . You have broken the Banks, the speculators, and the Manufacturers."[17] Even faced with destruction, the branches of the government failed to cooperate. The Confederate states refused to accept a federal system of government and opposed both legislative and executive attempts to consolidate control. Among the most severe problems in the country were dissatisfaction with and lack of confidence in the government. Yet, rather than ameliorate these fears, Wigfall exacerbated them.

For the final two years of the war, Wigfall turned his considerable talents at argument and created obstacles for the president. "Wigfall is strong . . . but erratic," an observer of the Congress noted. "When he gets a thing in his head, he pursues that alone, to the neglect of everything else, no matter how important. He can't control [himself]."[18] Wigfall used his powers to undermine the president by making sure that the legislative and executive branches worked against each other. The senator assured his colleagues that Davis could not be trusted with running the government or directing the war effort. Wigfall disparaged the president's military strategies, concluding that his own ideas were superior. In 1862 the Texan persuaded both houses to pass legislation limiting the president's power to select heads of armies and allowing generals, instead of Davis, the opportunity to select their own staff. Military leaders lauded his proposal and looked to him for legislation to help win the war.

When President Davis vetoed the bill, Wigfall attacked him as he had done with opponents in the past. He hosted parties and visited hotels throughout Richmond where he delivered scathing speeches. He blamed Davis for Confederate losses. The Senate joined Wigfall in rebuking the president by refusing to confirm his appointments. Instead of aiding Davis with his experience and support, Wigfall attacked him and undermined the people's confidence. The Wigfall-Davis feud (which eventually spread to include their spouses) hampered the Texan's lifelong quest for Southern nationalism. Even as the South faced destruction, Wigfall could not concentrate on realistic solutions to stave off defeat.

After the demise of the Confederacy, Wigfall turned his back on Texas and fled to England, where he tried in vain to stir up Anglo-American tensions. He finally returned and settled in Baltimore after concluding that Texas held little promise for the future. Even in the postwar years, Wigfall had misjudged the state. He failed to foresee the rise of the cattle industry. His mistake, however, was not surprising as he knew little of western affairs. Throughout his life his entire focus rested with the South—that is, the Old South with its institutions of slavery and commitment to agriculture. Wigfall once concluded, "My entire want of common sense damned near ruined me."[19] Once again he was wrong—it had ruined him completely. Regretting leaving Texas, he made a visit to Galveston in February 1874 in an effort to establish a law practice in the state when he died of an undisclosed illness.

The lasting contribution of the fire-eaters, including that of Wigfall, was driving Southern states toward extremism and secession. In the process these leaders protected regional interests over state ones. Wigfall moved Texas away from the heritage of independence and innovation earned during the Republic. Sam Houston's final, valiant effort to save the state failed because Texans were no longer interested in the ideals of Jacksonian democracy and the art of compromise. Houston once accurately depicted his rival, saying: "I should think more of the fellow than I do, if it were not that I regard him as a little demented, either from hard drink or from the troubles of a bad conscience."[20] Wigfall's drive for secession prevailed despite his personal flaws, but he did not have the sagacity or experience to establish an enduring government. His efforts to install Calhoun's principles of a limited national government with expanded powers for the states failed. Throughout his career, Wigfall looked to the past for inspiration and to the Old South for direction. The future of Texas, however, rested with the West. The state changed following Reconstruction as Texans returned to their unique ways and charted a course divergent from the South's.

Notes

1. Eric H. Walther, *The Fire-Eaters* (Baton Rouge, 1992), 164.

2. Alvy King, *Louis T. Wigfall: Southern Fire-eater* (Baton Rouge, 1970), 21–30.

3. *Congressional Globe*, 30th Cong., 1st Sess., 1301–1302 (first quotation); Walther, *Fire-Eaters*, 177 (second quotation).

4. King, *Wigfall*, 143.

5. A. W. Terrell, "Recollections of General Sam Houston," *Southwestern Historical Quarterly* 26 (October 1912): 118–19.

6. King, *Wigfall*, 70–74.

7. Walther, *Fire-Eaters*, 188.

8. Louis T. Wigfall, "Speech of Louis T. Wigfall, on the Pending Political Issues," delivered at Tyler, Smith County, Texas, September 3, 1860 (Washington, DC, 1860), 27–28.

9. William Howell Russell, *My Diary North and South, 1863* (Gloucester, MA, 1969), 73.

10. Ibid.

11. "Wigfall Speech," 27–28.

12. *Congressional Globe*, 36th Cong., 2d Sess., 14.

13. John Gabriel Hunt, ed., *The Inaugural Addresses of the Presidents* (New York, 1995), 187–97.

14. Walther, *Fire-Eaters*, 184–90.

15. Ibid., 190.

16. King, *Wigfall*, 153.

17. Walther, *Fire-Eaters*, 190 (both quotations).

18. King, *Wigfall*, 187.

19. Walther, *Fire-Eaters*, 163.

20. Ibid., 193.

Suggested Readings

Campbell, Randolph B. *A Southern Community in Crisis: Harrison County, Texas, 1850–1880*. Austin, 1983.

King, Alvy. *Louis T. Wigfall: Southern Fire-eater*. Baton Rouge, 1970.

Phillips, Ulrich B. *The Course of the South to Secession: An Interpretation*. New York, 1939.

Rable, George C. *The Confederate Republic: A Revolution against Politics*. Chapel Hill, 1994.

Walther, Eric H. *The Fire-Eaters*. Baton Rouge, 1992.

5

Captain Thomas Williams
The Path of Duty

Barry A. Crouch

Thomas Williams served in one of the most infamous organizations in Texas history, the State Police, yet his record is one of faithful service and attention to duty. As he saw it, however, duty involved a commitment to racial equality and the kind of law and order that was not popular with many former Confederates who were hoping to exploit the social and economic dislocation that followed the Civil War. Thwarted and rebuffed but never defeated, Williams threw himself methodically into his work. He pursued criminals, investigated murders, and protected suspects from lynch mobs. In every instance, "regular" Texans resisted his efforts out of a sense of political antipathy to the "Carpetbagger badge" and their own self-interests. Briefly, Williams tried his hand at politics, but, upon exhausting his money in a losing effort, he turned once again to law enforcement. Then, at a saloon in Lampasas, members of an outlaw gang whom Williams had come to subdue killed him instead.

Barry Crouch is professor of history at Gallaudet University in Washington, DC. He is the author of many books and articles on Texas history and is currently writing The "Governor's Hounds": The Texas State Police, 1870–1873.

In the aftermath of the Civil War, Texas experienced a decade and more of violent upheaval. Miscreants of every stripe inhabited the Lone Star State and bedeviled law-enforcement officials in their attempt to reduce the amount of mayhem prevalent in the region. The first elected administration during Reconstruction tended to ignore internal conflict in the state and focused upon the frontier, where the settlers required protection against Indians. When the U.S. Congress assumed control of the South in 1867 and enfranchised African-American males, political outrages continued to plague Texas. In 1870 the unpopular but victorious Republicans established a variety of militia units and a state force to combat the violence.

Governor E. J. Davis encouraged the Twelfth State Legislature to create the State Police under the direction of a Chief of Police, who also served as adjutant general, although ultimate authority remained in the hands of the chief executive. Thus, in July 1870, James Davidson became the first head of the State Police. In addition, state guard, reserve militia, and frontier forces were formed to stem the tide of lawlessness in Texas. The State Police would be a mobile unit designed to "follow up and arrest offenders" in areas where the authorities were either too weak to enforce respect or "indisposed to do so." The force would consist of 257 men: 4 captains, 8 lieutenants, 20 sergeants, and 225 privates.

During the existence of the State Police, often referred to as the "Governor's Hounds," violence saturated the Lone Star State. Nevertheless, citizen hostility toward the Davis administration and the deep hatred for the police themselves led residents either to cooperate with outlaws or shield them from apprehension. Although there would be exceptions, as a general rule the State Police performed rather credibly in the almost three years (1870–1873) that the force functioned. Their success came in the face of massive antipathy from white Texans. A contributing factor to this unyielding hostility was the fact that a large percentage of African Americans were on the force, which was unacceptable to those who supported the lost cause of the Confederacy.

Chief of Police Davidson provided the guidelines for the State Police in early July 1870 and began to select officers. One of the first lieutenants to qualify was Thomas Williams, who had served against the Confederates with Governor Davis during the Civil War. Although not a native Texan, for several years he had made his home in the Lone Star State. Opposed to secession, Williams had proved his abilities during the conflict and was the type of individual that the State Police needed. The story of Williams's service in the force is of interest to us because he was in and out of the organization from its inception and died while on duty. He advanced from lieutenant to captain and was often called on by Davis and Davidson in troublesome situations.

Although there is some debate about his name and background, Thomas Howard or Thomas G. Williams was born in Stone County, Missouri, on November 23, 1843, the son of Enoch and Emaline Williams. The family moved to Caldwell County, Texas, in the late 1840s, where Enoch earned a living as a farmer and millwright. Thomas's parents, who were strong Union supporters, would move to Newton County, Missouri, in 1867. Before 1861, Thomas was a stockraiser. His activities during the early part of the war are unknown, but on December 28, 1863, three days after his brother Samuel died in a New Orleans hospital, he enlisted in Company B of the North's 1st Texas Cavalry Volunteers at Brownsville. Thomas attained the rank of second lieutenant.

When hostilities ceased, Williams, a committed Republican, returned to Lockhart (Caldwell County) and dabbled in politics. Before he entered the State Police, in 1868 he married and had two children, Laura E. and Thomas. He served as county clerk and as an Assistant Assessor of Internal Revenue in the 2d Division in the 3d District of Texas. His first wife, Mattie, died in late 1870. A year later he wed Elizabeth "Lizzie" Baker. Tennessee born, she was the daughter of Thomas H. and Margaret Baker, who had moved to Texas in the early 1850s. Thomas Baker had carved out a small political career for himself, serving as county judge, Freedmen's Bureau agent, and state senator from Caldwell County.

Williams's first extensive State Police action occurred in Hill County, where Governor Davis would eventually declare martial law on January 10, 1871. Long before this date, desperadoes and outlaws such as John Wesley Hardin, a preacher's son, and Kinch West, a former member of William Clarke Quantrill's Missouri guerrillas, had been involved in killings in Hill County. The local population gave little assistance to the law enforcement officials, and thus violence continued to infest the area. After the formation of the State Police, this force attempted to eliminate disruptors to society, but they, too, encountered problems with the citizens. In August 1870 a private in the force was badly wounded by some disreputable elements, and Davis and Davidson decided to send in a contingent of police.

To command the Hill County State Police force, Davidson selected one of his best and most versatile men: Lt. Thomas Williams would consult with the legal and civil officers and then proceed to arrest the desperadoes roaming the areas as well as the adjoining counties. "If absolutely necessary," Williams had the authority "to summon citizens" to assist his unit in tracking down the badmen. He also had the right to call upon law enforcement officials in the counties surrounding Hill, and those in Hill itself. After making the arrests, Williams would return to his station and leave Sgt. George E. Haynie in charge at Waco.

Lieutenant Williams, along with two sergeants and thirteen privates, arrived at Hillsboro on the morning of September 28, 1870. The State Police remained for several hours to consult with the sheriff and other officers of the county, seeking information about the names of the desperadoes and the places to which they might retreat. Contrary to what the citizens declared, Williams received little help. Sheriff Evin Beauchamp relayed to Williams his knowledge about the Kinch West gang. The State Police detachment along with the sheriff proceeded to Peoria, where they expected to find the fourteen-member West band, as the desperadoes had been seen in the village the previous day.

The Williams group scouted Peoria but the West band had disappeared. On September 29 they located the residence of Kinch West and the Cox brothers, George W. and William. While searching the premises, West, the two Coxes, and a man named Mayfield attacked the State Police and Sheriff Beauchamp. The outlaws shouted insults and fired upon the five men present, the remainder having gone to another field to look for the criminals. The police returned the gunfire, but when the other policemen approached, West and his cohorts fled to the Cross Timbers, a dense grove of oaks that afforded many hiding places. A four-mile chase through the woods ensued, but the outlaws, with fresh horses and familiar with the region, disappeared. Williams returned to Waco and the other men went back to their stations.

After Williams left Hill County, an Austin newspaper interviewed the "accomplished and efficient officer." The lieutenant contended that the desperadoes numbered about fifteen men; while they operated in squads of four or five, they could "always concentrate when necessary." Well mounted and well armed with guns and revolvers, the desperadoes were able to deny the "civil authorities and have, in connection with their sympathizers, produced a reign of terror in Hill county" where anyone affiliated with the Davis regime excited the "ire of these men and their allies." Although Williams had about the same number in his group, only a few of them were equipped with long-range guns.[1]

As fall spread across central Texas, unrest continued to characterize Hill County. The State Police had begun to accomplish positive results. Governor Davis, always concerned about the high level of Texas violence, thought that action was required. He came to this decision after the return in September 1870 of Lieutenant Williams, who had failed to capture West and an assortment of other desperadoes. (His report was challenged by certain residents critical of the Republican regime.) Davis inquired of the sheriff and the citizens of Hill County what was happening with local law enforcement and why there was so much upheaval. The Hill County situation gave Davis the opportunity to demonstrate his commitment to racial equality and law and order.

Although the citizens denounced Williams's efforts in Hill County, he had carried out his duties responsibly and done as much as Chief of Police Davidson had expected. The lieutenant's presence was required in other areas, and his tenure in the county was necessarily temporary. He had proved unsuccessful in routing the outlaws because the local citizens refused to cooperate with the State Police, furnished the desperadoes with information, and helped them to evade arrest. For all his faults, even Sheriff Beauchamp confirmed the essence of Williams's observations. In the final analysis, Governor Davis imposed martial law because lawlessness went unchecked.

By late 1870, as the State Police became more completely mobilized and Williams completed his tour in Hill County, he assumed control of five counties in the 1st Police District in the vicinity of his home in Lockhart. Although he wanted to remain close to his hometown, more critical sections of the state needed attention, and he was ordered to Goliad. Circumstances, however, forced him to resign his commission in January 1871. What Williams did in his six-month hiatus from the State Police is unknown, but by mid-1871 he had been reinstated at his former rank. Almost immediately a crisis arose in Nacogdoches County that would require Williams's presence.

At 1 P.M. on Thursday, December 14, in the area of Linn Flat, fourteen miles northwest of Nacogdoches, State Policeman Columbus Y. "Bud" Hazlett (or Heaslett) and another policeman, William J. Grayson, for unknown reasons murdered David W. Harvell, a local resident. At midnight on December 19, they assassinated the town constable, John Birdwell. The killings "struck terror to the hearts of the people," declared a local writer; the "citizens felt as though they were left without any protection from the law." Although the State Police had existed for a year and a half, the Linn Flat affair brought increased criticism to an already beleaguered and Republican-sponsored agency.[2]

In late December, Davidson related to District Judge Mijamin Priest that Governor Davis wanted him to go to Nacogdoches with State Senator William H. Swift to investigate the troubles between the men "said to be policemen and the citizens." Because numerous stories and newspaper accounts circulated about what had happened at Linn Flat, there was much confusion about what had actually occurred, and contradictory accounts continued to appear. Davis wanted someone on the scene who could ascertain the course of events and, most important, he needed a man whom he could trust. He doubtless suggested to Chief of Police Davidson that Williams would be an ideal choice.

The call went out for Lieutenant Williams. Perhaps because he was the son-in-law of Thomas Baker, the prominent state legislator who may have garnered Williams's initial appointment to the force, he received a summons from Chief of Police Davidson. Williams was ordered to escort Hazlett and Grayson to Nacogdoches County and turn them over to the proper authorities. This situation was one that Williams could not resolve, although some observers have criticized his role in attempting to ensure that Hazlett and Grayson received a fair trial. Tensions within the area remained high, for two men had been murdered in cold blood.

On Monday, January 15, 1872, Williams and the other policemen escorted the prisoners into Linn Flat where they discovered armed and aroused citizens. He considered it "unsafe to go to trial." The lieutenant informed Sheriff Richard D. Orton that if the locals disbanded, he would furnish four policemen and the sheriff would be allowed four assistants to protect Hazlett and Grayson so that a trial could commence. The sheriff and his men rejected this proposal and demanded that Grayson and Hazlett be turned over to them. Williams refused, knowing that if he did so, the sheriff would likely turn the pair over to a lynch mob. Because of the increasing unrest in Nacogdoches County and the anger of the people, Williams and his unit returned to the safe confines of Rusk County.

Negotiations between Sheriff Orton and Lieutenant Williams resumed on Thursday, January 18. They reached a tentative agreement whereby Williams would escort the prisoners to Linn Flat for trial. But Williams changed his mind, and the next day the police left Nacogdoches County for Henderson, the Rusk County seat. It was conjectured that they intended to take the prisoners back to Austin by railroad or that they would appear at Linn Flat supported by a heavy guard of blacks and scalawags in an attempt to overawe the court and secure an acquittal. About 5 A.M., fifty to seventy-five men in search of Hazlett and Grayson, armed with double-barreled shotguns, "dashed" into Henderson, surrounded several houses, and created a general disturbance.

On Monday, January 29, Williams asserted that he would deliver the prisoners to Sheriff Orton in two days. Orton and Williams agreed that the former would provide a guard of eight men to take charge of Hazlett and Grayson. The trial began on February 1, with Judge Priest and District Attorney Jefferson Shook, but Williams again refused to deliver the prisoners and declared that he "would spill the last drop of blood in their defence [sic]." Priest assured Williams that the prisoners would be protected if they stood trial but Williams resisted. Justice of the Peace Gibson Dawson issued warrants for John J. "Jordan" King and J. M. Hazlett, Bud's brother, and ordered Williams to execute the writs. He refused.

While Madison G. Whitaker attempted to negotiate with Williams, a party of citizens rode into Rusk County seeking information about the State Police and the followers of Hazlett and Grayson. They were allegedly told that Hazlett, Grayson, and James Wallace were riding through the area summoning blacks to meet at the house of the Rusk County sheriff to aid them in resisting arrest. From many sources, Orton ascertained that a considerable number had assembled near the county line to protect the murderers. On Friday, February 2, a posse from Nacogdoches moved into Rusk County and learned that the resisters had gone toward Henderson that morning. With arrest warrants, this group followed them, but Williams had taken the two men to Austin.

Grayson and Hazlett, about whom "such an excitement" had been raging in Nacogdoches, stated the *Texas State Gazette*, were brought back to Austin by Williams and the other policemen who had them in charge. They contended that such a move was necessary because the two men could neither receive a fair trial nor be protected from the "mob that were determined to take their lives." Chief of Police Davidson turned the pair over to the Travis County sheriff for safekeeping. He planned in a few days to proceed with them to Nacogdoches with the "view of ascertaining the exact facts in this important case." The state government wanted the two men to be tried "under the laws of the land, and not by the bloody code of lynch."[3]

In the second week of February, Chief of Police Davidson ordered Lieutenant Williams, then in Lockhart, to report to Austin with his force. Governor Davis directed that Davidson assume custody of Hazlett and Grayson and transport them to Nacogdoches County, or to wherever Judge Priest could be found so they could undergo an examination on murder charges. "Great excitement" and "considerable feeling" existed against them, wrote Davidson. Governor Davis believed that Hazlett and Grayson's safety while waiting trial, and during the proceedings themselves, "would be better secured" if they were confined in "some county remote from the local prejudice."

In the meantime, Williams and his assistant had been indicted because they had removed Grayson and Hazlett from Nacogdoches County. The governor did not think that they could, "or should, be held to appear to answer any such charges as they undoubtedly thought they were doing their duty and that the course they adopted was essential to the safety of the prisoners." Davis admitted that the two men could have been in error, but, from what Judge Priest reported, the governor thought that their fears had a solid foundation. Davidson, when he arrived in Nacogdoches, would call the matter to the judge's attention so that such action might be taken that would not prevent the two men from "attending to their duties as required by law."[4]

On February 27, Williams and Sgt. William A. Baker, who had been ordered back to Nacogdoches, arrived in Nacogdoches. To their amazement, they discovered that Chief of Police Davidson and Sgt. Thomas G. Martin were already there. Davidson wanted to see the situation for himself. Sergeant Baker was not favorably impressed. He wrote that the people imagined they still "lived in a miniature Confederacy—they have no idea that the South has ever lost any of the prestige of its former glory, and any man differing with them in politics is in danger; of all the lawless counties in the State this leads; the sheriff with a mob thinks nothing of taking all the freedmen's arms and destroying them." At least twenty blacks had been disarmed and mistreated.[5]

Grayson and Hazlett were in jail. The rebels howled with rage because they could not hang them. The "whole enmity and hostility against these men exists in the fact that they are Union men," Baker continued, "[and] have been since 1861; they know the doings of all the villainous Ku-Klux [Klan] since that time, hence the desire to be rid of them." When arrangements were made with Sheriff Orton to deliver the prisoners, five hundred armed men surrounded the town. Williams "properly decided that something was wrong" and took them to Rusk County and then to Austin. Of all the "God forsaken counties in the State this beats all—disregard for law, for feelings of Republicans, for brutality towards the colored people, and violence generally."[6]

Grayson and Hazlett were tried at the June 1872 term of the District Court and found guilty of the murder of Birdwell. (They were not simultaneously tried for the Harvell killing.) Sentenced to life imprisonment, Hazlett escaped, but Grayson served fourteen years in the state penitentiary at Huntsville. He was granted a pardon by Governor John Ireland at the insistence of a number of Rusk and Nacogdoches County citizens along with the local state senator, because of his unusually "good conduct since his imprisonment." Moreover, it had never been alleged that he was the murderer. Hazlett, on the other hand, was killed, perhaps evading apprehension, near Woldron (Scott County), Arkansas, in 1877.

After the Linn Flat affair, Williams served in Mount Enterprise (Rusk County) and elsewhere apprehending criminals and attempting to reduce lawlessness. By April 1872, tired of constantly moving around, he applied once again to be stationed at Lockhart. His request was rejected by Governor Davis. He resigned and briefly entered politics. In this instance, he was pitted against some longtime stalwarts who had even more influence than his father-in-law. He declared for one of three state representative seats from the 27th District, which comprised Caldwell, Gonzales, and Guadalupe counties. Williams exhausted his bank account and finished a distant fifth out of six contestants.

Williams had cast his political lot at the wrong time, as a Republican backlash occurred across the state in 1872. Thus, because of his dire financial straits, he turned to the occupation he apparently knew best and requested that he once again be appointed to the State Police. In November 1872, "having lost greatly both in time and money in the past campaign," he was commissioned a captain by Chief of Police F. L. Britton, the governor's brother-in-law, who had recently assumed the position of adjutant general. Williams investigated lawlessness in McDade, Ledbetter, and Giddings, among other towns. When trouble occurred in Lampasas, he was ordered to the town to enforce the governor's directive on carrying guns. It was there that Williams's career came to an untimely end.

Many myths, distortions, and stories surround the killing of Capt. Thomas Williams, along with three other State Policemen, in Lampasas in March 1873. While invented conversations and unreliable sources may be blamed for much of the error-riddled accounts, the historical perspective that viewed Radical Reconstruction as a time of oppression and horror in Texas also pervades the writing about this incident. Until recently, most historians applauded the Texas Rangers for their aggressiveness in capturing criminals and keeping the peace. Although some critics may reject the comparison, the State Police performed the same function. Moreover, local law officials could not contain Lampasas's lawlessness and "begged" for assistance.

Constant turmoil in Lampasas led to the return of the State Police. A shortage of funds had forced the recall of a previous police force, but after their departure, the situation simply worsened. Cattle theft and "cowboy skylarking" brought the police back to Lampasas, a wide-open town. It was mistakenly reported that the sheriff had been killed before the arrival of Williams and this was the reason for dispatching him to the town. Some historians contend that to "old-time Texans" the Yankee government was "an abomination," and they sent word to Governor Davis "not to let any of his 'nigger police' show their faces" in the town. Thus, Williams chose six white policemen and only one black for the venture.[7]

As trouble continued to flourish in Lampasas, Governor Davis and Chief Britton pondered their choices. Even though there had been minimal support for declaring martial law, Davis had tried it in other counties but with mixed results. Williams may have been sent to strictly enforce the governor's earlier proclamation about bearing arms in town. Whatever the reason for Williams and his men being dispatched to Lampasas, there can be no doubt that the Horrell brothers along with several of their followers had become a general nuisance, breaking the law, and virtually taking control of the town. Many citizens became alarmed.

The local residents believed that something had to be done and insisted on receiving State Police reinforcements. Finally, on March 10, 1873, Adjutant General Britton ordered Captain Williams to proceed without delay to Lampasas and arrest any violators of a law that forbade the wearing of weapons inside the town limits. He was to be accompanied by a detachment of seven policemen armed with five Winchester carbines and fifty rounds of ammunition per gun. Further, Williams' mission was "to aid the local authorities in quelling a band of desperadoes who are committing outrages, and riding over the community" and attempting to murder Sheriff Shadrick T. ("Shade") Denson as well as end the "shooting into the citizen's houses" and prevent other illegal acts.[8] The Horrell band included: Thomas, Mart, Merritt, and Ben Horrell, Ben Turner, Joe Bolden, Allen Whitecraft, James D. Grizzell, Jerry Scott, Bill Bowen, Billy Gray, G. W. ("Wash") and Mart Short, Jim Jenkins, and Sam and Billy Sneed.

Later reminiscences of what occurred on the way to Lampasas and Williams's killing itself are at odds with contemporary sources and tend either to place the State Police in the worst light or blame them for creating a situation where they were likely to be murdered. For example, historians continue to repeat the story that while traveling to Lampasas, Williams and his men encountered some freighters: either John Means or Telford "Snap" Bean, or both. They asked them how far it was to Lampasas. Bean claimed that Williams had been drinking and had bragged that he was going to "clean up those damn Horrell boys." Considering Williams's character and past service to the State Police, this account does not ring true.

On the morning before Williams and his men reached Lampasas, the *Daily State Journal* later reported that the Horrells and their followers—"bloodthirsty wretches" and "monsters"—took up their usual posts at the saloon "with murder in their hearts." They tried to start a fight with Lt. A. P. Lee of a minutemen company on the same morning that Williams was shot. "But for the coolness of Lee the work of blood would have begun earlier in the day," the *Journal* suggested. The fugitives remained in town and had "consolidated with the Short band, another organization of outlaws, for mutual protection and to facilitate their objects of plunder and murder."[9]

As Williams and his men began their trek to Lampasas to meet their deadly fate, everything seemed to be calm on the surface. In fact, the local newspaper, perhaps with tongue in cheek, described an almost idyllic setting where peace reigned. The *Lampasas Dispatch* reported: "weather pleasant; health good; business flush; money getting plenty; times easy; town improving; country setting up; fishing parties common; boat riding frequent; school teachers busy; lawyers lazy; doctors idle; merchants pleasing; hotel keepers smiling; blacksmiths hammering; carpenters nailing; butchers flourishing; farmers plowing; old folks gardening and young folks courting."[10]

Williams and his seven-man escort arrived in Lampasas at about one o'clock on March 14. What transpired immediately afterward is not clear although there are various versions. When Williams rode into town he allegedly saw Bill Bowen, a Horrell brother-in-law, wearing a pistol and entering Scott's saloon. Adjutant General Britton reported that Williams arrested Bowen for carrying a six-shooter. "With breathtaking foolhardiness," according to one historian, "Williams decided to take on the clan on their own turf."[11] Accompanied by T. M. Daniels, Wesley Cherry, and Andrew Melville, they walked into the bar. Britton said that they were lured into the establishment "under some pretense."[12]

John Duff Green, born in Lampasas in 1873 and an admirer of the Horrells, gave this version. The policemen "boasted" that they would "clean up" the Horrells. Once in town, "they repaired to a saloon for a bracer" where they discovered the gang. Green, ignorant of the weapons law, has Williams attempting to arrest Bowen. "On the frontier and in the then-wild town of Lampasas, at that time, little if anything was thought about a man being armed." Mart told Bill that he had done nothing wrong. "For that short oration," wrote Green, "Mart Horrell tasted hot lead from Captain Williams's gun and his brothers and friends were not long in clearing the deck of the entire police force, though it made outlaws of them."[13]

Although former Texas Ranger James B. Gillett was not present in Lampasas, his account is rife with invented conversations. Williams, "an exceedingly brave but unwise man, took in the situation at a glance as he walked up to the bar and called for drinks." The captain supposedly turned to Bowen and said, "I believe you have a six-shooter. I arrest you." Mart told his brother-in-law that he had "done nothing and need not be arrested if you don't want to." Gillett claimed that "like a flash of lightning Captain Williams pulled his pistol and fired on Mart Horrell, wounding him badly."' (The evidence suggests that Mart was not injured until he went outside and encountered other policemen.[14])

C. L. Douglas described the scene in this manner. The policemen arrived and "one of the habitues" of Scott's saloon "swaggered from the doorway" wearing a Colt revolver. Williams (Douglas said he knew the man) exclaimed, "Wait a minute, Bill, aren't you forgetting something? You know as well as I do there's a state law now against totin' six-shooters in the streets." He had to arrest him. Bowen gave up his Colt and asked if he might return to the saloon for a brief word with a friend. Williams accompanied him and was "greeted by a barrage of Winchester fire from across the bar and from behind the tables." He "never knew what struck him." Cherry and Daniels were "riddled with carbine slugs" and died beside Williams.[15]

One of the major sources on the Lampasas troubles is John Nichols, who served as a county judge from 1897 to 1900 and as a justice of the peace, but he was not in Lampasas when the confrontation between the Horrells and the State Police occurred. Nichols, born in Missouri in 1841, arrived in Lampasas in the late 1850s. During the war he served with Samuel Horrell, senior and junior, in the Frontier Regiment of Mounted Volunteers, Captain J. J. Callan's company. Eighty-six years old when interviewed about his recollection of these happenings, Nichols lived in New Mexico when the Lampasas killings took place. He died in 1929.

In 1927, John Nichols recalled when the police went into the saloon, the "Horrells happened to be there." They left "a Nigger out to watch their horses." (Nichols believed there were "eight or ten" State Police). Williams, by Nichols's recollection, said that they had come after the Horrells. One of them replied that "they were there and they could take them if they wanted to, and began shooting." Mart was said to have shot Williams and Tom got one "as he ran off." The "Negro [Robert Jones] who had been left to hold their horses passed Dr. Andy Fields' residence, seventeen miles out on the road towards Austin and they said that he had never taken up his rope."[16]

Williams, Cherry, Daniels, and Melville never had a chance. Newspapers reported that when the troops arrived, the captain "heard of the presence" of a "number of men who were armed, and one man armed with a pistol displayed himself" and then went into the barroom. Williams sent "three of his men to different points," and along with the three privates entered the saloon to arrest Bowen. He ordered his men not to draw their weapons "or make any demonstrations, as he preferred to make a peaceable arrest."[17]

Williams stepped into the room, spotted Bowen, and "demanded his surrender." Bowen refused, and Williams "attempted to wrest his pistol from him, the rest of the men simply looking on, with their backs turned to the bar." At this point "a volley was fired into the police from behind, by at least eight or ten men." Williams was hit by three bullets; the first one entered the back of his head and exited "entirely through the face." When he turned, the second and third struck him in the chest. His "assassins must have been very near him when they fired." Daniels died instantly, taking several shots in the head and body, one of which passed "from one ear to the other." Cherry suffered a fatal chest wound as did Melville, but the latter lingered for almost a month before dying.[18]

With "twenty or more shots" fired from "Winchester carbines," it is not surprising that the State Policemen went down. Adjutant General Britton declared that the "manner in which the assassins were stationed and the accuracy of their fire, gave the policemen no chance to defend themselves against the cowardly attack."[19] What many previous writers have failed to realize about newspaper reports on the Lampasas incident is that the stories were based upon statements made by Melville in the weeks before he succumbed to his fatal wound. The twenty-five year old had been a member of the State Police for only three weeks when he met the Horrells.

According to Adjutant General Britton's account, Thomas, Mart, and Merritt Horrell along with Turner, Bolden, Whitecraft, Grizzell, Scott, Bowen, and Gray were in the saloon, and some of them had "secreted themselves behind screens and doors."[20] After the killing, the desperadoes came out and attacked the three remaining policemen. In an exchange of gunfire, Mart and Thomas Horrell were wounded, Mart in the back of the neck by Private Henry Eddy. At the inquest held on March 20, with Acting Coroner Thomas Pratt presiding, the verdict was that the policemen's death was caused by Thomas and Merritt Horrell, Turner, Bolden, Whitecraft, Grizzell, Scott, Bowen, and Gray.

The civil authorities were dismayed by the killings, although they probably did not fear the imposition of martial law because the legislature was moving toward eliminating the State Police. They quickly made arrangements for the funeral of the three dead State Policemen to take place the following day. On Saturday, March 15, "with honor and respect by the people of Lampasas," Williams, Cherry, and Daniels were buried in the local cemetery. Although the state never diligently pursued the killers of these three men and largely ignored the fact that they had been shot down in cold blood, a few of the assemblymen retained some dignity. On March 26 the Texas Senate appropriated $500 to have the men reinterred in the State Cemetery in Austin.

While Lampasas citizens paid their final respects to Williams, Cherry, and Daniels, Melville lingered near death at the Huling Hotel. Although "being kindly attended" to by Sgt. W. A. Johnson, his condition worsened and all "proved unavailing." Melville died on April 10 and was buried in Lampasas. Britton informed Melville's sister in Providence, Rhode Island, that her brother was a "brave and an efficient officer" killed by desperadoes. Any assistance that Britton could render either in removing Melville's remains or settling his affairs would be "proffered readily."

Williams's body did not arrive in Austin from Lampasas until April 9, almost a month after his death. An "eloquent" public funeral was held on April 11 at the United States District Court. Among those in attendance were Governor Davis, Attorney General Britton, the state treasurer, the superintendent of education, the black state senator George T. Ruby, and various other members of the legislature. The body was transported by wagon (the hearse was too small to receive his casket) to the State Cemetery, where the Odd Fellows read resolutions. The *Daily State Journal* left a fitting epitaph for Williams: he fell in the "path of duty" and "died in the defense of law and order, and his name deserves to be enrolled among the heroic dead."[21]

The *Daily State Journal* also extolled Williams's virtues. His murder would "cause a shock to our State, and sorrow to the entire community where he has lived most of his life." Known for "his bravery and excellent bearing," the newspaper wrote that the "disturbed condition" of Texas "would not permit a man of such activity to remain idle." He had proved through his efficiency the extent of his valuable talents. Williams had brought dedication to the State Police and "fallen in the path of duty, while enforcing the law, and protecting life and property." The *Journal* enthused that he was "so gallant, young, brave, [and] generous."[22]

Throughout his career as a State Policeman, Capt. Thomas Williams approached his duties conscientiously, judiciously, and responsibly. Unquestionably, he was one of the most respected members of the force, as evidenced by the confidence that Chiefs of Police Davidson and Britton along with Governor Davis placed in him when they called upon him in critical situations. During the existence of the State Police from 1870 to 1873, anti-administration newspapers excoriated its members as former convicts, corrupt and despotic, but maintained a deferential attitude toward Williams and his efforts. He may not have been a "typical" State Policeman, but, like others on the force, he performed his job capably and with honor.

Notes

1. *Weekly Austin Republican*, October 5, 1870; *Waco Register*, quoted in *Daily State Journal*, October 7, 1870.

2. Richard W. Haltom, *History and Description of Nacogdoches County, Texas* (Nacogdoches, 1880), 39.

3. *Texas State Gazette* (Austin), February 5, 1872.

4. E. J. Davis to James Davidson, February 19, 1872, E. J. Davis Letterpress Book (November 15, 1871–May 20, 1872), 305–6, Records of the Governor, Record Group 301, E. J. Davis Papers, Archives and Records Information Services, Texas State Library, Austin.

5. *Daily State Journal*, February 28, 1872; *Daily State Journal*, March 8, 1872.

6. Ibid.

7. C. L. Sonnichsen, *I'll Die Before I'll Run: The Story of the Great Feuds of Texas* (New York, 1951), 98.

8. P. L. Britton to E. J. Davis, March 24, 1873, Adjutant General Letterpress Book, 196–201, Ledger 401–619, Adjutant General Records, Archives and Records Information Services, Texas State Library, Austin.

9. *Daily State Journal*, March 19, 1873.

10. *Lampasas Dispatch*, quoted in *Houston Telegraph*, March 15, 1873.

11. James B. Gillett, *Six Years with the Texas Rangers* (Austin, 1921), 108.

12. Britton to Davis, March 24, 1873.

13. John Duff Green, "Recollections," ed. Joan Green Lawrence, unpublished MS, 91 (courtesy of Jeffrey Jackson, Lampasas).

14. Gillett, *Six Years*, 73–75.

15. C. L. Douglas, *Famous Texas Feuds* (Dallas, 1936), 131–32.

16. John Nichols to J. Evetts Haley, May 15, 1927, J. Evetts Haley Collection, Nita Stewart Haley Memorial Library, Midland, Texas.

17. *Norton's Union Intelligencer* (Dallas), March 29, 1873; *Daily Democratic States-man* (Austin), March 20, 1873; *Daily State Journal*, March 19, 1873.

18. Ibid.

19. Britton to Davis, March 24, 1873.

20. Ibid.

21. *Daily State Journal*, March 17, 1873.

22. Ibid.

Suggested Readings

Baenziger, Ann Patton. "The Texas State Police during Reconstruction: A Re-examination." *Southwestern Historical Quarterly* 72 (April 1969): 470–91.

Cantrell, Gregg. "Racial Violence and Reconstruction Politics in Texas, 1867–1868." *Southwestern Historical Quarterly* 93 (January 1990): 333–55.

Crouch, Barry A. "A Spirit of Lawlessness: White Violence, Texas Blacks, 1865–1868." *Journal of Social History* 18 (Winter 1984): 217–32.

_____. and Donaly E. Brice. " 'Dastardly Scoundrels': The State Police and the Linn Flat Affair." *East Texas Historical Journal* 37 (Spring 1999): 29–38.

Field, William T., Jr. "The Texas State Police, 1870–1873." *Texas Military History* 5 (Fall 1965): 131–41.

Nunn, W. C. *Texas under the Carpetbaggers* (Austin: University of Texas Press, 1962).

Singletary, Otis A. *Negro Militia and Reconstruction* (Austin: University of Texas Press, 1957).

Webb, Walter Prescott. *The Texas Rangers: A Century of Frontier Defense* (Boston: Houghton Mifflin, 1935).

_____. "The Texas Militia during Reconstruction." *Southwestern Historical Quarterly* 60 (July 1956): 21–35.

Wilkins, Frederick. *The Law Comes to Texas: The Texas Rangers, 1870–1901* (Austin: State House Press, 1999).

6

John B. Rayner
"No Outlet" on the Road of Hope

Gregg Cantrell

The life of John B. Rayner is one of great promise cut short. Born the son of a North Carolina congressman a decade before the Civil War, he was also the son of a slave woman, and in the eyes of Southern society that made him a black man. It also meant second-class citizenship for this well-rounded public figure whose education, capabilities, and resourcefulness under different circumstances could have taken him as far as opportunity and initiative would have allowed. Rayner came to Texas as a recruiter of black laborers and settled briefly into the life of a schoolteacher. Soon, however, he found his life's work in attempting to endow African Americans in Texas with a political voice that would improve their lot—a dream that he never saw realized. Often praised but more often vilified, he angered white Democrats by championing Populism and later earned the wrath of African Americans by writing humbling apologias for accommodation between the races. Ultimately he saw his influence wane and turned to composing militant tracts that accomplished little and went largely ignored.

Gregg Cantrell teaches at the University of North Texas. Among his many published works is *Kenneth and John B. Rayner and the Limits of Southern Dissent* (1993).

O n a late winter day in 1880 a train chugged into the station at Calvert, Texas. When the squealing brakes brought the great steam locomotive to a shuddering stop, out onto the platform leapt a well-dressed young man, obviously in a hurry. Of average height but built like a bull, he was the color of parchment, or perhaps coffee with a double dose of cream. The casual onlooker might have guessed him to be a Greek or Italian. But when he began barking instructions in his high, clear voice to dozens of passengers who followed him off the train, it was obvious that the accent belonged not to a foreigner but to an American. As it became clear that he was in charge of organizing the large number of black travelers who were leaving the train with their meager possessions, the careful observer might have concluded that he belonged to the category that the race-conscious South called mulattoes

87

—that is, people of mixed Caucasian and African-American heritage. In his case, the black portion of his genetic makeup could not have been much, perhaps one-eighth or less. But in the nineteenth-century South, the "one-drop" rule deemed a person a "Negro" if he or she had any "black blood" at all. Thus, this young man, John B. Rayner, found himself a second-class citizen in the eyes of society.

Rayner was born a slave in Raleigh, North Carolina, in 1850. His mother was a slave named Mary Ricks, probably a mulatto. His father was Kenneth Rayner, one of the state's leading white planters and politicians. The elder Rayner had served several terms in the North Carolina legislature and three in Congress, where he zealously promoted the agenda of the Whig Party. When that party had fallen apart in the mid-1850s, Kenneth Rayner had been one of the founders of the American Party, known by its detractors as the "Know-Nothings." For a while it had appeared that the Know-Nothing Party would become the new national opposition party to the dominant Democrats, and Kenneth Rayner's name was frequently mentioned as a potential candidate for high national office. The American Party ultimately failed to win the hearts and minds of voters, and in the North it was soon replaced by the antislavery Republican Party, which in 1860 elected its first president, Abraham Lincoln. Lincoln considered naming Kenneth Rayner—still a staunch Unionist and a former Whig like himself—to his cabinet, but finally he decided against it. It was just as well, because when the Civil War actually began, Kenneth Rayner reluctantly supported secession.

Although born and raised a slave, John B. Rayner received an upbringing that would set him apart from all but a tiny handful of his fellow slaves. He grew up in the servants' quarters of his father's mansion, a stone's throw from the North Carolina state capitol, where he would have heard his famous father make speeches and discuss the vital political issues of the day. Despite having a white family, Kenneth Rayner acknowledged his paternity of John and of another mulatto child, a girl named Cornelia. This argument was not as unusual as modern Americans might think. Sex between masters and slaves was not against the law, and white wives had little recourse when such liaisons were discovered. Moreover, peculiar southern notions of honor and duty—not to mention affection—often led the white fathers of mulatto children to take a certain responsibility for their illegitimate offspring and show them special favors.

Hence it was that when the Civil War came to an end in 1865, Kenneth Rayner saw to it that his son attended two newly established freedmen's schools in Raleigh, first at the Raleigh Theological Institute and thereafter at St. Augustine's University. At these institutions John received an education of surprising thoroughness, including the basics of English, history, mathematics, and the classics (Greek and Latin). This education would be reflected throughout his life in his writings and speeches.

Although he had not graduated, sometime between June 1870 and November 1872 young Rayner left Raleigh. His destination was Tarboro, in heavily black Edgecombe County. As elsewhere in the South, the Republican Party had swept to power there following the passage of the 1867 Reconstruction Acts. Rayner soon became involved in local Republican politics, and over the next five years he served as constable and justice of the peace. Despite the bitter resentment of most white Southerners toward the biracial Republican coalition, it appeared that a new era had arrived in southern politics.

In 1874, Rayner married a light-skinned mulatto named Susan Staten, and two years later the couple's first child was born. But just as his private life took this positive turn, his political career turned sour. The large Democratic majority elected to the state legislature in 1874 passed a bill calling for a convention to revise the state's 1868 Republican constitution. That convention took the right to elect justices of the peace away from the voters and gave it to the state legislature. North Carolina (in the terminology of the triumphant Democrats) had been "redeemed." As the local Democratic newspaper editor explained, "we consented to give up our much-loved right of electing Magistrates by the people, so that the incompetent carpet-baggers and negroes would have to stand aside." After his term expired in 1877, Rayner was no longer justice of the peace.[1]

Several circumstances seem to have led to his move to Texas. First, his private business interests suffered a setback. In 1875, Rayner had entered into a partnership with John Gant, a prominent white Republican, to operate what was probably a saloon. But two years later the city mounted a successful crusade to shut down the saloons and brothels in the area of the Rayner & Gant establishment, and they were put out of business. Then, three months later, Rayner attended a Baptist revival meeting and was baptized in the Tar River. Soon thereafter he was ordained to preach.

The political and economic conditions for black North Carolinians had deteriorated steadily throughout the 1870s as the vast majority found themselves hopelessly indebted to white landlords and politically powerless. In 1879, African Americans began to leave North Carolina and other southern states in substantial numbers. Soon the exodus reached such numbers that white planters, fearing the wholesale loss of their black labor force, became truly alarmed. While many blacks emigrated to Indiana and other midwestern destinations, some of the so-called Exodusters chose Texas.

Rayner's search for a fresh start coincided with the mounting exodus. In about 1879, Horatio "Rasche" Hearne, a wealthy planter from Robertson County, Texas, traveled to North Carolina with one of his plantation managers in an effort to recruit black laborers. With North Carolina planters working diligently to halt the emigration, men such as Hearne would have to find local intermediaries if they hoped to recruit black workers. He apparently hired Rayner to serve as such an intermediary. Oral tradition among Rayner's descendants places the number of Exodusters that he led to Texas at perhaps one thousand.

Rayner's new home in the Brazos Valley shared much in common with his old one in North Carolina. With half the population made up of former slaves and their families, Robertson County was heavily black by Texas standards, and it ranked in the top ten cotton-producing counties in the state. During Reconstruction, African Americans had played an important role in county government. But unlike Rayner's old North Carolina home, Republicans in Robertson County continued to elect black county officials well into the 1890s. Moreover, it had long been a hotbed of third-party activity. Rayner eventually came to lead the most important of these movements.

For his first few years in Texas, Rayner kept a low profile, concentrating on making a living by teaching school and perhaps occasionally preaching. But events in 1887 suddenly thrust him into the political spotlight. The occasion was a statewide prohibition referendum. The issue of banning alcohol deeply divided the state's Democrats, and Rayner sensed an opportunity. Anything that might turn Democrat against Democrat might give African Americans renewed political clout: when Democrats were evenly divided, blacks could hold the balance of power.

As Rayner followed the contest in the newspapers, he realized that the prohibition forces were making a mistake: They had made no plans for capturing the black vote. Accordingly, he wrote a confidential letter to Dr. B. H. Carroll, a prominent white Baptist minister who chaired the prohibitionist state executive committee. Avowing that he was "a prohibitionist from deep religious principle," Rayner offered some unsolicited advice on the grounds that he had "some little negro in my veins" and knew "the eccentricities of the negro." He then gave very specific instructions about how the prohibitionists could use the black press and employ influential black preachers in the cause. The editor of the state's most important black Baptist newspaper was to be paid $200 for the use of his paper, and a black Methodist bishop was to be brought to Texas to campaign in favor of the measure. This, Rayner told Carroll, would "silence all the old worthless and characterless Baptist preachers that will annoy you and your committee."[2]

Carroll heeded Rayner's advice, but soon there was trouble. In early June, Rayner's letter somehow fell into the hands of the opposition, who made its contents public. The exposure of the letter was "a devil of a mishap" for the prohibitionists, and immediately the "Rayner letter" became a major campaign document for the opposition. Anti-prohibitionists across the state read the letter at rallies, and it received widespread attention in the press.[3]

The letter badly embarrassed the prohibitionists, for it clearly indicated that they were following the instructions of a Negro. Anti-prohibition newspapers published Rayner's letter under the headline "Dark Tactics" and explained that Carroll had " 'tumbled' to Bro. Rayner's suggestions." "Rayner is a shrewd politician," added the *Waco Examiner*, "and understands to a dot how to organize a political campaign." By early July the *Examiner* could claim with some accuracy that "the success of the [anti-prohibition] cause has never been doubtful for one moment . . . since Parson Rayner came to Parson Carroll's help with advice as to how to run the campaign."[4]

On Election Day the voters buried prohibition by a 90,000-vote majority. Rayner had learned a hard lesson in Texas politics; cooperation among blacks and whites in a common political cause was a tricky business. But he remained convinced of one truth. When whites disagreed among themselves, blacks, if united in a bloc, could break the tie and place themselves in a position to demand greater rights.

By 1890 southern politics had reached a crossroads. For two decades the southern economy had worsened. Federal monetary policy (based upon the gold standard) resulted in chronic deflation, which meant that at the end of each year farmers were forced to repay their debts with dollars that were more valuable than those they had borrowed at the start of the year. Crop prices moved steadily downward, interest rates skyrocketed, and thousands of farmers lost their land to foreclosure and were driven into tenancy. Each year their debts mounted. Blacks were hit the hardest of all.

In the 1870s an organization known as the Farmers' Alliance was created, and in the 1880s it attracted hundreds of thousands of members. Among its political demands were government ownership of the railroads, a more equitable taxation system, and abandonment of the deflationary gold standard in favor of a flexible currency. At the heart of the Alliance program was the Subtreasury Plan, a proposed federal network of warehouses that would store farmers' crops, extend guaranteed low-interest farm loans, and release the crops onto the world market in an orderly fashion to prevent the usual market glut at harvest time.

In the early 1890s the Alliance formed its own independent political movement called the Populist, or People's, Party. Alliance demands would form the heart of its platform. At its first state convention in Dallas in 1891, the delegates debated whether to include African Americans. Some of the members opposed such a move, but one of the party's leaders, a charismatic orator named H. S. P. "Stump" Ashby, took the podium, saying, "We want to do good to every citizen of the country, and [the Negro] is a citizen just as much as we are, and the party that acts on that fact will gain the colored vote of the south." Ashby's call for "full representation" of blacks in the party's councils brought forth applause from the assembled delegates, who responded by electing two blacks to the state executive committee.[5]

Rayner soon began working for the Populist cause among the blacks of Robertson and the surrounding counties. When the 1892 state convention met to choose its first slate of candidates, a few black Populists brought encouraging stories of their success in recruiting African Americans to the party. "The colored people are coming into the new party in squads and companies," one black organizer reported. The Populists gave their gubernatorial nomination to Judge Thomas L. Nugent of Fort Worth, a quiet, scholarly man with an impeccable reputation as a champion of independent reform politics.[6]

Nugent lost to the popular Democrat James S. Hogg, who had run on a promise to regulate the railroads. The Populists failed to win the votes of significant numbers of African Americans. Although the Populist program clearly addressed the economic needs of all poor farmers, the 1892 state platform made no specific mention of blacks. African Americans might have been interested in the planks demanding a six-month public school term with state-furnished textbooks, a more equitable lien law, reforms in the notorious convict lease system, and fair elections, but the Populists kept silent on one of the most pressing of black concerns—lynching—and on the many other issues affecting African Americans. No mention was made of the Jim Crow railroad law, the blatant discrimination in state expenditures for black schools, and the right of blacks to sit on juries. The naming of blacks to the Populist state executive committee and a general appeal to economic self-interest were all that most blacks could see. These gestures were sufficient for Rayner in 1892, but they were not enough to convert the black masses to Populism.

The racial divides in Texas ran deep. Whites were reluctant to split their vote between the Populist and Democratic parties and risk putting blacks in office. Blacks were just as hesitant to desert the Republican Party. Populists had to find a way to make both blacks and whites place reform ahead of racial anxieties. The third party needed to show white farmers that their desperate financial plight would never improve under Democratic rule and that whites and blacks could honorably cooperate for the common good without inviting "social equality" for African Americans. Populists also had to convince blacks of their sincerity in offering meaningful political participation. There were good reasons to be optimistic about the chances of recruiting more white Populists as the agricultural depression deepened and cotton prices plummeted to a nickel per pound. Many whites were already familiar with Populist demands through the Farmers' Alliance and the reform press. But black "Pop clubs" could not organize themselves, and few blacks could read (or afford) newspapers that would instill in them the vital "education" of Populism. The party needed to address "black" issues more directly and find more blacks with leadership ability, courage, and dedication to travel and work as organizers and educators. Populists found their man in John B. Rayner.

As the 1894 campaign heated up, the press began to note the political activities of a "traveling negro named Rayner." In March the Populist state newspaper started publishing the speaking schedules of "Rev. J. B. Rayner, colored, our Populist orator." Typically, Rayner would visit a county and address the crowd at black barbecues, meetings, or conventions. Sometimes he made his speeches at the county courthouse or a local opera house, sometimes in tiny, off-the-beaten-path black settlements. He offered his services to any county Populist organization that needed them. "I will now gladly visit any part of the state," he announced, "and organize my people into Populist clubs." He invited "all who favor justice, liberty, a higher price for labor, and a better price for products." The response was overwhelming. In April, May, and June 1894, Rayner crisscrossed the eastern half of the state, speaking to crowds of all sizes and descriptions and leaving behind a trail of black Populist clubs. Rural Texans of both races gathered to hear the man billed as the "Silver-Tongued Orator of the Colored Race."[7]

Rayner worked closely with white orators and with the reform press, making recommendations to his white comrades about where their services were needed and helping poor blacks and whites to obtain Populist newspapers. He rarely hesitated to instruct his white colleagues on how to run a campaign, giving detailed directions in the state Farmers' Alliance paper, the *Southern Mercury*, for the benefit of county and precinct leaders. Above all, he stressed to white Populists the need to utilize his own services and to enlist local black leaders in the Populist cause. "Our county chairmen in counties where the negro vote is important, should have colored speakers to visit the county, and address and instruct the colored voters," Rayner wrote. "You must reach the negro through a negro."[8]

At the party's 1894 state convention in Waco, Rayner played a major role in the public proceedings and was elected to the state executive committee and the platform committee, where he exercised his influence in securing planks promising reforms in the brutal convict lease system and increased black control over African-American schools. He then commenced a wide-ranging speaking tour that threatened both his health and personal safety, traversing the state from the Red River to the Gulf Coast. "I am hard at work day and night for our party," he explained without exaggeration.[9]

Rayner's experiences on the campaign trail dramatically reveal the power of white supremacy and the lengths to which Democrats would go when they believed it to be endangered. The black orator displayed exceptional physical courage when he ventured into certain parts of East Texas, literally joking about the threats he encountered. In Morris County, Rayner spoke to a crowd of 450 white and black Populists and reported that drunken Democrats later "tried to frighten me and make me leave town. One poor little fellow wanted to know who would pay him to run 'that nigger' out of town." Rayner continued undeterred, adding that "the colored people of Morris county are doing their own thinking and will vote with the Populists. . . . Our party is growing daily and I am cheerful, hopeful and feel that victory is waiting to crown our efforts."[10]

The Populists lost again, but they had gained ground. In the 1894 gubernatorial race, Democrat Charles Culberson defeated Thomas Nugent by a vote of 216,373 to 159,676, but Populists carried dozens of counties and picked up numerous seats in the state legislature. The following year Rayner traveled extensively, making speeches, organizing black Populist clubs, and helping to arrange the enormous camp meetings that had become a third-party trademark. State chairman Stump Ashby appealed to "all patriotic Populists who can reasonably do so" to send a small donation to help defray the black committeeman's expenses. "The work I want Rayner to do," Ashby frankly explained, "no white man can do."[11]

One can scarcely overstate Rayner's power as a public speaker. Americans living in the age of microphones, amplifiers, and the electronic mass media cannot appreciate fully the degree to which nineteenth-century orators could mesmerize a crowd. Whites and blacks alike marveled at the forty-five-year-old Populist's power over an audience. A third-party partisan captured something of the flavor of an 1896 Rayner speech:

> What crowds of people, what throngs of people, by fours, by dozens, on foot, on horses, in buggies, in wagons, above the roars of applause and clapping of hands, you hear the sweet music of the voice of the illustrious Rayner. Now like a wild tornado, now like a summer evening breeze, pointed, logical, severe, yet soft and gentle, the spirit of God is plainly mirrored from his heart, carrying conviction at every breath. God speed his good work![12]

Rayner attracted listeners from both races. He would begin his speeches with a history lesson, Populist-style. The United States was "a great country, a giant with his head lathing in the ice water of the Arctic ocean, his feet in the turbid waters of the gulf, his left hand on the golden gate and his right in the billows of the Atlantic." This giant would rise "with the might of a Hercules and stamp the pigmies" (the Republican and Democratic parties) "into the deep, sad mud of defeat and the deep damnation of retribution," he thundered. Near the end he proceeded to the audience's favorite part of the speech, the roasting of the Democratic Party:

> The Democratic drag has held back the South, and she is raising a lot of empty-headed and empty-pocketed ninny-heads to vote the same old time-worn ticket of the father and grand-pap. . . . The best elements of the grand old Republican and Democratic parties [are] volunteers to help the Populists clean out the old stables and bury the occupants so deep in mundane mixture that Gabriel will need subsequent assistance to produce power to wind his horn loud enough to call them to Resurrection.[13]

When he "came in like a storm" to deliver this speech at Market Square in Houston, white hecklers tried to disrupt his talk. Undaunted, he "aroused the crowd to numerous applauses by his quick-witted thrusts," telling the hecklers that they were "unmanly" in trying to keep him from exercising the privilege of free speech. That Rayner dared to castigate white hecklers in public bears witness to his courage, and the fact that he could get away with it suggests that white Populists were willing to stand by their black ally. After his appearance a spectator told a reporter, "Houston has felt the storm and may take gracious comfort that a single house is left standing or that one lone official is left to tell the tale of political devastation."[14]

However, 1896 marked the end of the Populists' brave experiment in biracial politics in Texas. In that year the Democrats met in their national convention and nominated a surprise candidate, William Jennings Bryan, who supported one minor Populist demand, the coinage of silver. Many Populists outside of Texas naively believed that the Democrats had embraced reform, and when the Populist national convention met shortly thereafter, there was widespread support for the Populists to join forces with the Democrats and nominate Bryan as well. Rayner was among the 103 delegates whom the Texas party sent to the St. Louis convention, and to a man they opposed the Bryan nomination, understanding that it would mean the death of Populism.

Their prediction proved true. Returning home, Rayner and his fellow Populists fought an uphill battle to save Populism in Texas, but it was futile. Thoroughly demoralized by their party's nomination of a Democrat for president, thousands of Populists abandoned the movement. To ensure victory in November, Texas Democrats resorted to widespread voter fraud, intimidation, and violence. On Election Day in Rayner's home county, Democrats "quietly deposed" the town's black marshal in the county seat, Franklin, before the polls opened, and forty men with Winchester rifles stationed themselves at the courthouse to turn away all but Democratic voters.

In the lower end of the county, a large company of black voters was marching from their homes in the Brazos bottoms, accompanied by a brass band, to cast their votes in Hearne. An armed delegation of Democratic horsemen accosted them on the Little Brazos River bridge, throwing the band instruments into the river and dispersing the crowd. At Hearne, "a great number of pistol shots were fired in front of the polls when the negroes from the bottom came in to vote," and subsequently the ballot box polled six hundred fewer votes than in the previous election. In one rural precinct, the presiding officer reported that "a masked man took the box and returns away from him." In another the Democratic candidates for sheriff and tax collector stood at the door of the polling place, one with a gun and the other with a club, and held off black voters. About midafternoon, word reached the Democratic county judge that in spite of these efforts the election might hinge upon his home precinct. "I went down to the polls and took my six-shooter," he recalled. "I stayed there until the polls closed. Not a negro voted. After that they didn't any more in Robertson County." The judge boasted that he personally stood off one thousand African Americans that day. When asked many years later about his violent role in bringing white rule back to the county, he explained: "I only shot when I thought I had to. I know God pulled me through."[15]

After the defeat of Populism, John B. Rayner virtually disappeared from the record for several years. The Democratic Party was the only viable party left in Texas, and between 1896 and 1902 county after county adopted whites-only primary laws barring African Americans from voting in the Democratic primaries. In 1902 the voters of Texas approved a poll tax measure requiring the payment of a tax to vote, thus eliminating most remaining black voters as well as many poor whites.

In 1904, Rayner emerged from his seclusion to accept a position as financial agent for Conroe College, a new educational institution for African Americans forty miles north of Houston. It was to be modeled on the Tuskegee plan, stressing vocational training. The school's only chance of survival lay in Rayner's ability to tap potential sources of white philanthropy. It had worked for Booker T. Washington at the Tuskegee Institute; maybe it could happen at Conroe.

The new financial agent wasted no time in unveiling his scheme to raise money. If Populism had taught Rayner anything about conducting a successful crusade, it had taught him the importance of publicity. For the next two years he kept Conroe College almost constantly in the press, filling the columns of Texas newspapers with glowing reports of how the school was helping to solve the "race problem." "Scholars" at Conroe College were to be taught the science and art of politeness; how to obey the law and respect for public sentiment; how to resist temptation and be virtuous; that idleness is a sin—all labor is honorable; that a good character is the greatest wealth; that the white people in the South are the negro's best friends; and that Christianity means love and service.[16]

Two weeks after his appointment to the fund-raising post, Rayner began to publicize his most ambitious project at the school. He proposed that the white people of Texas donate money for a large, four-story, fireproof brick building to be dedicated "to the memory of the faithfulness of the slaves to their masters' families during the War between the States from 1861 to 1865." The building would be dubbed the Hall of Faithfulness, and over the main entrance would be placed an appropriate commemorative marker.[17]

Rayner also began contributing frequent editorials to Texas newspapers, particularly the *Houston Chronicle*. Nobody would have suspected that the author had been a militant politician a decade earlier. One typical essay read:

> Since some of the colored race have attempted to be protagonist in politics, we (negroes) have been deceived by iridescent visions of political power and idle ease, and misled by utopian promises, and we (negroes) as a race became so hallucinated . . . that we could not see the red flag of danger ahead, and when we came to our senses we found our political opportunities circumscribed, and our manhood proscribed; and what our fatuous presumption did in the past, our meekness and general moral worth must undo. The negro of today is not the negro of yesterday. Man must make himself worthy and admirable before he attempts by his vote to shape the policy and fix the destiny of states. . . . Politics has nothing to offer the negro.[18]

In 1909, having parted ways with Conroe College, Rayner accepted a similar position as financial agent for the Farmers Improvement Society college in Ladonia, another black vocational school. He renewed his Hall of Faithfulness scheme, and once again it seemed that no amount of groveling was beneath the dignity of the former Populist. Perhaps the low point came when Rayner wrote a letter to J. S. "K. Lamity" Bonner, editor of *K. Lamity's Harpoon*, a bitingly satirical newspaper published in Austin. Bonner was one of the most virulent racists in Texas, openly applauding the lynching of blacks. Yet, Rayner addressed him respectfully, agreeing that the racist editor had "well advertised the derelict negro" and meekly asking him to put in "a good word of commendation for the worthy negro." Bonner responded by defending his extreme racism and then presenting Rayner to his readers as "a worthy example for the negro race." What Rayner or his school gained from such an endorsement is at best questionable, but it no doubt came at great cost to the once-proud black leader.[19]

Rayner gained a sizable following among whites. One admirer declared that "Rayner is the most unselfish negro I ever knew" and pronounced him "the greatest negro on the American continent." Another wrote, "Not 200 miles from Houston an aged ex-slave resides. He is frequently called 'the white nigger.' At the risk of his life he stood by the whites during the crucial period of reconstruction, his work being like that of a mediator between the two races. To respect all in their several places and relations as superiors, inferiors, or equals is the solution of any social or race problem."[20]

Rayner's fellow African Americans, however, were not always so admiring. One black critic, Dallas minister A. S. Jackson, said that "no kind of building and school was worth the sacrifice of manhood that Raynor [*sic*] was making and that he would find that in trying to satisfy the white supremacists of Texas, he was attempting to feed a wolf—'the more you give him, the more he wants.' "[21] Rayner gradually was discovering the cruel truth in Jackson's words. The more concessions he made to white supremacy, the more strident that white supremacy became. For black leaders in the Progressive Era, temporary sacrifices of principle had a way of becoming permanent.

It would be easy to dismiss Rayner's dramatic retreat from militance as simply a sellout, a surrender to Uncle Tomism. But even as he humiliated himself before racist newspapermen and Confederate veterans' groups in his efforts to raise money for black education, behind the scenes he was desperately trying to maintain some semblance of a political voice for black Texans. After the exclusion of blacks from voting in the primaries, the only elections in which African Americans could cast their ballots were the general elections. But in order to do so, they had to pay their poll taxes, which most of them could not afford to do. There was one way around this problem, however, and Rayner was not above using it.

Since the winning candidates for most offices were chosen in the primaries, the only significant items on the fall ballot were local-option prohibition elections. In 1887, Rayner had championed the "dry" cause, but politics makes strange bedfellows, and now he cast his lot with the "wets." Rayner became a paid organizer for the Texas Brewers' Association, which furnished him funds to travel to counties where liquor elections were being held and to get out the black vote. Whatever Rayner believed personally about liquor, he now saw the brewers as his last opportunity to keep black Texans involved in politics. For several years he worked behind the scenes for the brewers, using their money to pay blacks' poll taxes and getting them to the polls on Election Day. But he gradually grew disillusioned with the whole business, and when he and the brewers could no longer agree on the terms of his compensation, they parted ways.

In his later years, Rayner occasionally wrote or spoke in favor of individual candidates in political races, but his influence had disappeared and his efforts were a waste of time. In a final irony, he accepted employment from John Henry Kirby, an ultraconservative lumber baron from Houston, to recruit laborers for Kirby's mills. Thus, Rayner, who in his Populist prime had championed the working man against greedy corporations, now found himself delivering working men into the arms of just such a corporation.

Rayner's health began to fail as the United States entered World War I. He spent much of his last years producing a group of writings that he entitled "Wise Sayings of J. B. Rayner"—bitter aphorisms that could not be published in the early twentieth-century South. In these writings, the old Populist could return to the themes of his militant years. "Commercialism," he wrote in one of them, "is a euphemistic word for artful preying: its motive is lustful covetousness, and it deals and exploits without a conscience or compunction." The religious emphasis, so prominent in the thought of southern Populists, emerges clearly in these writings: "The inordinate love for money, and ambition for power, are twin evils; whose father is Satan, and whose mother is selfishness." A number of the sayings were derived directly from the Populist diagnosis of the American economic system's ills: "When wealth concentrates, misery radiates." "No man can be charitable with money for which he did not give value received." "Interest on money invalidates the principal [*sic*] in man." "The man who takes usury from his fellow man, gives the devil a mortgage on his soul."[22]

The most prominent theme in the "Sayings," however, is not materialism, but racism: "God does not intend for one part of His people to feel that they are superior to another part." He pointed out that "the man or men who take from me the responsibilities of a full fledge citizen, take from me the opportunity to prove the true mettle of my virtues." The white southerner, he wrote, was "the most unreasonable of all men" because he "teaches the Negro to believe himself an inferior being, and at the same time requires of the Negro a character par excellent [*sic*]." If whites were superior, how was miscegenation to be explained? "A superior race never mixes their blood with the blood of an inferior race," Rayner reasoned.[23]

He never completely relinquished his faith in the American system of government. As badly as things had turned out for blacks in the South, the root values of American civilization nevertheless were "all the light the Negro has in the night of intolerance," Rayner suggested. It was "dark now," but perhaps "the hideous and horrible travail of the Negro through the valley of political and industrial intolerance" would signal "the birth of the day." However, Rayner was terribly pessimistic about the coming days, and he issued some dire warnings to whites. "The white race can only save itself by saving the black race," he cautioned. "If the Southerner keeps his sentiments, he will be sure to lose his land, his political power, and be eliminated from the commercial affairs of the country." The aging writer believed that white supremacy would "finally be [the white man's] undoing, because the Southern white man is impinging a law that no man wrote, and no legislative body enacted."[24]

To the old Populist hero, whites clearly had failed to use their power righteously. "The white people who say the most cruel things about the Negro," he declared, "are not morally nor mentally competent to write or express a thought that the future will pay any attention to." Turning his attention to the political institutions that undergirded the system of white supremacy, Rayner harshly indicted the Democratic Party. White southerners had imbued the party with a near-sacred infallibility, with tragic results. "The faith the South has in the Democratic party," he bitterly noted, was "stronger than the faith the South has in God."[25]

On July 14, 1918, Rayner died of congestive heart failure. In keeping with his wishes, there was no church funeral. The family held a simple service in his home, and few of the newspapers for which he had once written bothered to note his passing. On the next day he was laid to rest in the segregated Jim Crow cemetery on the outskirts of Calvert.

Notes

1. *Tarboro Southerner*, March 30, 1877.
2. John B. Rayner to B. H. Carroll, *San Antonio Express*, July 27, 1887.
3. *Waco Examiner*, June 19, 1887.
4. *Waco True Blue*, July 1, 1887 (first quotation); *Calvert Courier*, quoted in *Waco Examiner*, July 2, 1887 (second quotation); *Waco Examiner*, June 18, 1887 (third quotation), July 2, 1887 (fourth quotation).
5. *Dallas Morning News*, August 18, 1891.
6. *Galveston Daily News*, June 24, 1892.
7. *Dallas Morning News*, July 30, 1894 (first quotation); *Texas Advance* (Dallas), March 24, 1894 (second quotation), April 7, 1894 (third quotation); *Southern Mercury* (Dallas), July 5, 1894 (fourth quotation).
8. *Southern Mercury* (Dallas), August 11, 1894.
9. Ibid., October 4, 1894.
10. *Texas Advance* (Dallas), August 25, 1894.
11. *Southern Mercury* (Dallas), June 13, 1895.
12. Ibid., June 25, 1896.
13. *Houston Post*, October 22, 1896.

14. Ibid.

15. Norman L. McCarver and Norman L. McCarver, Jr., *Hearne on the Brazos* (San Antonio, 1956), 27 (first quotation); *Galveston Daily News*, November 7, 1896 (second quotation); *Bryan Eagle*, November 12, 1896 (third quotation); *Houston Press*, February 18, 1931 (fourth, fifth, and sixth quotations).

16. Clipping from *Houston Post*, dated November 7, 1904, in John B. Rayner Papers, Center for American History, University of Texas at Austin.

17. Ibid.

18. *Houston Chronicle*, October 20, 1912.

19. *K. Lamity's Harpoon*, clipping dated December 1911, in Rayner Papers.

20. *Houston Chronicle*, December 3, 1911 (first and second quotations), January 14, 1912 (third quotation).

21. A. S. Jackson, quoted in Melvin James Banks, "The Pursuit of Equality: The Movement for First Class Citizenship among Negroes in Texas, 1920–1950," Ph.D. diss., Syracuse University, 1962.

22. John B. Rayner, "Wise Sayings of J. B. Rayner," manuscript in Rayner Papers.

23. Ibid.

24. Ibid.

25. Ibid.

Suggested Readings

Barr, Alwyn. *Black Texans: A History of African Americans in Texas, 1528–1995.* 2d ed. Norman, OK, 1996.

Cantrell, Gregg. *Kenneth and John B. Rayner and the Limits of Southern Dissent.* Urbana and Chicago, 1993.

Cantrell, Gregg, and D. Scott Barton. "Texas Populists and the Failure of Biracial Politics." *Journal of Southern History* 55 (November 1989): 659–92.

Goodwyn, Lawrence. *Democratic Promise: The Populist Moment in America.* New York, 1976.

Martin, Roscoe C. *The People's Party in Texas.* Austin, 1933.

Williams, David A. *Bricks without Straw: A Comprehensive History of African Americans in Texas.* Austin, 1997.

Woodward, C. Vann. *Origins of the New South, 1877–1913.* Baton Rouge, 1951.

7

William Henry Bush
Panhandle Builder

Paul H. Carlson

The history of the Texas Panhandle might read differently had William Henry Bush not discovered the business potential that beckoned him early in the 1880s to the vast plains of that sparsely settled land. He lived the kind of rags-to-riches story that popular novels of his day made so familiar. Starting out in the business world as a clerk and general helper at a clothing store in Chicago, Bush rose to part ownership of the firm and branched out into other pursuits, including ranching. Traveling back and forth between Chicago and the Frying Pan Ranch in the heart of the Panhandle, he helped transform cattle raising from a risky adventure into a market-oriented enterprise. He also promoted farming on the high plains and became a doting founding father of Amarillo, encouraging railroad building and civic improvements. His keen business sense helped make Amarillo a significant social and economic center. Through his efforts in attracting midwestern grain farmers, the Panhandle also became a major wheat producer. Later, when helium was discovered on his ranch, Bush cooperated with the government in an operation that supplied the entire country. By the time he died in 1931, his mark on the land was everywhere.

Paul H. Carlson is professor of history at Texas Tech University and the author of *Empire Builder in the Texas Panhandle: William Henry Bush* (1996).

In the summer of 1928 young Joe Taylor traveled with his aunt to Chicago from his home in Amarillo in the Texas Panhandle. There was much for him to see in the great city. His aunt, who owned a millinery shop in Amarillo and was in Chicago to check on the latest women's fashions, led Joe through the famous Art Institute, around the busy downtown "Loop" district with its tall buildings, and along the Lake Michigan shoreline. And, like most Amarillo citizens who visited Chicago in the 1920s, his aunt also rode with Joe on one of the electric trolleys up North State Street where they saw the impressive home of William Henry Bush, a Chicagoan who had played a key role in developing early Amarillo and the greater Panhandle.

In the 1920s, Bush was a successful and well-connected, but re-tired, businessman who controlled extensive farm and ranch lands along Amarillo's western boundary. Because he also maintained a large and modern summer home on the edge of Amarillo about a mile north of the country club, Bush was sometimes called "a resident of Amarillo who [stayed] in Chicago."[1] In 1928, when Joe and his aunt rode by the Bush house in Chicago, they missed the wealthy entrepreneur, for that summer Bush had taken his family on a three-month-long tour of Europe, his fourteenth such trip.

William Henry Bush had taken a long and circuitous route to wealth and position. And his journey through life was often bumpy, with many of the same setbacks and hardships that all people endure. Born at Martinsburg in upstate New York in 1849, he went to work before he had finished school, and as a fourteen year old in 1863 he became a clerk in a general store, earning twelve dollars per month. Family memo-ries suggest that in 1864, during the Civil War, he left home to join a New York militia unit heading for the southern battlefields, but within a couple of weeks an uncle brought him home.

Over the next few years, Will Bush (as he was then called) clerked at small general stores in neighboring communities. In Constableville, about fourteen miles south of Martinsburg, he was paid two hundred dollars per year plus board. Then, in late 1868, he took a similar posi-tion in Lyons Falls, a village a little closer to his home. Five months later he left upstate New York for Chicago, where he went to work for Charles B. and Philo R. King, brothers from Martinsburg whom he had known as a youth. The Kings ran a large wholesale clothing business downtown, and Bush served them as a clerk and general helper, thus learning the business from the ground up. He received a wage of ten dollars per week and paid seven dollars for room and board at a room-ing house about seven blocks from his job.

Bush was nineteen years old. Although he had only a limited educa-tion, he was bright, persistent, and willing to work hard. Self-confident and determined, he had a friendly, open personality; his former em-ployer in Constableville called him a "pleasant, agreeable, and attentive young man." Tall and thin, he had a large, round head, high forehead, and prominent nose; his eyes were dark and narrow-set.

For more than two years Will Bush studied the wholesale clothing business with King Brothers and Company. As time passed, he gained the respect and confidence of the owners, who promoted him to more responsible positions. Then, in 1871, the Great Chicago Fire damaged much of the city, and Bush's life changed again. Pushed forward by high winds, the fire, which had started on October 8 in Patrick O'Leary's stable southwest of downtown, burned through the residential area and swept into the Loop, destroying everything before it, including the King Brothers building. The tiny municipal fire department had no chance.

As the fire raged out of control, Bush rushed from his rooming house near Lake Michigan to the company's property downtown. He broke into the burning building, grabbed a cash box and what company records he could carry, and with them under his arm raced north across the Rush Street Bridge over the Chicago River. Too late to reach safety in the lake or to keep ahead of the flames, Bush and hundreds of other panic-stricken people hunkered down in a wet, boggy spot of ground near today's Washington Square. As the fire roared around them, the nervous companions, with excited horses and frightened children all "trying to breathe in the suffocating heat," waited through the horrifying conflagration. Not until a light rain began falling late in the next afternoon, October 9, and the fire reached a cemetery near Lincoln Park did it finally burn itself out. Much of Chicago was destroyed.

Bush emerged from the fire tired and sore but otherwise uninjured. His prompt and heady action in saving the cash box and company records, however, marked him as an alert, quick-thinking young man. His experience and ability plus his foresight during the fire brought additional responsibility with King Brothers and Company. In 1872, after Charles had died, Philo King made Bush a partner. He was only twenty-three years old.

Bush was also a young entrepreneur who sought a variety of ways to manage and save his money. He invested in the burned-over area of the North Side by buying land and lots, and he enjoyed enough success in these ventures to purchase property elsewhere in the city. A few years later he wrote that in addition to his North Side property (Chicago's Gold Coast neighborhood, as it was called), he had secured "considerable real estate on the South and West sides" of the downtown district.

In the meantime, Bush in his capacity as a salesman for King Brothers and Company had met and courted Elva Glidden of DeKalb, Illinois, the daughter of Joseph F. Glidden, who in 1874 had patented a superior type of barbed wire. Elva was born in 1851. The young couple married in DeKalb in 1877 and moved to a large house that Bush had built on North State Street near Lincoln Park.

The marriage was fortuitous—for both Bush and his father-in-law. Glidden, sixty-four years old when his daughter married and made wealthy by the booming barbed-wire business, looked to his ambitious son-in-law for advice and direction with the large amounts of new money coming his way. Glidden invested in several DeKalb businesses and a bank, and with Bush's help over the next several years he bought Chicago real estate. For his part, Bush received financial backing when in 1885 he bought out King Brothers. With Francis Simmons, his brother-in-law, he established Bush, Simmons and Company, a wholesale clothing business.

Joseph Glidden, like Theodore Roosevelt and others, got caught up in the great western land and cattle boom that in the early 1880s was sweeping the country. In 1881, with Henry Sanborn, a slick promoter, successful salesman, and former Glidden employee, the barbed wire tycoon purchased nearly 200 sections of land (in alternating pieces, checkerboard fashion) in the Texas Panhandle and took possession by occupying the alternating sections that the state retained for future sale. When they enclosed the property with barbed wire, Glidden and Sanborn controlled some 240,000 acres, and Glidden convinced Bush to go to Texas to look after the Glidden interests.

Thus, in the late summer of 1881, W. H. Bush (as he was now called) headed for Texas. He went by train from Chicago to Springer, New Mexico. There he caught a stagecoach and rode east to Tascosa, a rough-edged supply center and cowboy watering hole about twenty-five miles northwest of Tecovas Spring, the ranch headquarters. After spending a restless night with a motley collection of outlaws, cowboys, and gunslingers in Tascosa, Bush hired a driver with a wagon and the two men started out, expecting to reach their destination by nightfall. Well after dark and with no moon to light their way, the men got lost. They pitched camp along a small creek, planning to find the headquarters in the morning. When the sun rose, however, they discovered that they had, in fact, arrived; the headquarters camp was only a few hundred yards farther up the creek.

His arrival at Tecovas Spring marked the beginning of one-half century of Bush activity in the Panhandle. In the early period, Bush from Chicago and Sanborn from his Sherman, Texas, property managed the ranch. Later, when Glidden decided to divest himself of many of his businesses, William and Elva Bush secured Glidden's half of the ranch, and on August 8, 1892, they bought Sanborn's share.

The Frying Pan Ranch, as the place was called, was located in Potter and Randall counties. It ran south from the Canadian River some thirty miles and extended westward from present Amarillo about fifteen miles. About half the large ranch was on the Llano Estacado, the high, flat plateau country of West Texas, with the northern half in the scarped and broken lands of the Canadian River Valley. For several years ranch cowboys moved the cattle between summer camps on the Llano Estacado and winter pastures in the Canadian breaks and away from cold northern winds. In 1894, Bush noted that the entire property was enclosed by barbed wire with two cross fences, and that it had a ranch house, corrals, and wells plus a large herd of cattle and some eighty horses.

Bush traveled to Texas once or twice per year. On one trip he got off the train at Dodge City, Kansas, and took a stagecoach south to Tascosa. A "fellow companion" on the stage, wrote Bush, was a "celebrated gambler by the name of Tom Emery. He had the most beautiful revolver with handle of pearl that I have ever seen." During the entire trip to Tascosa, Emery insisted on sitting on Bush's left in the stagecoach, Bush noted, "for the reason that if he happened to meet any cowboys he never allowed any of them to 'get the drop' on him."

Twice over the years Joseph Glidden accompanied Bush to Texas. On one trip in 1884, as Glidden stood on the plains looking over the wide expanse of grazing land, a strong gust of wind blew his hat off. The gust sent the black derby rolling over the prairie. A cowboy, when he saw the hat speeding away, mounted his horse, grabbed his rope, rode after the hat, lassoed it, and brought it back to the ranch owner.

Cowboys on the ranch worked hard, but they also found time for dances, trips to Tascosa, and less expensive forms of amusement. In one such instance they made Sam Dunn, a long-winded cowhand who "would talk your arm off," the target of a bunkhouse prank. A cowboy found a human skull on the ranch and, when the bunkhouse was empty, placed it in a prominent place in the building. On the skull he printed: "Talked to death by Sam Dunn."

Not all went well. Heavy investment in cattle, overstocked ranges, drought, and terribly cold winters in the period from 1885 to 1887 wrecked many ranching operations in the West. The winter of 1885–86 was rough on Panhandle livestock, and a hard drought the following summer did not allow grazing adequate for the cattle to recover. On the heels of the long drought came a second severe winter. In the spring of 1887, when cattlemen went to inspect their livestock, writes one historian, "they saw a sight they spent the rest of their lives trying to forget."[2] They found gaunt animals staggering along on frozen feet, dead animals heaped upon one another in every ravine, and piles of carcasses along the fences.

The Frying Pan survived, but many other ranching operations, including those of Theodore Roosevelt in the Dakotas, failed. The problems of the mid-1880s coupled with depressed prices and more drought in the 1890s changed the nature of cattle raising in the West. It became less an adventure and more a settled, market-oriented business. Bush, apparently, understood the changes. He moved in the early 1890s to get out of the cattle business but hold onto the land. Accordingly, he sold the cattle and succeeded in leasing to neighboring ranchers large tracts of grazing land in the Canadian breaks. With less success he leased smaller, four-section tracts on the Llano Estacado to farmer-stockmen who planted wheat or grain sorghum and raised a few head of cattle. To encourage others to lease Frying Pan land, he advertised its rich agricultural potential across much of the Midwest, but especially in Iowa and Illinois.

As his interests and investments in the Panhandle grew, Bush promoted the growth and development of Amarillo. Established in 1887 in southern Potter County just east of the Frying Pan, the town grew mainly on the strength of railroads and cattle shipping. The Fort Worth and Denver City Railroad reached the Amarillo area in 1887, and the railroad's presence was the key to the town's existence. When a year later a branch of the Santa Fe railroad entered Amarillo, its future was secure. By 1900, Bush had begun to take an active part in Amarillo's affairs. With Sanborn and others in 1899, for example, he helped to secure a third railroad for Amarillo, one that ran to Roswell, New Mexico. With the new rail line came a second depot. Soon afterward the Santa Fe Railroad built a roundhouse in Amarillo and moved its general offices for the region there.

In one of his most significant philanthropic efforts, Bush provided money and land on the north edge of town for a sanatorium, or hospital. In addition, he played a major role in encouraging the Sisters of Charity of the Order of the Incarnate Word of Saint Anthony to help support the facility. David Fly became the head physician, and seven Sisters of the Incarnate Word came from San Antonio to staff the hospital. Named Saint Anthony's Sanatorium, it opened in 1901, and for a decade the building served as the only hospital in the Panhandle.

Bush also supported a new library. In 1900 a women's club, which called itself Just Us Girls, began meeting weekly at the homes of its members. As time passed the women started study programs, and shortly afterward they determined to collect books to ease preparations for the programs. Such efforts led to plans for a club library. At a special meeting in March 1902 they gathered thirty-three books for their "library," and a short time later Margaret Wills, an elementary school teacher and the wife of Bush's Amarillo land and leasing agent, provided ninety books that Bush had given her to use as she wished. The club members, with 123 volumes, placed the collection in Mrs. Wills's home, and on October 4 their little library opened to the public. Through the years the Bush family continued to add to the library's holdings.

As these developments unfolded in Amarillo, Bush prospered in Chicago. He invested in banks and other businesses and continued his real estate interests. He owned rental property of all kinds as well as several farms, which he leased on a yearly basis. When in 1903 he and Francis Simmons dissolved their partnership, Bush established William H. Bush and Company, a wholesale hat and glove firm, with his brother Edwin as manager.

Not only a businessman and entrepreneur, Bush also had an engaging and wide-ranging mind. He joined the Chicago Historical Society and participated in its activities. He became a life member of the Art Institute of Chicago, contributed thousands of dollars to its trust fund, and in 1909 became one of its governing members. He collected and read a wide range of books, enjoying them for their content as well as for their design. This interest led him to become a member of the Caxton Club, a book and literary society that attracted writers, book lovers, and members of Chicago's intellectual community. And he joined the Cliff Dwellers, a group whose members pursued artistic and literary subjects.

Bush's interests were widespread. He promoted the preservation and expansion of Chicago's grand Lincoln Park. He enjoyed horses but later owned big, expensive automobiles and fancy touring cars. He played golf and held membership in three country clubs. He belonged to dinner clubs, businessmen's organizations, and the powerful Chicago Club, where he ate lunch each day with some of the city's most prominent business leaders. Except for an occasional glass of wine, he did not drink alcohol, but after lunch at the Chicago Club he sometimes smoked a cigar while he played whist or some other card game and talked politics.

A journey through life is not always smooth, and Bush had his troubles. After his father's death, for example, he assumed responsibility for his younger brother and four sisters. Some of his investments and some business ventures failed, including a large manufacturing plant in DeKalb. As his in-laws grew older and less alert, he and Elva managed the Gliddens' properties and tended to their needs, including their health care. There were setbacks in Amarillo, too. An attempt in the 1890s to diversify the Frying Pan operations by raising chickens failed, and Bush's plans for developing fruit and vegetable schemes foundered. He tried to grow eucalyptus trees, but that experiment went nowhere. After the turn of the century, he watched the adobe ranch house at Tecovas Spring crumble away. In a court fight over a tract of land in Amarillo he split with his longtime friend and partner, Henry Sanborn.

Greater tragedy struck on May 19, 1906, when Elva Bush died. She and W. H. had been married for twenty-nine years. Although they had no children, their relationship had been an intimate one, full of love and quiet pleasures. With no brothers or sisters, Elva had enjoyed her husband's family as her own, especially Hattie Simmons. Then, just four months after Elva's death, Joseph Glidden died, at the age of ninety-three. He and Bush had developed a close friendship that went beyond their business connections.

Fortunately, the human spirit has an enormous capacity to recover. On a visit to his sister Clara in Kansas City, Bush met Ruth Gentry, an intelligent, lively young Vassar College graduate. Although there was a considerable age difference between them, Ruth (twenty-seven) and Bush (fifty-eight) began courting almost from their first meeting, and on October 20, 1908, they were married in Kansas City. To Bush's great pleasure, Ruth took a more lively interest than Elva in the Texas Panhandle and the Frying Pan Ranch. Indeed, she accompanied Bush to the ranch and later encouraged him to build a new house on the property—one that was much closer to Amarillo than the original ranch house, buildings, and corrals at Tecovas Spring. She enjoyed playing golf with Bush and even "scandalized" many members at the Amarillo Country Club when she insisted that the club establish mixed foursomes.

Meanwhile, the Chicago, Rock Island, and Gulf Railroad entered Amarillo, and in the summer of 1908 it built westward through Bush's Frying Pan Ranch. When it reached Wildorado, just west of the Frying Pan, a businessman reported, "folks from the farms and ranches tuck [*sic*] out an' come to town to see the train go by."[3] A month later, on July 3, Bush dedicated the townsite of Bush Stop (Bushland) on Frying Pan land along the railroad between Amarillo and Wildorado. The community developed as a typical T-shape frontier village—that is, the railroad formed the top (crossed) part of the T, and the main street formed the post. Railroad shipping facilities lay across the tracks from the business and residential sections. Then, three days after the dedication of his namesake community, Bush formally opened the townsite of Soncy. Also located on Frying Pan land and along the Rock Island, the town stood six miles closer to Amarillo. In both communities, Bush named the streets for friends and family members. His plan was to sell business and residential lots and thus duplicate his success in Chicago.

By this time, Amarillo, which was just emerging from its pioneer past, had become the railroad and business center of the Panhandle. Its population was nearing 10,000, and Bush continued to seek ways to profit from his ranch land and to promote the Panhandle. He partici-pated with others in advertising the stock-farming and crop-raising po-tential of the area, and he sought, without much success, to develop dairy farming in the Panhandle.

As he helped to build Amarillo and by extension the greater Texas Panhandle, Bush moved into the large, stone house built just beyond the western edge of the growing community. Ruth improved the grounds with trees and shrubs, a shallow pool for swimming, and flower beds. She laid out a long curving driveway and bordered it with additional trees and shrubs.

Ruth also gave birth to two girls, Caroline in 1909 and Emeline in 1910, who came to Amarillo for the first time in 1914. "I was almost five," Caroline remembered. Upon arrival at the Santa Fe Railroad sta-tion early in the morning, two Harvey girls—waitresses hired by the Santa Fe's Harvey House restaurant chain—provided breakfast. After-ward, before they headed for the ranch house, their buggy driver took them "to the old Amarillo Hotel, where Mother and our maid were absolutely scandalized to see the number of drunks lying in armchairs in the halls."[4] Over the years the girls, who spent each summer in Ama-rillo, learned to love Texas. They rode horses, swam in the shallow pool behind the house, and walked downtown to visit with other children. The Panhandle became a place of grand adventure for them.

Bush, meanwhile, continued his active part in Amarillo affairs. He spoke each summer to the Amarillo Lions Club, helped to develop the Amarillo Country Club and the Tri-State Fair, and promoted additional railroads for his city. After one of his typical speeches in 1913 he told a reporter that "Amarillo has a good start on all the rest of the towns of the Panhandle as a railroad center." Pointing out that "Lubbock has had two railroads and is getting another since Amarillo has scored in that particular," he urged his fellow townspeople not to stop. Bush also noted

Plainview's "aspirations to build a city." Another line, he indicated, "will place Amarillo in the lead for all time, as the Panhandle's principal railroad and distributing center."[5] While he continued to maintain an office in downtown Chicago, in 1914, Bush retired from his hat and glove business and turned its operations over to his brother. Increasingly he turned his attention to Amarillo and the Panhandle.

During World War I, when the price of wheat jumped significantly, Bush pushed for its greater cultivation in the Panhandle. With many others he encouraged the plowing of his Llano Estacado lands, or "flat lands," as he called them, and continued his efforts to entice people from the Midwest to come to the Amarillo area to farm. The efforts were rewarded. The population of the Panhandle increased, Amarillo grew, and small towns appeared everywhere. By the end of the war in 1918, the Panhandle was no longer a frontier; it was an active rural commonwealth.

Then an oil boom hit. In December 1918 drillers struck natural gas in the Panhandle. Not long afterward, drillers struck oil in Carson and Hutchinson counties northeast of Amarillo. There was little interest in Potter County or in Bush's Frying Pan lands, however, for geologists speculated that no oil would be found there. They were right—in part. No oil was found on Frying Pan land until long after Bush's death, but drillers in the 1920s found plenty of helium—the world's largest known reserves at the time.

To encourage helium recovery, Bush provided the federal government with eighteen acres of land at Soncy for a helium extraction plant. When it opened in April 1929, the facility contained eight major buildings "together with their appurtenances, including roadways; water-cooling pond; water wells and tower; gas holders; water, steam, gas, electric and waste lines."[6] Pipelines carried natural gas from wells on the Bush property to the plant, and there workers extracted the helium. The government then shipped the helium to storage facilities on the East and West Coasts.

In the 1920s, as the oil and gas boom turned Amarillo into more than an agricultural town, Bush continued with his Frying Pan leases. As he had done for some twenty years, he rented grassland in the Canadian breaks to ranchers and farm land to wheat growers on the "flat lands." Moreover, he kept on buying and selling tracts on the Frying Pan. In 1930 the ranch comprised some 110,000 acres, about the same number that Joseph Glidden and Henry Sanborn had purchased in 1881.

In Chicago, likewise, Bush continued to buy, sell, and lease property. As he grew older, however, he instructed his agents to dispose of much of his farm acreage and to consolidate most of his real estate in the downtown area. He was now worth several million dollars. Then, suddenly, after a short illness, Bush died. He had contracted a cold that turned into pneumonia. Doctors indicated to his wife and daughters that little could be done, and on April 8, 1931, he passed away. With his death, Amarillo and the Texas Panhandle lost one of its most active community builders.

When in 1928 he viewed the Bush home in Chicago, Joe Taylor saw an impressive sight. Located near North Avenue and across from Lincoln Park (to the north) and across the street from the large residence and spacious grounds of the Catholic Archbishop (to the east), the house stood on the northern edge of the affluent Gold Coast. Moreover, the city had designated North State Street above Schiller Street as North State Parkway, a road that Lincoln Park officials maintained with special care, thus making the neighborhood even more elegant.

Back in Amarillo, had he chosen to do so, Joe Taylor could have driven out one of the main roads from town to the Bush summer residence on a small hill just west of the Frying Pan's eastern boundary, what is today Western Avenue. The house, one of the first in Amarillo to be wired with electricity, was sited with a grand view of the surrounding countryside. The long, curving driveway was lined with trees that Mrs. Bush had planted. According to contemporary newspaper accounts, the place was the scene each summer "of the season's outstanding social events in Amarillo."[7]

From young Joe Taylor's perspective in 1928, the life of William Henry Bush was (with apologies to Charles Dickens) "a tale of two cities." Bush enjoyed success in both places. In Chicago he remained in the wholesale hat and glove business for some forty-five years, from his arrival in 1869 until his retirement in 1914. In Amarillo, he stayed with the Frying Pan Ranch for fifty years, from his first visit to the Panhandle in 1881 until his death in 1931. He was, reported a local newspaper, "a tireless civic worker in Chicago, just as he was a builder in the Panhandle."[8] One of the Panhandle's most active boosters, Bush consistently engaged in enterprises crucial to the region's growth and prosperity. He was, suggested a local attorney, "a man whose vision of the future of this city and the Panhandle was greater than that of any [person] I ever knew."[9]

Notes

1. *Amarillo Daily News*, April 10, 1931.
2. Ray Allen Billington and Martin Ridge, *Westward Expansion: A History of the American Frontier*, 5th ed. (New York: Macmillan, 1982), 626.
3. *Amarillo Sunday News and Globe*, August 14, 1938.
4. Donna Flenniken, "Barbed Wire and the Frying Pan Ranch," *Accent West* 19 (February 1991): 19.
5. *Amarillo Daily News*, January 25, 1913.
6. C. W. Seibel, "The Government's New Helium Plant at Amarillo, Texas," *Chemical and Metallurgical Engineering* 37 (September 1930): 550–52.
7. *Amarillo Daily News*, April 10, 1931.
8. Ibid.
9. Ibid.

Suggested Readings

Carlson, Paul H. *Empire Builder in the Texas Panhandle: William Henry Bush*. College Station, TX, 1996.
Key, Della Tyler. *In the Cattle Country: History of Potter County*. Wichita Falls, TX, 1966.
Price, B. Byron, and Fred W. Rathjen. *The Golden Spread: An Illustrated History of Amarillo and the Texas Panhandle*. Northridge, CA, 1986.
Rathjen, Fred W. *The Texas Panhandle Frontier*. 2d ed. Lubbock, TX, 1998.

8

Hester Calvert
Farm Wife

Rebecca Sharpless

After the Civil War era, most Texans were likely to find themselves laboring under harsh conditions for little pay and with few prospects for improving their lot in life. Sharecropping and tenant farming remained the dominant arrangement on the average farm. Hester Calvert was typical of many Texas farm wives. Overburdened and undereducated, she toiled at many tasks to help her family make ends meet. In a cramped household that sheltered her, her husband, their eight children, and often the couple's aged parents, Hester was wife, mother, cook, seamstress, laborer, doctor, treasurer, and spiritual provider. For much of her adult life, this sharecropper/tenant family worked farms, mostly in the rural areas around Waco, on land that belonged to others. Societal traditions and economic imperatives endowed Hester with stoic resilience and a disciplined work ethic that helped her endure such an arduous life. Eventually the Calverts broke the cycle of poverty that trapped so many rural Texans by saving enough money to buy land on which they developed a dairy farm. A later move to Waco, from which Hester's husband commuted, provided the family with new advantages. For the first time they enjoyed a house with electricity and running water, access to shopping, and better schools for their children.

Rebecca Sharpless is the director of the Institute for Oral History at Baylor University and the author of *Fertile Ground, Narrow Choices: Women on Texas Cotton Farms, 1900–1940* (1999).

A husband, eight children, and the rhythms of cotton farming: these are the factors that shaped the life of Hester McClain Calvert. Daughter, wife, and sister of cotton farmers, Hester represents millions of Texas women at the turn of the twentieth century who led their lives in relationship to their families and rarely had existences away from the farm. But these women are important because their families depended on them. A rural household without a wife and mother had a difficult, if not impossible, time.

In the story of Texas, the farm woman is an unsung heroine. The efforts of these women ensured that Texas led the United States in cotton production before World War II, growing one-third to one-fourth of the raw cotton for the entire nation. The mythic Texas is that of oil and cowboys, but it was agriculture that supplied most Texans with their living before World War II. Entire families worked hard to bring in the cotton crop, and the women labored in the fields as well as took care of their families' needs for food, clothing, and housing.

Cotton farming dominated much of the Texas economy between the Civil War and World War II. The world wanted raw cotton from which to make cloth, and the Texas climate and soil brought forth huge harvests to satisfy the demand. One writer declared cotton to be "one of the most important, if not the most important, articles of the world's commerce."[1] Most of the region's farm families, however, were poor. In Central Texas the majority of cotton farmers in 1900 did not own the land that they spent their lives working, and many did not even own the plows and mules that they used to break the ground. A large number of these tenant farmers and sharecroppers remained constantly indebted to the people who owned the land. Some lived in relative comfort, but most tenants and sharecroppers existed in various stages of deprivation, lacking suitable housing, clothing, and food for themselves and their numerous children. They almost never had any cash, and they lived on credit from year to year.

Until at least 1940, millions of men, women, and children in Texas and elsewhere in the South worked to bring in the cotton crop. Within this system, women played several crucial roles. A majority of Central Texas women not only worked in the fields but also raised vegetables to feed their household; they sewed their families' clothing so that they would not have to spend much money for those items and go further into debt to the landowner. And they bore the children who would be valuable agricultural laborers before they were even old enough to begin school. Farm women's lives were filled with hard work and not much pleasure, but most of them tried in good faith to meet their considerable responsibilities to their families.

Hester McClain Calvert is a good example of a Central Texas farm woman. She was born in Falls County, Texas, on December 6, 1878, and received a sixth-grade education in the Mooreville area. Despite a lack of formal schooling, she was an intelligent woman who remained an avid reader all her life. In 1904, at the then-advanced age of twenty-six, she married Robert L. Calvert, a farmer four years younger than she, who also lived in the Mooreville area. Both of their families had migrated to Texas from Mississippi after the Civil War. While Hester was born in Texas, Robert had been born back east and migrated as a child. When Hester and Robert were still children, Central Texas had been settled less than forty years. Although the Native Americans had been gone for at least thirty years, the rich prairie sod had been broken only recently, and life on the prairies beckoned to families such as the Calverts who were fleeing the destruction of the Civil War. They soon found, however, that their hopes were dashed, as little of the rich land was available for purchase, and they wound up working on land owned by other people. They, and most of their neighbors, were extremely poor, and no amount of hard work could remedy their situation. But young people such as Robert and Hester set forth bravely, believing that they could make a life for themselves and their children on a Texas cotton farm.

Like most farm women, Hester became a mother shortly after her marriage. Women in the rural South had virtually no access to birth control until the 1920s, and their families were consistently larger in number than those in other parts of the United States. Hester bore nine children, beginning with Myrtle in 1905, followed by Lillian in 1906, Thelma in 1908, Clark in 1910, Milas in 1911, Carlos in 1913, Royce in 1916, and Nadine in 1918. Clarence, born prematurely, died as a newborn in 1912. As she grew older and developed thyroid problems, pregnancy became harder for Hester. At the age of forty, she almost miscarried her daughter, Nadine, and at the age of forty-five, she miscarried a tenth baby and nearly died from blood poisoning, more than fifteen years before the discovery of antibiotics. Throughout her difficult pregnancies, Hester remained on her feet. Her oldest daughter, Myrtle Calvert Dodd, remarked: "She couldn't stay in the bed. There was too many of us."[2]

Even with eight children, the Calvert household expanded to take in older relatives. The parents of Robert and Hester rotated among their adult children when they became too feeble to live alone. Growing too frail to farm, Robert's father, David Calvert, divided his farming tools among his sons. With his wife, Indiana, he left his farm in West Texas and returned to Central Texas. David and Indiana lived with Hester and Robert's family for the two years before David died in his late eighties. At that time, his wife, who was thirteen years younger, began circulating among her daughters' homes. Hester and her mother-in-law both worked hard at getting along despite the cramped quarters and the children bounding around them. Myrtle remembered, "Now, my grandmother knew to hold her tongue, but I've heard her say, 'If I's so-and-so, I wouldn't do so-and-so. I wouldn't let my younguns do so-and-so.' I've heard her say those things, but not to my mother. She knew when to say and when not to say. Very diplomatic." Hester's mother, Mary Adaline Strickland McClain, widowed years before, also rotated among her children. One grandparent often arrived shortly after the other had departed, making a congested household even more crowded.

Robert and Hester did not own land for the first twenty years of their marriage, and the family moved frequently. Sharecroppers and tenant farmers had little power within the economic system, but they often exercised their ability to change farms. The couple began their marriage on a farm near Lorena, in McLennan County. With their two oldest daughters, they followed his parents in 1908 to Jones County in West Texas, where cotton farming was opening up on the drier land. They remained there for two years, but, discouraged by a lack of rain, returned to Central Texas in 1910. Despite living next door to her in-laws, Hester missed her own family in Central Texas. Her widowed mother had bought a farm near the Woodlawn community near Bruceville, and two of Hester's brothers and sisters lived close by. When they came back, Hester was pleased to be among her people again.

With no land and few resources, the Calvert family continued to move for the next eighteen years across southern McLennan County. Their experiences show the range of situations available to a sharecropper or tenant farmer. They arrived back in Central Texas too late in the growing season of 1910 to find a suitable farm for the following year, and so they lived in a tiny house near Lorena owned by the Westbrooks, one of the wealthiest families in that part of Central Texas. Robert did odd jobs for the remainder of the crop year to support his family. The house on the Westbrook place was little more than an unpainted shack; Hester remained upset until her husband found screens to put on the windows to keep out flies and mosquitoes. Her daughter Myrtle recalled: "My mother just threw a fit when she saw that little house didn't have screens on it. . . . I can still remember when my mother said, 'Now listen, we're going to have screens. We can't live—my kids—with no screens.' " Like many of the houses in rural Texas, the Westbrook place had no electricity or running water; the family relied on kerosene lamps and brought water from a well.

The following year, they moved to the Attaway place near Hewitt, which had a large house, and remained there for two or three years. Robert then bought his own mules and tools and rose from the status of sharecropper to tenant farmer, and the family farmed for one year on the McLaughlin place near Eddy. They next spent two years on the

Connally farm at Long Branch, near Lorena, and then moved to the Stribling place at Hewitt, where they remained for five years, until 1921. The Stribling place was popular with the family, with its yellow paint, brown trim, carbide-burning electrical system, and indoor bathroom with a large tin bathtub. The Calverts fit eight children and two adults into three bedrooms: the two oldest girls in one, the parents and two youngest girls in the second one, and the four boys in the back room. When the Stribling farm came up for sale, the family urged Robert to buy it. He did not want to, however, declaring it not large enough. The Stribling farm passed to an outside buyer, and the family was forced to move once more.

To Hester's disappointment, they moved only a short distance to the Chapman place, which had more land but not as large or nice a house as the Stribling farm. The house on the Chapman place burned in the fall of 1927, with almost all of the Calverts' possessions. Neighbors donated food and furniture while the family lived in the basement of the vacant public school in Hewitt during the time that the Chapmans rebuilt the house. The next year, Robert and Hester bought a dairy farm near Bosqueville, five miles from Waco. They then moved to Waco, the county seat and a town of 56,000, in 1940, and Robert commuted to the dairy farm until his retirement in 1943.

With eight children, Hester spent almost all of her time meeting their needs. In this way, she was more fortunate than a number of women who had to balance child care with fieldwork. Keeping a growing family supplied with proper food and clothing was more than a full-time job. Inevitably, some of the children became ill or injured, and she cared for them without the benefit of antibiotics or other medicines. To ward off colds, Hester made poultices of lard and turpentine or ammonia, pinning them to her children's undershirts. As the eight children grew up, bumps and bruises were common and were usually treated with kerosene. When one child brought an illness home, most of the others would contract it. For one entire winter, for example, measles passed from child to child in sequence. According to her daughter, Hester said, "I declare, we had measles up till spring!" The Calverts raised all of their children to adulthood except Clarence, who, as mentioned earlier, died shortly after his premature birth. In this way they fared better than many of their peers, who commonly lost at least one in every five children.

As did many of her counterparts, Hester sewed almost everything that she and her eight children wore. In the first years of her marriage, she borrowed sewing machines from her relatives but acquired her own upon the family's return to Central Texas in 1910. For her daughters, she made everything from flannel nightgowns to underwear to bloomers made of black sateen. The oldest ones handed down their clothing to the next ones. Sometimes, Hester altered dresses for her daughters, making items over or dyeing them a different color. The boys wore store-bought denim overalls, but their mother sewed shirts and underwear. She even made costumes for her adolescent daughters to wear in a school program despite the fact that she considered the blue and green crinoline dresses far too skimpy for decency's sake. Hester also made items for the household, sewing sheets, pillow cases, and dishtowels from cotton yardgoods. From fabric scraps, she made two quilts per year, working in between daily tasks because the light was too dim at night for her to see her stitches. She kept geese and plucked their soft down feathers to fill pillows and mattresses.

Once it was made and worn, clothing had to be washed, and doing laundry was one of the heaviest, most unpleasant of farm women's tasks. At least once per year, the women cooked rancid lard, or rendered pork fat, with lye to make soap, boiling the lard in an open kettle over an open fire. They sometimes scented it with sweet-smelling spices. They poured the soft soap into pans and cut it into squares after it hardened. (Some of the poorest families even bathed with lye soap; others, like the Calverts, bought less harsh soap.) On washday, the women hauled water from a well or a creek to the yard of the house. They heated the water in a wash pot over an open flame and rubbed the clothes on a washboard. Each item then went through several tubs of rinse water. Men's heavy denim overalls, caked with mud and sweat from the cotton fields, were especially difficult to wash.

Like many Anglo women in Central Texas, Hester spent some of her family's hard-earned cash to hire help with the laundry. Across the region, African-American women worked for low wages doing wash. When the Calverts lived on the Chapman place, an African American named Ada Richardson did their laundry, bringing her young son with her while she worked. Most women did their ironing with flat irons, or "sad irons," heated on the kitchen stove. Using the sad irons required some skill because the ironer could scorch the clean clothes or get soot on them from the stove. Most rural women did not have access to the electric irons that their city sisters enjoyed, and yearned for nicer possessions. As Myrtle said, "I didn't have things that I'd hear about. You know, I read the paper and read books, the [things] that they had. Of course, we all had the idea of going to town and having better things, and that's what most of us did."

Like virtually all southern farm women, Hester thought a great deal about meals for her family. The Calverts lived on the typical southern diet known as the three Ms: meat, meal, and molasses. The meat came mostly from hogs, which could be fed table scraps; it did not spoil as easily as beef or chicken. In every rural area, the men butchered hogs at the time of the first cold snap, using nature's refrigeration to keep the pork fresh. The women and children ground some of the meat and mixed it with salt, pepper, and sage, stuffing it into cloth casings or the butchered hog's intestines to make sausage.

Sausage casings were another of Hester's sewing tasks, made from wheat flour sacks. Her daughter said, "We didn't care for the sausage that was put in the intestines, so Mother made sacks. You saved your flour sacks from one year to the other, so she would have flour sacks to tear up and make sausage sacks out of them." The pork, particularly hams and bacon, would then be smoked or preserved with salt. Sometimes the supply lasted until the next year; at other times, families were left with no meat in their diet. As Myrtle commented, "When the sausage were gone, why, you did without."

Families used every part of the hog, pickling the feet and making loaves of jellied, chopped meat from the head. After the butchering, the next task was rendering lard. Hog fat was cooked into lard, which was stored from year to year and used for frying and for making biscuits and other baked goods. As poor as the Calverts were, they were better off than their African-American neighbors. According to Myrtle, "They used to come and [say], 'Mrs. Calvert, you got any old grease?' You know, she would save old grease for the woman that washed for us. It would get kind of rancid, but, you know, she'd re-cook it and use it."

The "meal" of the three Ms was cornmeal. Southern farmers raised corn to feed their mules as well as their families. The men took part of their crop to a gristmill, sometimes paying the miller with a share of the ground meal. Families kept large amounts of cornmeal on hand, trying to store it in ways that would keep out weevils. Most farm women cooked cornbread at least once per day, a simple, hearty bread that could be made plain or elaborate depending on supplies of milk, eggs, and other ingredients. Hester also fried patties of cornmeal, which her children loved: "When she'd fry cornbread patties for supper, she couldn't hardly make enough. We kids loved them. . . . And you can imagine, especially when my grandparents were there, trying to make cornbread patties for supper. . . . I don't know how she stood it in the summertime, to get stuff ready over that hot stove, but she did." At the times of the year when the food supply was thinnest, the Calvert family lived on these cornmeal patties. And "molasses" was a variety of syrup made from sugarcane or sorghum.

Hester Calvert worked diligently to increase her family's diet beyond the three Ms. She supervised the planting of a large vegetable garden near the house, choosing beans, Irish potatoes, tomatoes, okra, turnips (used more for the greens than for the root), collard greens, and onions. Myrtle observed: "I remember my mother would say, 'We're going to plant this and plant that and plant the other thing.' Usually my mother bossed it, told what she wanted. If my father planted it, she would always say, 'Well, he planted too much of this or too much of that, or not enough of the other.' "

Families like the Calverts also depended upon wild fruits such as plums, grapes, and blackberries. While many owners had orchards of peach and plum trees, most tenants did not have access to them. The farmer who was lucky enough to be hired on a place with peach trees was ensured a rare treat for his family. "If we had one peach tree and plum tree, they were always so glad," Myrtle recalled. Her mother made jelly from the fruits that grew wild on the farm, standing over a woodstove in the summer heat. She also bought dried fruit. The stereotypical image of the farm wife with rows of canned goods on her pantry shelves did not ring true in Central Texas; most women canned nothing until after World War I, and Hester did not have any equipment for canning until the late 1920s. Families ate vegetables in season; there were no more until the next crop came in.

Farm women such as Hester also supplemented their families' diets by raising chickens for both eggs and meat. Chickens were easy to feed and water, and even the poorest households kept a few. They did not lay all year round, and families looked forward to the spring laying time, when eggs were plentiful. As the Calvert children grew, they had the task of gathering eggs each day and bringing them to their mother. Myrtle remembered an overabundance during the spring: "Mama would boil them and stuff them and fry them and any way in the world to get rid of them because you couldn't keep them very long." When farm women had a surplus of eggs, they often bartered them with traveling peddlers or town merchants for merchandise.

Hester raised turkeys as well—not an easy task, for they were stupid and easily injured. Myrtle told one of the family's favorite stories about their turkeys:

> When I was born, it was in May. And Mama had some turkey to come off with little turkeys, and you know, you put a little meat grease on top of their head to keep lice off. And my mother couldn't get out and do it, had my father to do it, and every one of them died. And my uncles just laughed so, said Papa had the idea, if a little bit did good, a lot would do more good, and he put too much on there and they died. He lost a whole setting of little turkeys. They laughed about that as long as most of them lived, about Bob greasing the turkeys.

When the turkeys survived, Robert took the doomed birds into Waco, the nearest town, to sell at holiday time. Hester used her turkey money to purchase Christmas gifts for the children.

Most rural families ate beef only occasionally; it spoiled easily. For the Calverts, roast beef remained a rare treat. Having dairy and meat products was difficult because most farm families had no refrigeration. They kept milk and butter cold by storing it in their well or in a cooler, a device with canvas-covered shelves that absorbed water from a pan; with a breeze, evaporation cooled the items. The Calverts eventually acquired a commercially manufactured icebox; even though they had to go into the nearby village of Hewitt to buy ice, they were extremely pleased to have it.

Until they bought the dairy farm, the Calverts usually had one or two cows, which made them more fortunate than many families in rural Texas and kept them supplied with milk, cream, and butter. However, butter making was a tedious chore, which the females in the house shared and despised. Myrtle observed: "My mother hated it. Nobody liked to churn. My sister Thelma used to read and churn and if Grandma's there, she'd say, 'Thelma, you're just slowing down. You've got to keep paying attention. Just get busy and churn! Get through with it!' " Extra butter also was taken by Robert to Waco to sell. With the proceeds, he bought rice, raisins, apples, and canned fruit such as peaches. The family loved the variety that store-bought food brought to their meals.

Hester prepared two hot meals per day. She cooked on a woodstove for most of her early marriage, with wood brought from the river bottom some distance away from the farm on the grassy prairie. For breakfast each morning, she made dozens of hot biscuits, served with homemade butter and jelly or syrup, bacon or ham, and sometimes scrambled eggs. Farm breakfasts were hearty, planned to sustain the family workers on their way to the fields. Dinner, the main meal of the day, was at noon. Robert always looked forward to dinner; relatives teased him about his punctuality in leaving the fields for the house at 11:30, when the nearby train blew its whistle. The midday meal usually consisted of some type of pork, cornbread, and whatever fresh vegetables were available, and sometimes dried beans. For supper, the evening meal, the Calverts ate bean or potato soup or a salad picked from the garden, with a fresh batch of cornbread. For some farm families, supper was cornbread crumbled into buttermilk. Cooking with children nearby sometimes was difficult. Myrtle remembered that one of her sisters accidentally knocked a sliver of Ivory soap into the soup: "And somebody got soup and said, 'Mama! What's the matter? This soup foams!' And we found out what had happened, couldn't eat it. Ruined the whole pot."

In the early part of the twentieth century, few families ate yeast bread or "light bread." Yeast was tricky to store, and breadmaking with yeast was time-consuming. Hester's sister-in-law made yeast bread, which her family consumed within a day or two. Robert also bought it in town as a treat for his family. The children all adored "light bread," but it had to be reserved for special occasions. Hester sometimes made chocolate pie or a flat, cookie-like cake known as a tea cake. She also baked a great deal at Christmas, hoarding eggs for her coconut and lemon cakes and various pies. From peaches, apples, and fresh or preserved berries, she made cobblers.

Life in rural Central Texas revolved around the seasons of the cotton crop. As a young woman, Hester worked in her parents' fields. The tasks of cotton cultivation changed little between the Civil War and World War II, and Hester's chores were identical to those done by her daughters thirty years later. As an adult, Hester did not take part in the actual field work, looking after her numerous children instead, but her daughters worked in the fields from the time that they were six or seven years old.

Hester labored diligently, however, to support the work of those out in the fields, cooking and caring for them. Cotton farming was extremely labor intensive, and it would not be completely mechanized until the 1950s. Robert, later assisted by his sons, prepared the land for planting in the late winter, then sowed the seed in early April. By late May, the young cotton would be ready for thinning and weeding in a process known as "chopping." The Calvert children began to help as soon as they could safely handle a sharp hoe, at the age of ten or eleven.

As the summer progressed, the cotton grew and ripened, moving toward the harvest that could start as early as August and might last as late as December, according to the weather. Hester began preparing for the harvest by sewing cotton-picking sacks. The pickers pulled long canvas sacks, secured with a strap over their shoulders, behind them as they moved down the long rows of cotton, pulling the white fibers from the hard boll. Hester also sewed fingerless gloves for her daughters to protect their hands from the prickly bolls.

Cotton picking was the time when the Calverts worked hardest, trying to bring in the harvest before rain could ruin the crop or other calamities befell it. They worked from first light until dark, with a meal break at the hottest part of the day. If a farm family could afford to, they hired help. African Americans and Mexicans, in particular, welcomed the wages, however meager, that picking cotton brought. Pickers were paid by the pound, and a good picker could average several hundred pounds per day. In many families, a daughter who was good at arithmetic waited by the cotton wagon and kept track of the pickers' daily yield. Once the wagon was full, the men took the cotton to the gin, and the women waited patiently at home for the news of what the family's income for the year would be. A poor harvest or low cotton prices meant a year of scraping by, making old clothes last a while longer, and not buying anything new for the house.

Life on the farm was more than hard work. Much of the farm people's socializing took place at church. Hester grew up as a Freewill Baptist but became a Methodist upon her marriage. As an adult, she sent her children to church regularly, but she herself attended only on special occasions. Her eardrum had burst when she was a child, and her hearing was significantly impaired. As a result, she remained at home much of the time, although she did attend the annual revival meetings sponsored by the Christian churches—Baptist, Methodist, Church of Christ—in the Hewitt area. She took Sunday as her respite from cooking, preparing a meal on Saturday to serve on Sunday. Many rural women enjoyed belonging to the women's groups in their churches, but Hester's deafness prevented her from taking part. The Calverts hosted parties for their children, however, serving ice cream, cookies, and lemonade to the young people who lived in the area of their farm. The family loved music, and Hester played the organ despite her hearing loss.

Hester also liked trips into town. Before World War I, her trips were infrequent, perhaps only once per month or less. After the family bought a car, they traveled to Waco more regularly; the twenty-mile trip lasted about an hour. Once, Robert and Hester took all eight of their children to Waco to see a baseball game. They dressed in their Sunday clothes for the adventure. Myrtle remembered: "[Mama] probably wore her best dress and hat. Some of them said, why did she dress up so to come to the park? Well, I guess we thought you was supposed to. I don't know. But we wore our very best to go to the ballpark."

Robert began buying land in the 1920s, and the family moved to a dairy farm near Bosqueville in 1928. The family lived there until 1940, when they moved into Waco. Hester, who had lived in the country all of her life, adjusted immediately to living in Waco, with its shopping as well as electricity and running water. She enjoyed freedom from the responsibility of caring for livestock and raising crops. Myrtle confirmed that "she was thrilled. She was just ready to move to town. . . . She had a cousin just a few blocks from her that was real close, and they visited and she could walk to the little store and do things like that that was good for her." Her pleasure was short-lived, however, for Robert died in 1947. Hester then moved in with her oldest daughter, Myrtle Dodd, and lived in the Dodd household until her death on May 24, 1964.

As a Texas farm wife, Hester Calvert never gained fame or fortune. For her husband and eight children, however, her efforts made a significant impact on their lives. The food that she cooked, the clothing that she sewed, and the care that she gave her family made the difference in the quality of their lives. The contributions of women like Hester made it possible for their children and grandchildren to grow and thrive amid the harsh circumstances of life in rural Texas.

Notes

1. William Bennett Bizzell, *Rural Texas* (New York, 1924), 156.
2. This and subsequent quotations are from Myrtle Calvert Dodd, *Oral Memoirs of Myrtle Calvert Dodd* (series of interviews by Rebecca Sharpless, August 14–September 19, 1990, Waco, Texas; The Texas Collection, Baylor University).

Suggested Readings

Allen, Ruth. *The Labor of Women in the Production of Cotton.* Austin, 1931.
Bizzell, William Bennett. *Rural Texas.* New York, 1924.

Foley, Neil. *The White Scourge: Mexicans, Blacks, and Poor Whites in Texas Cotton Culture.* Berkeley, 1997.

Hagood, Margaret Jarman. *Mothers of the South: Portraiture of the White Tenant Farm Woman.* Chapel Hill, NC, 1977.

Sharpless, Rebecca. *Fertile Ground, Narrow Choices: Women on Texas Cotton Farms, 1900–1940.* Chapel Hill, NC, 1999.

Stimpson, Eddie, Jr. *My Remembers: A Black Sharecropper's Recollections of the Depression.* Denton, TX, 1996.

9

Thomas Mitchell Campbell
Reform Governor of the People

Janet Schmelzer

The Progressive Era, it has been said, represented the spirit of an age. The improvements that Texans enjoyed during that period were a part of a nationwide phenomenon. Thomas Mitchell Campbell established himself as a liberal progressive in a state that was otherwise dominated by conservative politics. A middle-class background and lifelong friendship with fellow "man of the people" James Stephen Hogg helped shape Campbell's outlook. As an attorney he built a respectable practice, but it was his work reorganizing the affairs of the troubled International and Great Northern Railroad that earned him a reputation for high moral standards and ethical business conduct. Coupled with a concern for the average Texan, his record propelled him into the Governor's Mansion in 1906. The legislation that he championed resulted in social, economic, and political reforms that significantly improved the general welfare of ordinary Texans. Campbell's crusade affected such areas as health and education, the state prison system, and big business, especially railroads. His reforms came at a critical time and helped Texas adjust to the rapid change that emerged in the twentieth century.

Janet Schmelzer is professor of history at Tarleton State University and is currently working on a biography of Tom Campbell.

The beginning of the twentieth century in Texas was a time of political change. The Democrats, the largest and most powerful party, completely dominated state elections and governmental patronage. The Republican Party, associated with the chaos of Reconstruction, was too weak and unpopular to be much of a challenger. More formidable were third-party movements such as the Populist Party, which had threatened the dominance of the Democrats in the 1890s. But by the turn of the century many Populist ideas, such as antitrust reform, direct election of U.S. senators, and the free and unlimited coinage of silver, had been stolen by the Democrats. Now progressivism, the newest reform movement, was spreading across the state, and the Democrats could not ignore popular demands for social, economic, and political reform.

What was driving the demand for reform? In the post-Civil War period, Texas was beginning a transformation from an agricultural to an industrial economy. This industrial revolution would change the way people lived and worked. Human needs and social concerns were swept aside. Instead, the machine became the most important component of industrialization: they could run all day, every day, without food or rest, and machines never complained about pay and working conditions. In the industrial age the machine would control the work habits of men, women, and children, dictate work schedules, determine pay, and set the pace of production.

Factory workers were at the mercy of the machine. They labored long hours for low, subsistence pay. Concerned only with production schedules and making money, most factory executives viewed workers as expendable, even easier to replace than a part in a machine. If a man, woman, or child died in a factory accident or in a mineshaft, employers simply hired someone else. Safe and comfortable workplaces were unnecessary expenses because corporations cared only about profits. Monopolies such as the railroads, for example, would charge customers inflated prices or deny service to people and towns altogether. Banks showed little compassion for debtors, especially for farmers who struggled to raise a meager income from their land. Human conditions were not important to the success of businesses, corporations, and banks.

Unable to protect themselves from such unfair and unjust business practices, usually independent-minded Texans looked to the state government for help. The governor and state legislature were the keys to whatever remedies and regulations were needed in order to improve the quality of their lives. Since the Texas Democrats were the party in power, they were expected to provide for the general welfare of the state's citizens. If the Democrats failed, many Texans would turn to others, to some new third party as they had earlier done with the Populists.

In 1906, however, the Democrats in Texas were determined as usual to remain the dominant party. The reform demands of restless citizens could not be ignored. Party leaders looked for a gubernatorial candidate to attract those who wanted progressive reform, targeting especially those who had recently defected to the Populists. They needed someone who would appeal to the old agrarian causes of railroad regulation, free silver, and distrust of corporations and banks. This man must also be an unwavering, loyal Hogg Democrat, so-called for the affection that Texans still had for the late nineteenth-century reform governor, James Stephen Hogg. Moreover, he must believe in progressive ideas such as antitrust legislation, conservation programs, labor safe-guards, and education reforms. And he must defend prohibition.

Into the political arena stepped Thomas Mitchell Campbell, whose background made him the perfect Democratic candidate in the political environment of 1906. Born on April 22, 1856, Campbell was from Cherokee County in rural East Texas. A typical country boy, he grew up helping his father, Thomas Duncan Campbell, work their farm as well as doing odd jobs for him at a local hotel. Hard work taught him self-respect and pride. The constant struggle with rural poverty made him realize that life could be harsh and unforgiving, but it also made him strong in character and spirit. Life's rewards, he learned, came from truth, fairness, justice, and love of family.

And if farm life were not hard enough, growing up during the Civil War and Reconstruction years caused Tom Campbell even greater pain and unhappiness. Like everyone else, he soon discovered that the war would tear at the fabric of life in Cherokee County. Shortages of food, medicine, farm implements, and other necessities taxed the resourceful-ness of every family. Fear and uncertainty were common. Every day Tom saw men from the county—fathers, sons, and brothers—join the Confederate Army. In 1862 his own father left for the war. And in his small community, sorrow was everywhere as many soldiers, men whom he had once known, were reported killed on the battlefield. Even his boyhood friend, that same James Stephen Hogg who would later set the standard for Texas reformers, lost his father. But what Campbell was totally unprepared for as a young boy was the death of his beloved mother, Rachel, in 1864.

Only with the return of his father and the end of the war was some normality restored. Tom went back to his daily chores, feeding chickens and milking cows, instead of running the farm. Once more he had time to roam the hills, playing war and hunting varmints with his friends. And, although public education was not yet available, he earned money so that he could attend the Rusk Male and Female Academy. There he studied reading, writing, logic, arithmetic, and the classics. He loved to pull pranks on his classmates and sometimes got a reprimand from the schoolmaster.

In 1868 his father married Cynthia Carroll. Soon, Tom had four more siblings from his stepmother's previous marriage. Graciously, she treated him like her own son and helped him adjust to the loss of his mother. Cynthia instilled in him, he often insisted, his best attributes: compassion, strength, and gentleness. As a young man, Campbell turned to a professional career, read law, and was admitted to the bar in 1878. Establishing his practice in Longview, he opened an office in the county courthouse. Then he met and fell in love with Fannie Bruner of Shreveport, Louisiana. He loved her desperately, writing affectionately to "My Dear Dear Fannie, Darling of All."[1] While his letters dripped honey, hers in return were more proper and friendly. Finally, she accepted his proposal. On December 24, 1878, the couple married and made Longview their home for the next fourteen years.

A successful lawyer, Campbell became a partner with S. A. "Gus" McMeans, an active leader of the Democratic Party and a political ally of Jim Hogg. For Campbell, politics had been a way of life in his family since the 1870s. His father had run for minor posts in several elections in his home county and had won most of them. Tom would sit for hours and listen to his father and friends discuss political issues—the Grange, the Farmers' Alliance, railroads, and money.

Although at first involved only in local politics with his father, Tom Campbell would begin his significant role in the state Democratic Party in the 1880s and 1890s. In 1886, Hogg was running for attorney general. When Hogg wanted someone whom he could trust to sit on the Platform Committee of the State Democratic Convention, he had to look no farther than his old boyhood friend. Alongside the highly visible leaders of the party, Campbell was quickly identified as a rising young Democrat who supported the platform, "Hogg and Reform."

Over the next few years he would loyally serve Hogg and the party in a number of ways. Of course, he was active in political campaigns, especially those involving the gubernatorial candidacy of the ascending Hogg in 1890 and 1892. Texans loved Hogg, who had come to symbolize "the people." He was known especially for his attacks on railroad malpractice and was the author of the state's most important piece of railroad legislation, the Railroad Commission Act.

Campbell and Hogg were lifelong friends. As children, they had played together in Cherokee County: hunting rabbits, swimming in the creek, playing games, and swapping stories. Not surprisingly, Campbell would benefit from his friendship with Hogg. In 1889, when Hogg was attorney general, and then in 1891, when he was governor, Campbell was his choice to represent the state's interests in the litigation with the International and Great Northern Railroad, owned by railroad mogul Jay Gould. Serving first as a court-appointed master in chancery and then as a receiver, his work with the IGN gave him the opportunity to run a railroad "the right way." Profit would be important but not as important as good service, fair rates, and safe employment conditions. He quickly accepted the responsibility for the daily business and the reorganization of the railroad to avoid bankruptcy.

When the receivership ended in 1892, Campbell's business skills were readily recognized by Gould, who offered him the position of general manager. This job would mean working for Gould, who was infamous for the kinds of shady and unprincipled business deals that Campbell had fought so hard against. Moreover, he would have to be separated from his family for a time until they could be moved to Palestine, southeast of Dallas, where his office was located, so he was unsure whether he should accept.

After seeking advice and counsel from Fannie and friends such as Hogg, he decided to take the offer. He would, in contrast to the common business dealings of a Gould general manager, run the IGN properly and successfully without violating any of his own lifelong principles or ethics. He would provide good service, maintain financial solvency, and operate under fair business practices. From 1892 to 1897 he worked diligently to eliminate many inappropriate practices that were common in the railroad industry. He ordered that fraud, favoritism, free passes, and unfair freight charges cease. At the same time he managed to keep the railroad out of bankruptcy during the Panic of 1893 and the subsequent depression, a period during which many rail lines folded.

Campbell's relationship with Gould and the IGN finally ended, however, when he could no longer tolerate the standard business practices of a Gould-run railroad. Moreover, Campbell had remained an active Democrat, which had not endeared him to Gould, who preferred the Republicans. In 1896, against the wishes of the IGN management, Campbell openly supported the Democratic presidential candidate, William Jennings Bryan, an advocate of railroad and corporate regulation. Many friends applauded him for holding "principles above power, money, and wealth."[2] In 1897 he resigned as general manager and left the lucrative position with no regrets.

Returning to private law practice in 1897, Campbell was ready to devote more time to Fannie and his remaining four children—Fannie, Thomas Jr., Sammie Belle, and Maydelle. His family had always been important to him, even more so after the death of the oldest child, Mary, at age four. His work with the IGN had been time consuming and had separated him from Fannie and the children at various times. That separation had always bothered him. Whatever ambitions he had, his family had to receive first consideration.

Instead, after 1897, he found most of his time and energy going to the Democratic Party. Like Hogg, he was distressed by the defection of Democrats to the Populist Party over the past decade. In 1898 he, along with other party leaders, devised a "test" to identify the true and loyal Democrats—the same kind of true and loyal Democrat that he saw in himself. Any member who had defected to the Populist Party would, after 1898, be barred from participating in Democratic elections. Campbell and others were intolerant and angry that anyone would leave the party, support another one, and, in so doing, contribute to the destruction of "the one true party" in Texas. Their mood left no compassion for defectors.

In 1902, Campbell decided to run for governor and restore reform principles to the Democrats and to the state government, but the Hogg Democrats did not have the numbers to alter the conservative direction of the party. The person who controlled party affairs was Colonel Edward M. House, the closest to a state party boss in Texas. And House did not want such rabid reformers as Campbell, or any Hogg Democrat for that matter, in the governor's chair. His support of S. W. T. Lanham ended any hopes for Campbell in 1902. Angry, Campbell announced his withdrawal from the race because "the hidden hand of the machine" was pulling the party's strings.[3]

This 1902 gubernatorial race now inspired Campbell to put into place plans that would assure his life's ambition—to become governor. Following his old friend's leadership, he seized the opportunity to rebuild and recharacterize the Hogg Democrats. Together they set out to entice old-time Populists back to the Democratic Party. No longer would they punish those Democrats who had abandoned the party for the Populists. Working as allies, they would have the numbers and power to take control of the Democratic Party.

Hogg's fervent advocacy for railroad regulation was the magnet that attracted Populists. After all, Populists had made railroad reform one of the cornerstones of their party. If this plan could be carried out successfully, the Hogg Democrats would be able to restore the Democratic Party as the party of reform, much of which had been lost during the more conservative administrations of Joseph D. Sayers and Lanham.

The plan worked. By 1906 the time was right for Campbell to run for governor. The former Populists and Hogg Democrats were working in concert. Campbell was endorsed by many of the erstwhile members of the People's Party as the closest to old-time Populism, and Hogg Democrats lined up behind him. Labor unions and social reformers found Campbell to be the man who could best represent their interests. His reform principles also attracted those who believed in progressivism. And being a temperance advocate, he was a favorite of those who wanted a prohibition amendment added to the state constitution. As a consequence, at the state convention, with the band playing "The Campbells Are Coming," he accepted the party's nomination. In November 1906 he was elected governor.

Campbell, Fannie, and the children quickly moved into the Governor's Mansion. For the first time in many years the sounds of children playing and laughing could be heard throughout the house. Soon the yard was filled with flowers and gardens. In 1908 electricity was finally brought into the house. Fannie was the perfect First Lady, entertaining dignitaries, lunching with members of women's clubs and charities, and hosting many public and social events. As governor from 1907 to 1911, Campbell had reached his highest ambition. Determined to keep his promises to the people, he announced that the "public interest and the welfare of the State are of first importance to us all."[4] His demands for social, economic, and political reform were progressive ideas, just like the progressive ideas in other states and across the country.

Very much a product of his time, Campbell appeared to be formal, even stiff, but within him was a warm, compassionate person who wanted to do the best for the people of Texas. A family man who cherished his children, Campbell was supremely conscious of the need for the kinds of reforms that would benefit and protect other families like his own. Indeed, such sympathies were the driving force behind much of his social legislation. One area of concern to Campbell was education. "The cause of education is cherished by the people," he explained, but, he argued, Texas had not dedicated enough resources to provide adequate schooling.[5] His passion for better education was soon translated into legislation that increased funding to schools through a maximum ad valorem tax, extended the school term from four months to seven, and raised the minimum teachers' annual pay to $390.

Public education was not the only priority of Campbell's social reform agenda. In the food and drug industries few standards existed. Inspectors found ether, opium, and chloroform in medicines, cocaine in soft drinks, and bacteria or decayed food in canned goods. At meat-packing plants, flies, rats, and roaches covered slabs of meat, processed beef came from tuberculosis-infected cows, butchers did not scrub their hands or tools, and inspection for trichina and other parasites were not even afterthoughts. The new governor was appalled to read such reports on food and drug production. After all, children were at the greatest risk from careless and uncaring practices. He stated that he did not want any children in Texas to suffer illness or death because he had not done everything in his power to correct these abuses. With the backing of the legislature, Campbell approved the Pure Food and Drug Act in 1907 that authorized the Dairy and Food Commission to regulate food and drug standards as well as inspect processors and report violations of standards.

Much closer to him was the heartbreaking prospect that someone would suffer the needless death of a child. Having lost Mary to illness, Campbell did not want other parents to share the experience that he and Fannie had endured. Children needed to be protected from health dangers. Threatening the well-being of many Texans at the turn of the century were leprosy and tuberculosis. The number of cases was on the rise, with some Texas cities reporting a 300 percent increase in fatal cases of tuberculosis. Campbell thus urged the legislature to create the State Board of Health, which would enforce quarantines and sanitation regulations and study and prevent the spread of diseases. In 1910 the board issued its first Sanitary Code that required pure drinking water along with ear, nose, and throat examinations for schoolchildren and clean public bathrooms. Local physicians were now required to impose quarantines and inform state authorities of outbreaks of typhus, small-pox, anthrax, and cholera.

For Campbell, reforms for the general welfare also meant better treatment for prison inmates. While dedicated to the principle that "the object of punishment is to suppress crime and reform the offender," he also demanded humane treatment for the incarcerated, declaring:

> The reformation of offenders can progress only under such favorable prison conditions as to include humane handling, hope of reward for good conduct, wholesome discipline, reasonable employment and moral influences around them. Experience teaches that in every condition of life wholesome environments make good men better while unhappy examples with their untoward influences make all men worse.[6]

At the governor's request, the legislature initiated an investigation into prison conditions. The report was a sad commentary on the primitive conditions in Texas: housing was poor and antiquated; the sewage system consisted merely of buckets; prisoners bathed in outside troughs; food, often moldy, was routinely contaminated by roaches or maggots; and lice infested the inmate population.

Almost immediately newspapers such as the *San Antonio Daily Express* were filled with articles critical of the governor and the prison system. Campbell was accused of poor management and labeled a Johnny-come-lately who had to be pressured into pushing for prison reform. Some editorials compared the administration of prisons to the Spanish Inquisition. Far from being coerced into adopting prison reform, Campbell had been outspoken on this issue for years. Essentially he was now taking the heat for other men in the legislature who had been slow to respond. Criticism was a kind of political game that came with the territory. In fact, when his successor, Oscar Colquitt, found himself under attack for his own prison problems, the new governor simply threw the blame back on Campbell.

Campbell, however, could at least point to some accomplishments that have long outlasted his critics. In 1910 he signed into law the Prison Reform Act that changed much of the system's operations. The hated practice of leasing prisoners as laborers to private companies was halted. All facilities were to be renovated with indoor plumbing and running water. Education, religion, and medical care were mandatory.

Like most progressives, Campbell was also an advocate of conservation. A child of rural East Texas, he often recalled in fond terms the natural beauty that had surrounded him in Cherokee County. He was an outspoken advocate for legislation that would protect the state's forests, waterways, and wildlife. In a land with a growing population and new extraction industries such as oil and sulfur, the preservation of natural resources in Texas could not be delayed or ignored but required immediate action. Already by 1900 the state timber supply was in jeopardy because of the lack of a reforestation program. The loss of forested land would mean not only a loss of profits, but also more important, a loss of wildlife habitats and natural protection against wind and water erosion. Then, in 1908, the Trinity River flooded 500,000 acres in Dallas County, a tragedy that could have been avoided with flood-control programs.

In response, Campbell supported the State Levee and Drainage Act that would reclaim land for cultivation, survey and map rivers and flood plains, and implement irrigation programs. Bird and game experts had already declared turkeys, bison, elk, antelopes, and wood ducks as endangered because former controls and enforcement were ineffectual. Robins and doves, their populations suffering rapid declines, were still unprotected. In the Gulf of Mexico, fishermen were contaminating oyster beds by dumping refuse over them.

Campbell's reforms extended to human resources as well. He had already been recognized for his work to secure a child labor law in 1903 that prohibited children under twelve from working with machinery, and children under sixteen from working in mines and breweries. No child should be forced to labor, he argued, and thus be deprived of a childhood and a public school education. To further these ends, Campbell vigorously supported the creation of the Bureau of Labor Statistics and the State Mining Board. As enacted by the legislature, both agencies began compiling statistics, issuing reports, and inspecting work conditions. It did not take long before the newly created State Mining Board had uncovered sixty-nine violations of the 1903 Child Labor Law.

Still, critics charged that the laws cut too deeply into the workforce and actually penalized some prospective workers, even if those voices remained silent. In the rural areas, on Texas farms and ranches, citizens were more vocal. Campbell, the farm boy from East Texas, was acutely aware of the difficulties that families endured because of low crop prices and indebtedness to banks. Farmers and ranchers who knew the governor counted on him to help them deal with their ongoing problems. Old-time Grange members and Populists had voted for him in 1906, and farm spokesmen such as James Harvey Cyclone Davis had even campaigned on his behalf. Now it was time for the reform governor to come to their aid, and Campbell did not disappoint them. With the creation of the state Department of Agriculture, headed by a commissioner, farmers received new information on plant diseases, insects, crops, and livestock production. Just as important was the prohibition on price fixing by grain speculators, a process that had deprived farmers of fair market prices and profits.

For all the legislation that had been enacted during his administration, Campbell still had some promises to fulfill. For much of his life he had seen the evils of unregulated corporate power. "Organized corporate greed confronted the people's representatives at every turn," he warned, "but victory has been on the side of the people in every contest."[7] In a battle that he viewed as good versus evil, Campbell was not going to surrender to the power or will of big business.

In his 1908 reelection campaign, Campbell came face-to-face with his avowed enemy. His opponents, referred to as the "corporations gang," put up their candidate, Robert R. Williams, a blacksmith from the Northeast Texas town of Cumby. Backed by a war chest put together by oil, lumber, and railroad interests, Williams's strategy was to play up voter dissatisfaction with Campbell. While concerned early on with the Williams campaign, Campbell soon discovered that his reelection faced little serious risk. Fortunately, Williams proved to be a poor campaigner, which earned him the nickname "the Old Simpleton." Moreover, many people considered Williams's supporters to be the "slick crowd" with a "slimy trail." In contrast, Campbell had many friends and allies who praised him as an opponent of corporate domination who offered the people of Texas "a square deal."[8]

Campbell's record on corporate and antitrust regulation clearly reflected his determination to carry through with reform. The challenge was aided by an able attorney general who exercised the power to examine and subpoena corporate records. By 1909, Campbell announced proudly that twenty-one antitrust cases had been prosecuted and that the state had collected almost two million dollars in fines and penalties.

His old nemesis, the railroad, was also a target for reform. Because of his experience with the International and Great Northern, Campbell knew firsthand about the many abuses of this industry. One was the mistreatment of railroad employees. Long workdays and unsafe and uncomfortable working conditions had caused hundreds of Texans to suffer dismemberment, injury, or death. Passenger and freight cars, for example, did not have grab irons or foot stirrups for conductors who had to jump aboard moving trains. Improvements as elementary as electric lights on engines or modern braking systems had been resisted by railroad management. The result was that in 1907 alone, 289 people died and 4,200 others suffered injuries. To reform this industry, Campbell signed bills requiring new safety equipment and instituting the eight-hour workday.

Equally exploitative were the railroads' unregulated business practices. Campbell's old friend, Jim Hogg, had died in 1906 without seeing three of his most cherished reforms enacted. Campbell had promised Hogg and the people of Texas that the "Hogg Amendments"— prohibition of corporate insolvency, of free passes, and of corporate political contributions—would become law. As expected, business and corporate interests flooded the legislature in a frantic effort to defeat these reforms, but Campbell did not back down. He fought the interests by condemning their influence peddling. He aimed his harshest condemnations at lobbyists who were "the hired instrument of selfish schemes" and "a public enemy."[9] To keep his promise to the "immortal Hogg," Campbell fought against the corporate interests and signed bills that finally helped make the Hogg Amendments the law of the land.

Campbell's successes let big business know that reform was a force with which to contend. His admirers insisted that when he was in the right, he would not give up, no matter who was trying to strong-arm him. Even the legislature learned this lesson when its members refused to pass the proposed Bank Guaranty Bill in 1909. Campbell was loath to see the session end without such a measure, and in April he delivered an angry speech that became known as the "Easter Egg Message." Calling the activities of the legislature "a sham and a fraud," he vowed to keep the legislature in special session until its members had finished this banking measure.[10] Under such extreme pressure from the governor and an energized public, the legislature enacted the banking law.

By the fall of 1910, Campbell was finishing his second term as governor. In his last speech to the legislature he spoke of his pride in having been able to serve the people of Texas. Since the general welfare of Texas and Texans had been his goal, he proudly pointed to a wide range of social, economic, and political reforms that had answered the hopes of Democrats, Populists, and progressives. By fighting for the people, he had guided the enactment of a wealth of progressive legislation that echoed laws on the national level and in other states. Pure food and drug standards, railroad regulation, child labor prohibitions and labor protection, conservation of wildlife and other resources, and educational improvement were just a few of his reforms. He had accepted the challenge to care for their welfare. As a result, his years as governor were the most progressive in Texas since the days of Jim Hogg. Under his leadership an extraordinary volume of reform and forward-looking legislation had been enacted.

In January 1911, Campbell returned to his home in Palestine, where he resumed his law practice as the senior partner of Campbell, Greenwood and Barton. And he welcomed the opportunity to enjoy the company of his family, now greatly enlarged with grandchildren. But his retirement from politics was short-lived. The issue that would draw him back was prohibition. Although local options had been in force since 1876, "drys" such as Campbell were not satisfied. They wanted statewide prohibition. As governor, Campbell had encouraged the passage of laws placing regulations on the manufacturers of alcohol and applauded those counties opting to be dry. Once in retirement, however, he became an outspoken proponent of prohibition. "A law prohibiting the sale of liquor," he admonished the legislature, was imperative "for the protection of our young men against the evil influences of saloons, dens, and dives."[11] As a member of the Campaign Executive

Committee of the State Prohibition Mass Convention, organized in 1910, he stumped the state for a prohibition amendment to the Texas constitution.

By 1912 the prohibition fight had become even more deeply entwined in Texas politics. Democrats, both "wets" and "drys," were working on the presidential race. One of the national Democratic frontrunners was Woodrow Wilson, the progressive governor of New Jersey. While not originally a Wilson man, Campbell became one early in 1912. At the State Democratic Convention he was elected to be a delegate-at-large to the Democratic National Convention in Baltimore. After Wilson was nominated, he gave speeches for him and cheered his election in November.

Although national politics had preoccupied him in 1912, Campbell again focused on the state gubernatorial race in 1914. Like many prohibitionists in Texas, he rallied behind Thomas Ball of Houston, a "dry." The opposition candidate for the Democratic nomination was James E. "Pa" Ferguson of Temple. On Election Day voters chose Ferguson, much to the dismay of Campbell and other prohibitionists.

In 1916, Campbell finally decided to give political office one more chance, so he entered the race for U.S. senator. He faced a strong field that included incumbent Senator Charles Culberson, former Governor Colquitt, Baylor University President Samuel P. Brooks, and two other men. Of the four leading candidates, Campbell and Brooks were ardent prohibitionists while Culberson was lukewarm and Colquitt was "wet." But Campbell believed that he had a real opportunity to win with votes from prohibitionists, progressives, and Wilsonites.

As the day of the primary approached, Campbell's chances of winning dwindled. The prohibitionists would be splitting their votes among three candidates, one of which was Campbell, while the antiprohibitionists would be unified behind Colquitt. The primary race reflected this dilemma for the prohibitionists, and Campbell, who tallied the fewest votes, was out of the race. Moreover, he was competing with a popular incumbent, Culberson, whose charisma could not be matched by Campbell. For all of the accolades that Campbell had earned for his reform agenda, it was a program whose success wearied voters who were preoccupied with present issues.

The 1916 campaign was Campbell's last race. Over the next four years he would work for other candidates. His last presidential campaign was in 1920; afterward, he retired from any active role in politics. He had accomplished everything that he could for prohibition and progressivism since the end of his governorship in 1911. His work for prohibition had persisted until the passage of a prohibition amendment to the state constitution in 1919 and the ratification of the Eighteenth Amendment to the U.S. Constitution in 1920. He had campaigned successfully for a progressive president, Woodrow Wilson, and with limited success for state candidates.

His decision to retire was based more on poor health than disappointment with the recent elections. At home in Palestine his physical condition declined. In 1923 he learned that he had leukemia and entered John Sealy Hospital in Galveston, but nothing could be done for him. On April 1, 1923, Campbell died at the age of sixty-six and was buried in Palestine. In memorials to him, he was remembered as "one of Texas' most distinguished sons" and was "beloved by Texans because of his devotion to their interest."[12]

Notes

1. Mary D. Farrell and Elizabeth Silverthorne, *First Ladies of Texas: The First One Hundred Years, 1836–1936, A History* (Temple, TX, 1976), 242.
2. William Jennings Bryan to George Carden, September 22, 1896, Thomas Mitchell Campbell Papers, Center for American History, University of Texas, Austin (hereafter cited as Campbell Papers).
3. *Austin Statesman*, January 26, 1902.
4. Ibid., January 16, 1907.
5. State of Texas, *House Journal*, 30th Legislature, Regular Session, 1907, 123.
6. Ibid., 32d Legislature, Regular Session, 1911, 51.
7. Ibid., 32.
8. "Opening Campaign for Re-election," Campbell Papers.
9. Ibid., 30th Legislature, Regular Session, 118.
10. Ibid., 32d Legislature, Regular Session, 66.
11. Pat M. Neff to Mrs. Campbell, April 2, 1923; Edward M. House to Mrs. Campbell, April 2, 1923, Campbell Papers.
12. Ibid., 32d Legislature, Regular Session, 66.

Suggested Readings

Barr, Alwyn. *Reconstruction to Reform: Texas Politics, 1876–1906.* Austin, 1971.
Cotner, Robert C. *James Stephen Hogg: A Biography.* Austin, 1959.
Farrell, Mary D., and Elizabeth Silverthorne. *First Ladies of Texas: The First One Hundred Years, 1836–1936, A History.* Temple, TX, 1976.
Gould, Lewis L. *Progressives and Prohibitionists: Texas Democrats in the Wilson Era.* Austin, 1973.

Martin, Roscoe C. *The People's Party in Texas: A Study in Third Party Politics.* Austin, 1933.

Richardson, Rupert Norval. *Colonel Edward M. House: The Texas Years, 1858–1912.* Abilene, TX, 1964.

10

Ormer Leslie Locklear
The *"Epoch of Flying" Has Arrived*

J'Nell L. Pate

Texans, like other Americans, marveled at the inventions of the modern age. From film and radio to automobiles and airplanes, the introduction of almost every innovative technology brought an excited response from an eager public. The life of Ormer Leslie Locklear illustrates the excitement of living on the brink of this new age. He was a born daredevil who showed no fear in performing life-risking stunts. Attracted to flying even as a boy, he was often seen around Fort Worth in the homemade glider that he and his brother pulled behind their father's automobile. Given his chance to train in a Jenny during World War I, the young barnstormer went on to help popularize flying by touring the country with two fellow pilots. Wherever he made an appearance, towns all but shut down as crowds by the thousands came to witness his stunt flying or to watch him perform such aerial acrobatics as wing walking, hopping from one plane to another, or standing on his head. Soon, Hollywood came calling, which put Locklear on the big screen. Other flight enthusiasts such as Lawrence Bell (Bell Helicopter), the Loughead brothers (Lockheed), and Jack Northrop (Northrop Aviation) went on to revolutionize the business of flying and become leading industrialists. Locklear, however, never got the chance. His luck ran out when he crashed while filming the last scene in a long-forgotten silent movie.

J'Nell Pate is professor of history, retired, at Tarrant County College, Fort Worth, and the author of numerous books and articles on Texas history. Currently she is researching the impact of aircraft and the defense industry on North Texas.

Huge crowds met a Southern Pacific Railroad train as it rolled into Fort Worth on Saturday afternoon, August 7, 1920. On hand was a marching band composed of Armour and Company workers from the stockyards and a platoon of city policemen. Probably no one in the crowd thought of the event as one defining moment of a new age of air flight that would explode in Fort Worth, in North Texas, and in the nation in the coming decade, but the event could qualify at that moment.

Texas, as aviation experts discovered, represented an excellent place for air flight and air flight training. West of Fort Worth the land was flat and virtually treeless. Moreover, the warm climate allowed more days of flying for pilot training than more northern sites would permit. One need not worry about ice forming on the wings or propellers very many days per year. Even the Canadians, allies of the British in World War I, selected North Texas for three flight training fields. Once the United States joined the war effort, Ormer Leslie Locklear trained at one of these.

The train arriving in Fort Worth transported a coffin carrying the body of twenty-eight-year-old Locklear, a young man who grew up in Fort Worth, who learned to love airplanes, and who had been killed five days earlier in an air crash in the last scene of a Hollywood silent movie. During a nighttime scene in *The Skywayman*, Locklear was to take a nosedive and pull out just before he reached the ground. Lights were to go off to signal to him that he was near the ground so he could quickly end the dive. Somehow a mixup occurred; the lights did not make the correct signal, and Locklear and his friend and passenger, Melton "Skeets" Elliott died.

Nearly 50,000 people attempted to attend Locklear's funeral at Mulkey Memorial Methodist Church in Fort Worth on Sunday, August 8. Crowds surrounded the area so completely that it took ninety minutes for the procession to travel a mile from the funeral home to the church. Later, in the procession to Greenwood Cemetery, one hundred U.S. Army fliers, two hundred soldiers, and some pilots of the Royal Canadian Air Service joined the solemn funeral cortege. Four airplanes flew over the scene and dropped rose petals. Who was this young man whose short life inspired such outpourings of devotion and whose actions typified the new air age to come? His biographer, Art Ronnie, claims that Locklear "did as much in his own way to further the cause of aviation as did [Charles] Lindbergh," and articles during his own time called Locklear "the greatest daredevil of modern times."[1]

A decade or two after the Civil War five Locklear brothers came to Texas from North Carolina; one eventually traveled on to California. Back in North Carolina the Scots-Irish Locklears had intermarried with the Cherokee and Roanoke Native American tribes. Locklear's grandfather apparently had been one of these mixed-race Native American-Scots-Irish brothers who migrated to Texas. Locklear was born on October 28, 1891, in Greenville, Texas, one of ten children of James and Odessa Locklear. He was still a youngster when his father moved the family to the south side of Fort Worth where the elder Locklear could work as a building contractor. Even as a kid creating his own fun with pals during summers and free time from school, young Ormer revealed the daredevil nature that later would dictate his career. He would ride his bicycle up planks to the roof of a barn and then leap off to a platform fifteen feet below. His mother later told of his continually climbing to the top of trees and having to be lured down.

Events in Fort Worth encouraged by *Star-Telegram* owner Amon G. Carter and city officials kept interest in those new-fangled airplanes high. Some international fliers, mostly French, made an appearance in Dallas, so Fort Worth businessmen invited them to come thirty miles west to perform on Thursday and Friday, January 12–13, 1911. Stores closed; schools declared a half-day holiday; streetcar companies offered cheap rides to the site on West Seventh Street just west of the Clear Fork of the Trinity River where the Montgomery Ward store later would be built. Ormer Locklear and his friends were in the crowd of 15,000 as the pilots took off and landed on the open field.

In that same year, on October 17, Calbraith Perry Rodgers, the great-grandson of Commander Matthew Calbraith Perry who had opened Japan for trade with the United States in 1854, landed in Fort Worth. He was making an attempt to win a $50,000 prize offered by William Randolph Hearst to the first pilot to fly cross-country from New York to Los Angeles in thirty days. Again, Locklear was in the crowd, this time sitting on the Hattie Street Bridge with his brothers. One of them remembered years later that Ormer commented that some day he wanted to do that. Hero of the 1911 spectacle, Cal Rodgers did not make it across the United States in thirty days; he reached Pasadena in forty-nine.

These exciting events no doubt inspired Ormer and his brothers to build a crude glider with fifteen-foot wings from bamboo fishing poles. They covered it with linen and shellacked it to draw the cloth taut. When they pulled it behind an automobile, it would go up in the air 150 feet as each Locklear brother took a turn to ride. The glider had no controls so, if set free of the rope, whoever was riding it had to use the weight of his body to guide the craft. The boys toted it around on their father's Maxwell to likely places around Fort Worth to glide. As a youngster, Locklear read everything he could get his hands on about airplanes.

Locklear graduated from bicycles to a motorcycle and raced around the city doing the same daredevil tricks that he had done with his bicycle earlier. He joined the Panther City Motorcycle Club in 1914, jumping ramps with the best of them. Once, he sped his motorcycle across one of the main streets of downtown Fort Worth and ran into the front door of a saloon, making headlines in the local newspapers with that escapade. On a race track behind the Montgomery Ward site, Locklear would complete fifty-mile races on his cycle. Locklear worked part-time for his father in construction and would climb to the top of buildings without any fear of heights. After high school he obtained a job as a mechanic and shop foreman at the Massie Motor Supply and Key Company in Fort Worth where he worked for three years. Locklear's carefree life became somewhat curtailed in April 1915 when he married Ruby Graves, also of Fort Worth. Ruby did not approve of his friends or of his motorcycle daredevil antics. To her, they were not only dangerous but childish, too. Her objections did not prevent Locklear from hiring himself out to escape artist Harry Houdini in January 1916, when the famous performer appeared at the Majestic Theater in Fort Worth. Behind his motorcycle Locklear dragged Houdini, who wore a hood and padded overalls and had his hands tied behind him. The stunt down Main Street clearly worked because Houdini played to a packed house for the remainder of his run in Fort Worth.

The United States declared war on Germany on April 2, 1917, as the nation entered the World War. After Locklear enlisted in the Air Service on October 25, he wanted to celebrate by riding his motorcycle around a narrow wall topping off the roof of a newly constructed building in downtown Fort Worth. The night before, he secretly built a small platform at the corners of the wall so he could turn easier. He had informed the local newspapers of his intended stunt, so several hundred people came to watch. The Humane Society stopped him.

After reporting for active duty, Locklear took his flight training at Fort Sam Houston in San Antonio. Of twenty pilots who took one particular pretraining flight test, only Locklear and one other young man passed. Descriptions of the twenty-six-year-old airman made him 5'10" tall at 145 pounds, with blond hair, gray-green eyes, large ears, and a crooked grin. After ground school at the Texas School of Military Aeronautics in Austin, he was commissioned a second lieutenant. Most likely, Locklear's family and Ruby were happy to learn that he was ordered to one of the three airfields located in Tarrant County on the outside fringes of Fort Worth. These airfields, occupied first in October 1917 by the Canadians for pilot training, were in present Saginaw to the north, Everman to the south, and Benbrook to the southwest. Although the Canadians named them Taliaferro I, II, and III, the Americans renamed them Taliaferro, Barron, and Caruthers, respectively. Locklear was ordered to Barron Field near Everman to complete his flight training with Service Squadron B, formerly the 106th Flying Squadron.

Even in the military, Second Lieutenant Locklear remained a daredevil and, according to his biographer, often stayed just one step ahead of a court-martial. He flew a Canadian version of a Curtiss JN4D biplane called a Jenny, which had a 90 horsepower OX-5 engine and could go ninety miles per hour. The first instance of Locklear as army daredevil involved a test in which student pilots were required to read ten words flashed from the ground while flying at 5,000 feet. No student made a perfect score because the wing obscured the view below. Locklear solved the problem by climbing out on the wing while his instructor flew the airplane and was the first to receive a perfect score. When the other cadets did the same stunt, they all were reprimanded and confined to barracks.

On another flight a radiator cap came loose and was hanging by a short chain as Locklear and an instructor flew their airplane. As the front pilot in tandem, Locklear was getting sprayed in the face with hot water. He unbuckled his safety belt, climbed forward, straddled the fuselage, replaced the cap, and then inched his way back to the cockpit. At another time a spark plug wire disconnected, so Locklear scrambled onto a wing, leaned forward into the prop wash, and replaced it. These impromptu reactions gave Locklear and a couple of his companions— James Frew of Newcastle, Pennsylvania, and Skeets Elliott of Gadsden, Alabama—the idea for stunt flying. With two different airplanes, the men began stunting on a regular basis on flights away from the field. Frew would fly the airplane, and Locklear would walk on a wing or balance himself while standing. Locklear later told interviewers that the cross-country flights from Barron Field were boring, so he did his stunts and antics to amuse himself and other flyers.

Eventually someone told the Barron Field's commanding officer, Colonel Thomas C. Turner, about the stunts, and he ventured out to see them himself. Instead of punishing the three men, he asked them to fly demonstrations to illustrate the stability of the Jenny, rather like the present-day Blue Angels of the U.S. Navy or the Thunderbirds of the Air Force. Thus, Locklear and his daredevil friends remained at Barron Field as instructors and were not sent overseas to fight in France in the World War where they might have become aces. The young men were disappointed and complained, requesting transfers which they were not given. One Fort Worth pilot, Lt. Fred Brewster, who shot down four German planes, returned home to watch Locklear and his buddies stunt.

He reported that their antics surpassed any flying he saw in France: "If given a chance, it seems a certainty he [Locklear] would have ranked with the greatest pilots of the big war."[2]

Given the permission to continue their stunting, Locklear, Elliott, and Frew stretched it as far as possible. They buzzed the Adolphus Hotel in Dallas, the Westbrook in Fort Worth, and an all-women's college in Denton (now Texas Woman's University). Sometimes a landing on school grounds would result in a takeoff with a giggling college girl in the front cockpit. A stunt that Locklear pioneered with his friends took place on November 8, 1918, when he jumped from Frew's airplane to a similar one piloted by Elliott, with Frew's airplane flying directly above Elliott's—the midair transfer of a passenger from one airplane to another. He would jump from the frame of the top airplane to a spot in the middle of the wing of the lower craft.

When the war ended, Frew accepted his discharge and went home, but Locklear and Elliott remained in the Air Service for a short time longer. In December 1918, Locklear became the commanding officer of Squadron B and Elliott of Squadron C. They found an instructor, Lt. George L. Alexander, to replace Frew in the stunts, but he only flew with them a short time before returning to civilian life. Then they asked another instructor, Lt. Shirley J. Short of Goldfield, Iowa, to join them, and he remained a longtime part of the team. The number of Locklear's transfers from one airplane to another in midair increased. He would do so by way of the landing gear, the wing skid, or just by stepping across a couple of feet of space from one wing to another. During this time a small news article appeared in a Fort Worth newspaper: "Lieut. Omar [*sic*] Locklear, Squadron B, Barron Field, has originated a number of airplane stunts new to the world of aviation."[3]

Colonel Turner sent Locklear to Chicago on April 22, 1919, to participate in the Fifth Victory Loan Drive. Apparently it was in that city that Locklear first began to think seriously of doing stunt flying professionally. Back in Fort Worth, he met William Hickman Pickens, a promoter who had already been showcasing pilots before the World War. These early pilots simply were called "barnstormers" and in a group "flying circuses." Locklear insisted that his buddies Elliott and Short be a part of the promotion. Pickens's contract called for a 50 percent cut for himself.

Some accounts report that Ruby could take no more. When Locklear went off to make a living at stunt flying, they split up. Neither sought a divorce. Then, after he became famous, reporters interviewed her and she stated that she was not worried about his flying. In fact, she told them that she wanted to learn to fly herself. Ruby and her family later denied that the couple was separated.

Within two weeks after being discharged from the Air Service on May 5, 1919, Locklear joined Pickens in New York. The promoter traveled to Canada to buy new airplanes for Elliott and Short. In his advertising for Locklear's Flying Circus, Pickens called the young daredevil "the man who always takes a chance," while his biographer called him "the man who walked on wings." As Locklear continued to jump from one airplane to another, he was described by a leading aviation magazine as "the foremost aerial acrobat in the world"; by a writer in *Billboard* magazine as "the limit of human adventure"; and in a *New York Times* cutline in March 1919 as "the world's only aviator, so far as is known to transfer from one airplane to another."[4] He performed his stunts at 5,000 feet; any lower, and the flight would be too bumpy, he explained to reporters. If a day was foggy, however, his pilots flew lower so that spectators could see the stunts. Surprisingly, the young daredevil was superstitious and never flew on Sunday if he could help it. Although he did not attend church services regularly, his young days in Sunday School at Broadway Baptist Church in Fort Worth apparently had influenced him.

In every big city where Locklear and his team of pilots flew, promotional articles appeared in newspapers hyping the coming event, and reporters sought out the stuntman for exclusive interviews. As one might expect, the news stories sometimes contained erroneous and conflicting copy. "I certainly am not a fatalist and never was," he told one reporter while explaining how careful and calculating he remained during each performance. Other accounts made him sound as though he knew that he would never reach old age. When asked if he was superstitious, he told one reporter that he "couldn't afford to be." "I believe that everyone has a certain time to die and that one is in as much danger crossing the street as performing stunts in an airplane." He added that he probably would be killed "falling off a curb in front of a car or even being hit by a wheelbarrow."[5]

According to an Oakland newspaper, in one performance Locklear hopped out of his seat and walked along the lower wing, holding onto nothing; let himself down at the very tip of the wing and hung on by one hand; pulled himself up to the topmost wing, walking rapidly to its end where he stood with his arms outspread; stood on his head on the engine casing with his legs forming a "Y" in front of his pilot; and, in "perhaps the most dangerous of all feats," strolled to the tail of his plane and, standing upright, rode with his arms calmly folded. One reporter called him "lithe and quick as a cat." Others said that he "moves with the agility of a monkey" and at the same time the "firmness of a cat."[6] Locklear would sometimes take twenty minutes to climb from the bottom airplane to the top one on a rope ladder. Several women in New York apparently fainted during the rope ladder stunt.

In some performances his final stunt was to hang by his knees from the landing gear and toss roses one by one at the crowd with one hand from a bouquet he held in the other hand. For the roses stunt his pilot flew the airplane only 100 feet from the ground. Sometimes when he dangled from his knees the plane was traveling eighty miles per hour. An Atlantic City journalist called Locklear "the ace of the aerial acrobats," and a Syracuse newspaper reported that "all Central New York seemed to be turning out for the second day of the fair" at which he was performing.[7] Locklear once explained to a reporter, "When I am standing on the plane, the wind is so strong that I can lean against it just as if it were a brick wall."[8] Of course, he had to be careful about changes in air patterns.

An ad in *Billboard* in September 1919, no doubt written by Pickens, proclaimed: "Dozens of figures stood out in the world of 'dare-devils' (as the public has become accustomed to name all men who are just a bit more daring or more brave than the other fellow) for a period of years AND THEN CAME LOCKLEAR! What were considered thrilling feats before his arrival appeared tawdry by comparison after he began to change from one airplane to another."[9] With this growing fame, Hollywood called, or perhaps Promoter Pickens called Hollywood. At any rate, Locklear starred in a silent movie called *The Great Air Robbery* in July 1919 with co-star Francelia Billington. The twenty-seven-year-old movie hero had added an abbreviated mustache to his mischievous smile. When interviewed about heading to Hollywood for his first film, Locklear said, "I am not expecting to make Douglas Fairbanks retire."[10]

He resented being called a "nut aviator" by some newspapers, and he admitted that he had ambitions beyond his county fair tours. He wanted to attempt a nonstop transcontinental flight by refueling in the air. He also planned to manufacture commercial airplanes, incorporating the engineering principles that he had learned while flying and performing. Locklear tried to get sponsorship in June 1919 for a transatlantic flight from Newfoundland to Ireland to compete for the *Daily Mail* prize. He figured that it would take nineteen hours for the trip for which the Curtiss airplane people had offered him a craft. Lindbergh's history-making flight from New York to Paris would succeed eight years after Locklear's oceanic flight hopes came to nothing because of his early death.

Following the completion of the film and until its release, Locklear and his two stunt buddies returned to county fairs and other such appearances between August and November 1919. Sometimes he made $1,000 per day, and sometimes $3,000 for a half-hour appearance. In Milwaukee a wealthy businessman sponsored Locklear's show by paying $7,000 per week for airplanes and pilots. Also engaged as stunt pilots on the county fair circuit were other young men. Among them either prior to the World War or afterward were Glenn L. Martin, who supported his building of airplanes in California with the money that he was earning by stunt flying. Lawrence Bell as a nineteen year old prior to the war worked as a factory hand for Martin and also helped him with his exhibitions. Two brothers, Malcolm and Allen Loughead (later changed to Lockheed), performed in carnivals when they became interested in aviation before the war and set up a small aircraft plant in the back of a garage in Santa Barbara, California, calling themselves the Loughead Aircraft Manufacturing Company. They hired young John ("Jack") Northrop, a recent graduate of Santa Barbara High School, as chief engineer.

Historians of the air industry who tell stories of these early stunt pilots often credit Locklear as an inspiration to others, thus leading to a great deal of stunting and barnstorming in the 1920s. To set the record straight, it should be noted that Martin, Bell, and the Lockheeds attracted attention before the World War. In their day, however, the public considered that simply flying one of those flimsy contraptions was a stunt in itself. Their antics did not approach the dangerous stunts of Locklear, who did help to inspire the barnstorming of the 1920s.

The Locklear Flying Circus owned three airplanes. One was kept as a spare, although sometimes after a changing-planes act Locklear would fly the third craft and do loops with Elliott and Short. Two mechanics went with the trio to state fairs and other engagements, everyone traveling by train, dismantling the airplanes and taking them along. Pickens went ahead to publicize the events. On Friday October 17, 1919, 75,000 spectators at Fair Park Racetrack watched Locklear at the State Fair in Dallas. "Texas Boy Thrills Multitude at Fair," the newspaper headlines trumpeted.[11] "Locklear Day" crowds turned out for the hometown boy, even if the hometown was Fort Worth, a city thirty miles west of Dallas and its perennial rival. Locklear's mother, father, two of his brothers, and two sisters for the first time saw him perform his plane-changing feat. Ruby was there, too. Locklear Day that year outshone the traditional Texas-Oklahoma football game that was scheduled the next day. To make the local boy look good, reporters stated that he attended Sunday School, was adverse to bootlegging, was "opposed to government control of railroads," and did not use "that kind of language."[12]

While in the Dallas area for the State Fair, the Fort Worth Chamber of Commerce hosted a luncheon in Locklear's honor. In saying a few words of thanks, he admitted that he was more afraid of standing and speaking to a small gathering than he was of doing his stunts. He said that he hoped to inspire an aerial club and to see Fort Worth as the center of an aerial postal route. At the luncheon his former Sunday School teacher from Broadway Baptist Church, Mrs. M. W. Potts, called him a "soldier of the cross as well as of the air."[13]

Locklear and his team continued their county and state fair circuit all over the country after his Dallas engagement. In a four-day stint at the Michigan State Fair in Grand Rapids, he broke attendance records. Whether separated from Ruby or not, Locklear apparently met a young actress, Viola Dana, in Hollywood while filming *The Great Air Robbery*. During the three months of his barnstorming in the midwest after finishing the movie, he called her daily or sent frequent telegrams. Many years later, in 1975, Viola wrote to Ormer's brother James in Fort Worth that "the happiest time of his life was with me."[14]

Late in the fall of 1919, Locklear returned to Hollywood to await the opening of his first movie. Dressed in a Santa Claus suit, on December 13 he stood on top of an airplane and rode into San Francisco to advertise a benefit performance the following afternoon for the *San Francisco Examiner*'s Cheer Fund. Locklear earlier told reporters that he hoped to make his San Francisco show the "best he has ever given." "The fact that this is a benefit and that the people of San Francisco are taking so much interest in seeing large returns makes me more anxious than ever to give them more than they anticipate."[15]

One of the newspaper promotions for the San Francisco show reported: "It is not that he is a reckless daredevil who might kill himself to entertain a crowd, but that he has planned and carefully worked out an amazing demonstration of using the aeroplane in combination with his own magnificent physical development and confidence to prove that the epoch of flying has arrived."[16] His trying to outdo himself for the San Francisco crowd, however, meant that he would hang by one hand from a skid beneath the airplane and wave with the other, the plane flying low so people could see the grin on his face. In imitation of the "Flying Mercury" statue, he went out to the tip of the upper wing and balanced on one toe! Even his friends and manager were aghast at that one, for he had not told anyone in advance what he planned to do; he only promised a "better" show for the Santa Claus crowd.

Pickens booked him and his partners for air shows in California until the movie premiere on December 28. For the next two months he went on tour to promote the movie. In Chicago, one hundred thousand circulars advertising the film were dropped by air. Ads proclaimed, "A big six reel super feature. Thrills Sensation and Excitement!" [17] The film was the first aerial feature ever made, but, unfortunately, no copies of it have been preserved.

By the spring of 1920 young Locklear began hobnobbing with the Hollywood crowd: Jack Pickford (brother of Mary), Charlie Chaplin, Cecil B. DeMille (who liked flying, owned an airport and Mercury Aviation), Douglas Fairbanks, Wallace Reid, Buster Keaton, and Rudolph Valentino. It was pretty heady stuff for a young man who had grown up in Fort Worth, raced motorcycles with his friends, and flown airplanes over Barron Field. At this time, Locklear wrote to his family in Fort Worth: "It won't be long now 'til I will have to start east again on my tours which I surely dread as I feel I can do well out here in Pictures now." [18] In late April the William Fox Studio asked him to star in an air thriller, *The Skywayman*, and offered him $1,650 per week. His costar for the new movie was Louise Lovely, a young actress from Australia.

Other stunt pilots had copied Locklear's feats in the air, changing from one airplane to another. Now, he was tired of stunt flying. He preferred to stay in Hollywood and make movies. Viola Dana was there, too. The pilot-turned-Hollywood-star seemed torn during the filming of *The Skywayman* in several ways. Ruby, his estranged wife, tried to reconcile with him, but he still was seeing Viola. Other stunt pilots were planning their summer tours, so Locklear convinced Elliott and Short to go with him at night to do his stunts to prove to himself that he still could manage them. This flight was in violation of orders from the studio. The producer had told him that he did not have to do the tricks for the movie live, that they could be staged or doubles could be used, but Locklear insisted on the real thing.

His friends believed that he was depressed and feared the summer stunt circuit that Pickens had lined up. However, Locklear did not want other aerialists to get ahead of him. Fort Worth flier Arthur Oakley, leader of the Oakley Aerial Escadrille, created the stunt of jumping from a moving airplane to a moving train in May 1920 at Ellington Field, Texas. No one had made a transfer from a train to a plane, so Locklear wanted to be the first. Before he could do so, someone beat him to it, but Locklear was the first to do the stunt in a movie. Locklear should have been satisfied. After all, he had performed his plane-changing antic 262 times, by his and his friends' calculations, and survived, with Elliott as his pilot each time.

On the night of August 2, 1920, Locklear had a premonition that he should not fly. He was filming the last scene of *The Skywayman*, which was to end in a nosedive and crash. When ground lights flashed off to signal him to pull up he was to pull out of the spin, but they did not go off. Locklear and Elliott, who was in the other seat of the airplane, both died. Some accounts said that the lights blinded Locklear and that he dove into the ground at an estimated 150 miles per hour. His friend Jack Pickford called Ruby to tell her that Locklear was dead; she took the news very hard and collapsed. Newspapers all over the country carried the story of his death. Hollywood had never seen a funeral procession like the one staged for Locklear and Elliott as the bodies traveled to the Southern Pacific depot, nor was it equalled until Valentino's death a few years later.

Work halted at all the movie studios for five minutes in tribute and a band played "The Star-Spangled Banner" at the station as the coffins were transferred into railroad cars. Locklear's body was returned to Fort Worth to the largest funeral crowd his hometown had ever known. One newspaper reported that a charred letter to Locklear's mother was found on his body, a farewell that he supposedly always carried, just in case! Fox Studios rushed copies of *The Skywayman* into print, and it reached the theaters by September 12. The scene and the movie were not ruined because a crash was to end the film. Locklear's name was displayed above the title.

Almost immediately following Locklear's death there was a problem. His parents filed a protest in the Tarrant County Probate Court in Fort Worth about two weeks after his death to prevent his estranged wife from being temporary administratrix of his estate. They showed a letter from their son leaving $5,000 to his mother and $5,000 to a brother, which the probate judge admitted. The elder Locklears informed the court that the bulk of his estate was in Los Angeles and that Title Insurance and Trust Company of that city had been named administrator. Ruby acknowledged that his estate in Tarrant County amounted only to various articles of personal property worth about $300. On the other hand, his estate in California probably was worth about $15,000 in personal property, a significant sum in 1920 when a brand-new Ford rolled off the assembly line at $240 or a new frame house cost about $2,000. In addition, Ruby was expecting royalties from *The Skywayman*. The case dragged on until November 1921 when the probate judge forced Ruby and Odessa Locklear to settle. Ruby had to pay the court costs and give her former mother-in-law $1,850. When all the claims were settled, Ruby received less than $10,000.

The life and death of Ormer Leslie Locklear exemplified an entry into the age of flight for Fort Worth citizens and Texans. Not only were three airfields constructed near Fort Worth during the World War, including Barron where Locklear trained, but other Texas installations included Love Field in Dallas as well as Kelly and Brooks in San Antonio. After it was built in 1928, Randolph Field in San Antonio would be called the "West Point of the Air" because so many pilots were trained there.

In Locklear's own home town of Fort Worth, commercial air travel began through the auspices of the Federal Model Airway System in which the government encouraged municipalities all across the country to set up airfields. On Main Street some four miles north of the Tarrant County Courthouse a 170-acre field opened on May 23, 1925—the Fort Worth Airport. A young army officer, William Fuller, set up Love Field in Dallas. Following the war he came to Fort Worth to manage the airport that later became Meacham Field, named after the local mayor. It was at this field that Southern Air Transport (getting the aerial postal contract as Locklear had hoped) would later merge with other airlines to become the Fort Worth-based American Airlines. Lighter-than-air craft, dirigibles, were tethered at North Fort Worth at a facility that would later house the Federal Aviation Authority. In the mid-1920s the state's helium industry moved to Amarillo where additional deposits of the gas had been found.

Events and people in places outside Texas during the 1920s nevertheless shaped the coming air industry in the state. Maj. Reuben Fleet, a World War I veteran, formed Consolidated Aircraft Corporation in 1923 after buying and merging two fledgling companies on the East Coast. He soon moved his business to Buffalo, then in 1935 to San Diego. World War II expansion brought Consolidated to Fort Worth; the company became Convair, then General Dynamics, and later Lockheed-Martin. The latter was the merger of Malcolm and Allen Lockheed's company with that of Glenn L. Martin, a fellow stunt pilot in the early days of the industry. The young fellow, Larry Bell, who worked as a mechanic for Martin in California in the 1910s, took a job with Major Fleet in Buffalo, later started his own aircraft plant there, and then began making helicopters in Hurst, Texas, in the 1950s.

While Ormer Locklear was doing his stunts, a daredevil kid was growing up on the North Side of Fort Worth, racing his bicycle, motorcycle, and car. He, too, would die in an airplane crash at age twenty-eight, but his craft was a B-24 that was shot down by the Japanese as he bombed their fleet in the South China Sea in 1944. The young man was Horace S. Carswell, Jr. An Air Force base in the western part of Fort Worth bore his name for forty-five years.

Even Locklear's younger sister, Anita Mae (called Nita Mae by her family and friends), eventually took up flying due largely to the influence of her older brother's fame. Only ten years old in 1920 when he died, Nita Mae remembered Locklear Day at the Dallas Fair in October 1919 and that he had promised her a ride at the end of the day. Deteriorating weather prevented it. After graduating from Paschal High School, Nita Mae worked for Interstate Theaters, a Texas movie chain, as a cashier in two of their Fort Worth movie houses for over a decade. In April 1941, Nita Mae began taking private flying lessons. She told a reporter who sought her out because of her famous brother that she planned no fancy stuff; she only wanted to be a good pilot. However, she admitted that flying brought her an "unexplainable thrill."[19]

In February 1943, Nita Mae, an attractive brunette, quit her job as assistant manager of the Hollywood Theater in downtown Fort Worth and joined a group of women pilots organized by Jacqueline Cochran to relieve men for combat assignments in the war effort. She attended the Army Air Forces Contract Pilot School at Avenger Field near Sweetwater, Texas, which had been set up solely to train women pilots. Eventually the group became known as the Women's Airforce Service Pilots, or WASPs. During the remainder of World War II they served as flight instructors and aircraft ferry pilots.

Over fifty years after the death of Ormer Locklear his legend and that of the stunt pilots of those flying circuses of the 1910s and 1920s inspired a movie starring Robert Redford, *The Great Waldo Pepper*. Producers of the film dedicated it to Locklear and his acrobats of the air. Perhaps in response to the attention drawn to stunt piloting by the movie, the Smithsonian Institution's National Air and Space Museum in Washington, DC, opened an exhibit in May 1974 that featured Locklear's barnstorming career. Also included in the exhibit were Lincoln Beachey, Roscoe Turner, Jimmy Doolittle, Art Goebel, and Al Williams. Thus, the nation's premier museum dedicated to flight acknowledged that with the life and career of Texas soldier, stuntman, and film star Ormer Leslie Locklear the "epoch of flying" had arrived.

Notes

1. Art Ronnie, *Locklear: The Man Who Walked on Wings* (New York, 1973), 23; *Fort Worth Record*, June 8, 1919, Locklear Collection, Pate Museum of Transportation, Cresson, Texas.

2. *Fort Worth Star-Telegram* (no date), Locklear Collection.

3. Ibid.

4. Ibid.

5. *Fort Worth Record*, June 8, 1919.

6. Ibid.

7. *Syracuse Journal*, September 9, 1919, Locklear Collection.

8. *San Francisco Examiner*, September 12, 1919, Locklear Collection.

9. Advertisement in *Billboard*, September 1919, Locklear Collection.

10. *Fort Worth Star-Telegram*, June 13, 1919, Locklear Collection.

11. "Texas Boy Thrills Multitude at Fair," unattributed article, October 17, 1919, Locklear Collection.

12. *Daily Times Herald* (Dallas), October 17, 1919, Locklear Collection.

13. "Says Locklear Is Soldier of Cross and Air" (unattributed article), Locklear Collection.

14. Viola Dana to James Locklear, April 1, 1975, Locklear Collection.

15. " 'Impossible' in Locklear's Tricks Today," San Francisco newspaper (no other identification), Locklear Collection.

16. Robert H. Willson, *San Francisco Examiner*, December 15, 1919, Locklear Collection.

17. *San Francisco Chronicle*, January 19, 1920, Locklear Collection.

18. Ronnie, *Locklear*, 223.

19. *Fort Worth Star-Telegram*, April 10, 1941, Clipping File, Special Collections Library, University of Texas at Arlington, Arlington.

Suggested Readings

Biddle, Wayne. *Barons of the Sky*. New York, 1991.

Bilstein, Roger, and Jay Miller. *Aviation in Texas*. Austin, 1985.

Coleman, Ted, with Robert Wenkam. *Jack Northrop and the Flying Wing*. New York, 1988.

Jary, William E. Jr. *Camp Bowie, Fort Worth, 1917–18: An Illustrated History of the 36th Division in the First World War*. Fort Worth, 1975.

Norton, Donald J. *Larry: A Biography of Lawrence D. Bell.* Chicago, 1981.
Ronnie, Art. *Locklear: The Man Who Walked on Wings.* New York, 1973.
Wagner, William. *Reuben Fleet and the Story of Consolidated Aircraft.* Fallbrook, CA, 1976.

11

Carter Wesley
Sounding the Ram's Horn for Human Rights

Amilcar Shabazz

The life of Carter Wesley attests to the persistence of the human spirit. Wesley grew up and reached manhood in a state where he was effectively barred from voting, where he could not go to a school of his own choosing, nor could he eat at most cafés, swim in public pools, or even enter certain lobbies at many train stations. A combat veteran of World War I, he left the battlefields of Europe only to return home and face the same old prejudices. Eventually, Wesley rose to a level of prominence in the black community as an attorney and newspaper publisher. He turned the bar and the press into a bully pulpit for attacking racism, especially in the area of higher education. Working with such leading lights as Thurgood Marshall, Wesley helped devise strategies that opened to black students the doors of college campuses that Jim Crow and the "separate but equal" doctrine had long closed. Like those of Hermine Tobolowsky (see Chapter 14), Wesley's efforts have gone largely unheralded, despite the pivotal role he played in achieving legal equality for African Americans in Texas and despite his emergence at the forefront of the civil rights movement before it became a popular crusade.

Amilcar Shabazz is professor of American Studies and the director of the African American Studies Program at the University of Alabama. He is the author of *Saving the Race and Advancing the Cause of Democracy: The Struggle for Access and Equity in Texas Higher Education* (forthcoming).

Texas has contributed in many ways to the human story in the twentieth century. Its wildcatters propelled the world into the petrochemical age; its young left home to fight wars in every corner of the globe; its scientists helped to make space travel and the computer age possible; its activists changed society through landmark Supreme Court decisions and mass demonstrations; its business leaders developed such architectural wonders as the Astrodome; and, tragically, one assassin in Dallas changed the course of history. To the American political culture, the Lone Star State has given presidents, vice presidents, war hero generals, influential congressional leaders, and foreign policymakers—and the list goes on. In terms of securing human rights for all persons and the betterment of human relations, however, the state that adopted the motto "The Friendship State" appears to have no such legacy at all.

A big state too proud ever to be humble, Texas says to the world that perfection has no flaws, and thus it learns no lessons from its mistakes. Texas, however, is not perfect. Some of its best sons and daughters sacrificed themselves in the struggle for freedom and human rights. We mock the human tradition of "friendship" to the extent that we fail to pay homage to our ancestors who had to fight to make Texas a decent place to live for all human beings. This essay, about one of those ancestors, tells a story as a way of keeping alive the spirit of all those who, when they saw injustice, refused "to go along to get along."

Houston provides one of the most dynamic places in the state to study the emergence of the human rights struggle. By 1940 it had become the New South's largest and fastest-growing city. Burgeoning economic opportunities and an expanding urban population influenced social philosophy, and the notion began to circulate that it was not foolish to be optimistic about the future. The resurgent Ku Klux Klan of the 1920s had cannibalized itself and ceased to parade down Main Street, U.S.A. The city's people dared to believe that the Great Depression would end, that better days lay ahead. Some recalled the words of Frederick Douglass, the great African-American leader of the nineteenth century: "If there is struggle, there will be progress."

Something else was also burned into their memory. After the Bill of Rights in the U.S. Constitution was ratified, it was not until the 1830s that all white men would win their rights as citizens of the republic and be able to participate fully in the body politic and to be heard. In 1861 the Civil War split the Union, but in the ensuing Reconstruction Era came a great victory for democracy and human liberty with the extension of citizenship rights to African Americans in the passage of the 13th, 14th, and 15th Amendments to the U.S. Constitution. Sadly, the advance that these amendments symbolized was only a paper victory, and it took many decades of agitating, educating, organizing, and resisting to make the rights in the written Constitution a reality.

Carter Wesley, a product of African-American life and culture in Houston, was one example of a Texan who stood up for his rights and for those of his fellows. His activism and professional career, especially in the 1940s, reveal the mainsprings of the movement of black people for human rights. Take Wesley out of history, and we pull out a part of Thurgood Marshall, Rosa Parks, and Martin Luther King Jr. It is difficult to imagine an individual making so great an impact on his times when only a few history books mention him. Not one school building, park, or street is named for him, nor any statue or monument erected in his honor, even in his hometown. Almost completely forgotten today, the legacy of Wesley nonetheless demands remembrance.

Carter, born on April 29, 1892, in Freedmen's Town, Houston, was one of three sons of Mabel Green Wesley and Harry Wesley. Thirty years before Carter's birth, Mabel was the firstborn of Lettitia and Frederick Green, both enslaved Africans on a plantation in Montgomery County. Historians Patricia Smith Prather and Bob Lee note that she, like her ancestors in the Americas, had among their white neighbors no commonly accepted "right to an education." The opportunity for an education had to be seized, and education as a basic human value was scrupulously cultivated in the Wesley household. When Carter was born, his mother had already established her name as a teacher in the schools of Houston. The education available to African Americans usually stressed religious or technical training, with an emphasis on humility and obedience. Mabel Wesley, however, knew that education could and should serve to produce democratic citizens—free human beings who would rather die than be enslaved.

She gained this knowledge from her parents who, as soon as they could, made an exodus from slave plantation life. Yet, after the so-called Juneteenth emancipation, slavery in many ways would be renamed "sharecropping," for it was, in substance, the same old system. About forty miles north of Houston, the 1860 census put Montgomery County's black population at slightly larger than the white. Under postwar Reconstruction this meant that black men and white Republicans dominated the political offices of the area. By the early 1870s, however, white supremacist elites had used tactics ranging from sporadic acts of violence, threats of harm, literacy tests, and the white primary to effectively strip blacks of the vote and of virtually any influence in the political arena. The white primary barred blacks from voting in the Democratic Party primaries strictly on the basis of race. This practice would become the first issue on which the young Carter Wesley would cut his political teeth. The same practice that helped spur his grandparents to migrate out of Montgomery County and take their chances in Houston, fifty years later, would move him to challenge by all legal means available the white primary as an unconstitutional, racist tactic. The intergenerational tradition of struggle within the Wesley family, then, progressed from migration to education and then to political action via litigation and public agitation.

Through their decision to vote with their feet and move to Houston, the Greens taught their daughter to resist the dehumanization of slavery in all its forms. Mabel, in her own way, took up education as a weapon of struggle and became one of the first students at the major school in Freedmen's Town, the Gregory Institute. At eighteen years of age, she began to teach at Oats Prairie School, the Chaneyville School, and the First Ward School. She so impressed Houston school district officials that in 1917 they named her principal of the newly opened Crawford Elementary School. Without a college degree, she became the first of four African-American women to assume a leadership position that customarily went to men. Throughout this time she continued her postsecondary education by attending school at the sole state-supported college restricted by law to blacks only, Prairie View A&M University. She studied in the summer months until in 1930 she earned her bachelor's degree.

Carter Wesley's schooling was not as protracted as his mother's education had been, but his promising future was nearly cut short. In 1910, during his senior year of high school, Carter and a young woman conceived a child. The details of the child's birth in 1911, outside of wedlock, are unknown. What is significant, however, is that Carter and his family assumed responsibility for the baby boy. Thanks to his parents, Wesley was able to go on with his college plans.

Houston at this time had no institution of higher education that accepted African Americans. Prairie View, about fifty miles away, was the state college for black students, but its academic program was limited to little more than a good high school and teacher training. Fisk University in Nashville was one of the leading private universities for African Americans, and it was there that Wesley dreamed of going. When his dream came true, he did not take it for granted, but excelled. He graduated in 1917 with a bachelor's degree, magna cum laude. As important to him as getting good grades, Wesley also searched for an intellectual understanding of his world and of his future as a person of African descent in an anti-African country and a European-dominated world. His chief influence was Fisk's greatest former student, W. E. B. DuBois. Having graduated from Fisk almost forty years before Wesley arrived there, DuBois had become the most widely known and respected African-American man of letters. His classic *The Souls of Black Folks* (1903) and his editorship of *The Crisis*, the monthly magazine of the National Association for the Advancement of Colored People (NAACP), which he had created, brought him to the pinnacle of renown by 1915 when

Wesley was still an undergraduate. With a circulation of more than 30,000, DuBois defined in an April 1915 issue of *The Crisis*, "The Immediate Program of the American Negro." He wrote that "the American Negro demands equality—political equality, industrial equality and social equality; and he is never going to rest satisfied with anything less."[1] Such simple yet bold words became the guiding light of Wesley's adult life.

Second only in importance to DuBois in Wesley's life and thought was James Weldon Johnson. Wesley admired the great poet, scholar, and writer (who also had been a lawyer) and was attracted to the NAACP when Johnson was the national secretary. Johnson's novel, *The Autobiography of an Ex-Colored Man* (1912), stimulated in Wesley the desire to become a race man—that is, a person who fights racial injustice and works to improve the conditions of African-American people through their life vocation and civic activism. The malevolent winds of war in Europe and racial violence in the United States, however, would interrupt Wesley's plans even as they steeled his youthful idealism into a lifelong crusade.

In June 1917, Wesley enrolled at a black officers' training camp at Fort Des Moines, Iowa. In a few months he completed the program and was commissioned a first lieutenant, making him one of the first black junior officers since Colonel Charles Young led black troops of the 10th Cavalry into combat during John "Black Jack" Pershing's pursuit of Pancho Villa into Mexico in 1916. As Wesley neared the completion of officers' training, an event occurred in his hometown that must have sorely tested his faith in DuBois's "close ranks" appeal: that wartime service should mark the pathway to equal rights and justice at home and abroad. On August 23, 1917, a black soldier of the 3rd Battalion, 24th Infantry Regiment, stationed on the outskirts of the city to guard the construction of Camp Logan, came upon a Houston police officer mercilessly beating a black woman whom he suspected of withholding information about a crapshooter he was looking for. When the soldier interfered by asking what was the matter, the policeman beat him with his billy club and had him arrested and taken to jail. The soldier was soon released, but when a black corporal went to inquire of the arresting police officers about the matter he was chased, shot at, beaten, arrested, and locked up. When the news of the second incident reached Camp Logan, some hundred or more soldiers mutinied, taking ammunition and weapons as they marched into the city to confront and "punish" the hated Houston police force. In the wake of their attack, twenty-five policemen were killed, along with two white soldiers, nine white or Hispanic civilians, and four of the black mutineers. Of great concern to Wesley and his companions at Fort Des Moines was the fate of the soldiers who had mutinied. Would they be tried fairly? Would the sentences of those court-martialed take into consideration the racism and the long train of abuses that blacks, civilians and soldiers alike, had endured in Heavenly Houston, as the local Chambers of Commerce dubbed the Bayou City?

The army assigned Wesley to the 92nd Division, organized in November 1917, at Camp Funston, Kansas; and, on December 22, as a newly commissioned officer, he learned the court's decision. Out of sixty-three men charged with mutiny in a time of war and with premeditated murder, thirteen were sentenced to death and were hanged in a camp adjacent to Fort Sam Houston that same day. Five men were freed, four were found guilty on lesser charges, and forty-one men were given a sentence of life at hard labor. In the aftermath of the mutiny, Wesley not only felt concern for the legal predicament of the soldiers, but he also worried about the welfare of his family and friends in a city where already poor relations between the races had degenerated to such an abysmal state. Despite the fact that Houston's civilian black community took no part in the day of fighting, the attitude of the city's police and white men in general were outmoded, and a policy of collective punishment became the order of the day.

Somehow, Wesley had to put his apprehensions on hold. Upon shipping out to France, he served in the 372nd Infantry Regiment which, under the command of the French Army, fought in the Argonne and at Verdun in major battles of the World War. After being transferred to the 370th, Wesley took part in the battle of the Oise-Aisne on September 27, 1918. When the white captain of his company was severely wounded in the fighting, Wesley took command. The armistice that ended the war denied Wesley a chance at a significant combat command and, in February 1919, he returned to the United States and was happy to receive his discharge a few months later. In the fall of that year he was again a student, this time at the law school of predominately white Northwestern University in Illinois.

Wesley's choice of the legal profession, instead of following in his mother's footsteps and becoming a teacher, reflected his belief that his people needed men and women educated in the law to fight for human and civil rights. At the time there were few African-American lawyers, and for most of them the law was not the high-paying profession that it was for many whites. White lawyers and judges united to restrict the legal practice of African-American attorneys to an all-black clientele, dealing mostly in family and other civil matters. In the 1920s the law offered a talented and risk-taking person a cutting-edge lifestyle. Wesley, truly a man of the modern age, wanted to be on that edge, leading society toward progressive change.

When Wesley graduated from law school, he looked for a job that would also put a little cash in his pocket. Oklahoma was the place. Jasper Alston ("Jack") Atkins, Wesley's friend from his Fisk University days, had earned his J.D. degree from Yale and was practicing law in Tulsa. He later joined Wesley in Muskogee to set up a partnership. Their practice hit it big from successfully representing Afro-Native Americans on whose land oil or "black gold" had been found, but whites, their so-called guardians, had been taking the profits. Between 1922 and 1925, Wesley had prospered enough to marry a young woman he knew from Fisk, Gladys Dunbar of Ohio, and he brought to live with them his twelve-year-old son from Houston. In 1925, Gladys Wesley died in childbirth. The double blow of losing his wife and their baby hurt Wesley deeply. He sent his son back to Houston, but, in 1927, Wesley joined him and convinced the Atkins family to relocate there as well.

In the Bayou City, he and Atkins found a business, political, and social environment very different from Oklahoma. Dodging complaints that they had overcharged their Afro-Native American clients to amass their own fortunes, Wesley and Atkins arrived in Houston ready to make a fresh start. They launched their careers as entrepreneurs in the construction business, brokered land deals through the Safety Loan and Brokerage Company, and made a sizable capital investment in Clifton F. Richardson's Houston *Informer*, a black community newspaper. In 1931 their law practice took on another partner to become a three-man firm: James Madison Nabrit Jr., an honors graduate of the Northwestern University School of Law and the first black student there to be elected to the prestigious Order of the Coif. Nabrit not only shared a solid legal education with Wesley and Atkins, but a deep commitment to public interest litigation as well. In 1930 there were only twenty black lawyers in the entire state of Texas.

Wesley, the native Houstonian in the firm, quickly became a major player in the black renaissance in the city's social, political, and economic life. Before Wesley's arrival, Francis Scott Key Whittaker ran the principal black law office in Houston. A Harvard University Law School graduate, Whittaker opened his office in 1923. In unrelated actions,

Richard D. Evans, trained in the law at Howard University, moved to Waco in 1912 and became the first lawyer in Texas to put white supremacy/black disfranchisement on trial. In 1919 he launched a systematic legal campaign against the exclusion of blacks from voting in primary elections in Waco. When Wesley and Nabrit joined in the black struggle in Texas for full voting rights, numerous lawsuits from Beaumont to El Paso had been filed and lost by other lawyers, both black and white. It seemed a hopeless cause, but they had faith that if they could bring a case before the U.S. Supreme Court, righteousness would prevail.

The NAACP, however, from its headquarters in New York, considered itself the pioneer in and leader of the constitutional law fight for the rights of African Americans. Although Texas activists and the NAACP's national office shared common goals of wanting to defeat white supremacist laws and practices in the courts, the leadership issue would be a thorny and recurring problem. Wesley and his partners did not flinch from a head-on collision with the NAACP legal team. They particularly objected to its reliance on white lawyers in the early years of the legal campaign when capable black lawyers such as themselves were available in the state where the NAACP filed a lawsuit. Partly as a result of their objections, the NAACP's national office hired the dean of Howard University's law school, Charles Hamilton Houston, an African-American graduate of Harvard University, to direct its legal campaign. From that step toward embracing diversity and supporting a greater African-American presence at the bar, Houston's own student, Thurgood Marshall, would become the NAACP's chief counsel and eventually the first African-American justice on the Supreme Court.

The conflict between Wesley and the NAACP also extended to the area of legal tactics and strategies in the fight against the for-whites-only primary elections, but ultimately unity prevailed. After almost one-quarter century of lawsuits, black Texans finally won the battle in 1944 in *Smith vs. Allwright*. In this case named for a black dentist in Houston, Lonnie Smith, Wesley, and Marshall worked together to urge the Supreme Court to rule that blacks could not be barred from voting in the Democratic Party primary in Texas or in any number of other states where white party officials practiced such exclusion. It was in Wesley's office that he and Marshall prepared the brief that convinced the Court to strike a blow for the voting rights of African Americans.

Wesley's work with Marshall on the *Smith* case was as a consultant and as a political and financial backer. For almost a decade before the

Court's decision he had retired from the practice of law and had become increasingly involved in the publishing of the Houston *Informer*. His rise to control of the paper required him to outmaneuver owner Clifton Richardson, which Wesley had no qualms about doing. After learning the financial ins and outs of the paper by becoming its auditor in 1929, he moved the next year to become vice president, followed by general manager and treasurer before the end of 1932. Wesley also bought out Richardson's interest in the paper after a bitter dispute over the paper's journalistic and financial policies. In 1933 another aspect of Wesley's life changed. He married Doris Wooten and soon had two infants in his household. Wooten had been his partner in running the newspaper business after 1932. When Atkins left Houston in 1936 to join the faculty of Howard University's law school, Wesley had become more a publisher than a lawyer.

Two very different sources speak to Wesley's character and how he was viewed in his time. The first, Lorenzo Greene, a graduate of Howard and Columbia Universities with degrees in history, went to work for Carter G. Woodson, the Harvard-trained historian who established the Association for the Study of Negro Life and History and is best known today as the founder of February as Black History Month. In 1930 he and two students loaded an old Model T Ford with black history books that Dr. Woodson had published and traveled across the country from town to town selling the books and promoting historical consciousness among African Americans. Greene kept a diary of his travels and, during his pass through Houston, wrote about meeting Carter Wesley. He estimated Wesley's age a few years younger than it actually was, and he was deeply impressed that a man still in his thirties was so business-minded, successful, and prominent. Marveling over what a "progressive young man" Wesley was, Greene stated that the publisher "made a fine publicity man for me" by telling others about his work with Dr. Woodson. In trying to sell books to Wesley, he observed that after much persuasive sales talk Wesley "finally succumbed when I appealed to his ego. [I] told him that his name listed [among the purchasers] would induce others to do likewise."[2] Many people who knew Wesley regarded him as being rather full of himself, but they also recognized that he was a man in full, a true leader.

The other source on Wesley is John Gunther, a journalist whose reports as a foreign correspondent around the world were bestsellers. In his 1947 book *Inside U.S.A.* he wrote about the Lone Star State and included some remarks on the "Negro issue" in Texas. In this passage he commented: "The most interesting Negro in Texas . . . is probably a moderate named Carter Wesley, the publisher of a string of newspapers including the Houston *Defender* and *Informer*, the Fort Worth *Mind*, the Dallas *Express*, the oldest Negro paper in the state. All told, Wesley's papers have a circulation of about sixty thousand; they are intelligently edited and vigorously outspoken on most issues. Wesley is now fifty-three."[3]

The comments of Greene and Gunther present Wesley as a force to be reckoned with. The height of his influence as a newspaper publisher and human rights activist came in the period following the *Smith* victory and the end of World War II. Besides the cities that Gunther noted, Wesley also published papers or local editions in San Antonio and San Diego, California, and as far to the east as New Orleans, Mobile, and Memphis. In 1945, moreover, Wesley's paper, in terms of the number of people it employed and its gross income and property, was the largest black-owned business in Houston. On the national level, Wesley was a founder of Associated Publishers, Inc., a black advertising business; a recognized leader in the National Newspaper Publishers Association; and one among an elite group of black newspaper editors who met during the war in the White House with President Franklin D. Roosevelt. In 1948 the U.S. government sent him and ten other black publishers to Germany as part of an investigation of the claims of black servicemen that they were victims of racial discrimination. Closer to home, however, Wesley's major campaign was the fight for African-American access to and equality in education.

The "all-out war for democracy" in education, as he and other blacks described their struggle, was multifaceted and complex. In a word, Wesley wanted equalization of the educational opportunities and resources afforded by the state to whites with that afforded to blacks. In principle and in the long run, he supported integration of the races; but in practice and immediately, he demanded improvements and increased resources for the schools that the state restricted to black students only. In 1945, at the postsecondary level, that meant the college at Prairie View, and any increase in state funding for Prairie View had two aspects. First, the state constitution for more than seven decades had promised to create a second university for blacks that would be the equivalent of the University of Texas (UT) at Austin. The state never acted to fulfill its constitutional mandate and black Texans never forgot the original promise. Second, a limited campaign to persuade legislators in Austin to improve Prairie View consistently met with failure. The state refused to heed pleas for funding increases regardless of whether they came from blacks or even from whites within the Department of Education. The legislative majority was concerned only with improving white institutions of higher education and could care less about the needs of the disfranchised black minority.

In response, Wesley advocated a two-pronged strategy: a direct assault on segregation while at the same time pleading, demanding, and taking whatever monies could be wrung out of the lily-white legislature for the benefit of Prairie View or toward the creation of the long-promised black UT. He recognized that the direct assault on the whites-only admissions policy could finally push whites toward appropriations to upgrade black schools. Along the first line of attack Wesley raised thousands of dollars to fund the protracted litigation. Through articles and columns in his newspapers, he influenced public opinion, especially in making the black community believe that it was possible to force whites to admit blacks into universities defined as exclusively theirs.

Wesley also supported and protected the man who would file the major test case against segregated higher education. Heman Sweatt, a native Houstonian qualified in every way for admission to UT's law school except that he was racially identified as a Negro, filed suit in 1946. While the suit worked its way to the Supreme Court, Wesley placed Sweatt on the payroll as an employee of the Houston *Informer*. No one—besides men and women such as Sweatt who braved white reaction by applying to universities where whites banned them—did more for the struggle to eradicate segregation in Texas education than Carter Wesley.

At the same time, Wesley was one of the greatest backers of the existing all-black Texas schools. Prairie View, the Houston College for Negroes (established as a municipal junior college in 1927), and the eleven black private colleges across the state had no better friend than Wesley. His newspapers boosted the image of these institutions by recording and trumpeting their successes and victories, however great or small. He personally donated time and energy toward various projects, especially major fundraising campaigns. As a relentless and incisive critic of the state and the white majority for their hypocrisy, duplicity, inertia, and apathy toward black institutions, Wesley fought for these colleges in the pages of his newspapers, at the state capitol, and in the courtrooms.

Notwithstanding the relative inadequacy of resources and lack of standing, he recognized that black colleges did the work of providing higher education to the majority of African-American undergraduates. He foresaw that such schools would continue to be the only institutions available to most black students for the many years that it would take to overturn the Supreme Court's 1896 *Plessy* decision, which gave federal sanction to the practice of racial discrimination across the United States on the basis that "separate but equal" treatment did not violate the equal protection clause of the 14th Amendment to the U.S. Constitution. Wesley refused to abandon altogether black colleges and universities in the name of integration.

Lulu Belle White, a prominent human rights activist in Houston and a friend of Wesley's through the many years of the fight against black exclusion from the Democratic Party primaries, took issue with the publisher's two-line strategy regarding educational equalization. Consistent with the position which Marshall and the central leadership of the NAACP took in the late 1940s, White adopted the view that segregated black schools were no more than monuments to Jim Crow racism. A graduate of Prairie View, she rejected as too little, too late Texas's compromise measures of increased funding to black higher education that arose in response to Sweatt's lawsuit. A militant from her college days, the fight against fascism in Europe and Asia concomitant with the battle for human rights in the United States pushed White to go beyond a service role in the black freedom struggle and to accept a leadership position as the executive secretary of the NAACP's Houston branch. In 1943 she was the only woman in the South to hold such a full-time salaried position.

When the difference between Wesley and Marshall on political tactics crystallized, White put to work her acid tongue behind the NAACP position and against Wesley. She lambasted him before members of the movement and in broader public discourse as clinging to the posture of yesterday's Negro, the stooping, eyes-to-the-ground, hat-in-hand, Stepin' Fetchit stereotype. Wesley, never such a man, did not accept white men who disrespectfully honked their automobile horns at black women as they walked to church or school, nor did he accept their addressing black women without using the courtesy titles of "Miss" or "Mrs." He never accepted whites calling an adult black man "boy" or white soldiers in the U.S. military refusing to salute black officers who outranked them. Thus, when White portrayed him as a sellout to his race over a tactical dispute, he did not turn the other cheek. He charged her and the NAACP generally with wanting to monopolize the equal rights and justice battlefield and of fomenting division within the united front that leaders of black organizations in Texas had forged since the 1930s. Moreover, in the postwar period when anti-Red hysteria was rising, Wesley claimed that White was a Communist sympathetic to Marxism-Leninism. Marshall, as NAACP chief counsel, joined in the attack on Wesley and expanded the conflict into a national brouhaha for a period of several months. Ultimately, the Wesley-White feud ended in defeat for White, the Wesley-Marshall shoot-out in a draw. In June 1949, White resigned from her position with the Houston branch. Soon thereafter the NAACP's national leadership focused its public statements more on the side of the benefits that would accrue to society from the elimination of segregation and refrained from wholesale condemnations of historically black colleges and universities.

Wesley, for his part, never wavered in his full and overt support for Sweatt's right to attend UT and for the fight against segregation. On July 2, shortly after White's resignation, he maintained in his newspaper column, "The Ram's Horn," his stance from the beginning: "Even if Sweatt enters the University of Texas, we will not want to get rid of Texas State University for Negroes . . . the Texas Constitution decrees separation provided it is equal; why shouldn't we make them carry out the Constitution and equalize Texas State University in toto with the University of Texas?" A year later, the Supreme Court ordered Texas to admit Sweatt into UT's law school.

African Americans began entering UT in the summer of 1950, but only in graduate programs and professional schools. W. D. McClennan, a faculty member at Austin's Samuel Huston College, was admitted to the graduate program in mathematics and John Chase was admitted to the School of Architecture. UT officials continued, however, to turn away black applicants to its undergraduate school until the middle of the decade following the Court's landmark ruling in the 1954 *Brown vs. Board of Education* case. Even with that decision, which overturned *Plessy* and the white supremacist doctrine of racial hierarchy that it legitimized, Texas did not mandate the elimination of race as a requirement of admission at all its state-supported institutions of higher learning until 1965. Wesley was a pivotal figure in the social revolution that brought on many changes in Texas and beyond. He acted behind the scenes to help blacks take to court school districts and other state universities and junior colleges to equalize black institutions or to admit blacks into schools that barred whites. In his newspapers he supported efforts to improve education in both segregated and integrated contexts, always while emphasizing that legally enforced separation of the races was a crime against humanity.

In 1969, Wesley died—a man who was as honorable as Martin Luther King Jr., and as committed to social change and as tireless in pursuit of human rights and justice as any of the great martyrs of the twentieth century. Despite his associations with labor unions and the black working class, Wesley's political worldview remained procapitalist, although mildly anti-imperialist. Just as DuBois said of himself before he died as a citizen of the new African nation of Ghana in 1963, Wesley must be judged by history as a "bourgeois democrat." As he stood on the strong shoulders of his mother and father, on the genius of Du Bois, Johnson, and militant journalists such as Ida B. Wells, so, too, have many men and women stood on Wesley's shoulders and climbed to greater heights. Every lawyer trained at Texas Southern University and the University of Texas as well as anyone who supports the rule of law owes him respect and gratitude. Through his work, immoral and unjust laws were dealt a deathblow. A shrewd entrepreneur, keen publisher, and champion of human rights and self-determination, Wesley blew his ram's horn to call men and women to challenge the power structures of their day, which were preserving oppression and injustice. Texas will be a greater state when it better appreciates the lives of history makers such as Carter Wesley.

Notes

1. *The Crisis* 9 (April 1915): 310, reprinted in Cary D. Wintz, ed., *African American Political Thought, 1890–1930: Washington, Du Bois, Garvey, and Randolph* (Armonk, NY: M. E. Sharpe, 1996), 109.

2. Howard Beeth and Cary D. Wintz, eds., *Black Dixie: Afro-Texan History and Culture in Houston* (College Station: Texas A&M Press, 1992), 149, 140.

3. John Gunther, *Inside U.S.A.* (New York: Harper & Bros., 1947), 868.

Suggested Readings

Beeth, Howard, and Cary D. Wintz, eds. *Black Dixie: Afro-Texan History and Culture in Houston.* College Station, TX, 1992.

Gunther, John. *Inside U.S.A.* New York, 1947.

Hine, Darlene Clark. *Black Victory: The Rise and Fall of the White Primary in Texas.* Millwood, NY, 1979.

Obadele-Starks, Ernest. *Black Unionism in the Industrial South.* College Station, TX, 2000.

Pitre, Merline. *In Struggle against Jim Crow: Lulu B. White and the NAACP, 1900–1957*. College Station, TX, 1999.

Prather, Patricia Smith, and Bob Lee, eds. *Texas Trailblazer Series*. Houston, 1997.

Smith, J. Clay, Jr. *Emancipation: The Making of the Black Lawyer, 1844–1944*. Philadelphia, 1993.

12

Bob Wills
The Enduring Magic of His Music

Charles R. Townsend

Music reflects the society that makes it. In this regard, Bob Wills was a product of his place, time, and circumstances. He took an ordinary fiddle and transformed what had been a folk instrument into a piece that commanded center stage in popular dance music of the twentieth century. Western swing, the new sound that Wills created during the Great Depression, continues to influence country music today. A born fiddler, Bob Wills played his first dance as an eight year old. He learned from his father, an accomplished fiddler in his own right, but was equally influenced by the music and culture of African Americans who lived on the farms that surrounded his childhood home in East Texas. Soon he began to perfect his sound, adding to traditional white fiddle music the rhythm, timing, and beat of the blues and jazz that he had borrowed from his black neighbors. Wills first gained prominence at the head of the Light Crust Doughboys, who played on the statewide radio show of future governor W. Lee "Pappy" O'Daniel. It was as founder of the Texas Playboys, however, for which he is best remembered. As popular music changed, Wills continued to grow. He is one of only a handful of musicians to be enshrined in both the Country Music and Rock and Roll Halls of Fame.

Charles R. Townsend is professor emeritus at West Texas A&M University in Canyon and the author of *San Antonio Rose: The Life and Music of Bob Wills* (1976).

One night in the mid-1930s, Bob Wills and His Texas Playboys had played a dance that was attended by a very large crowd. As was their custom, they went to a local restaurant for dinner or an early breakfast before driving back to their home base in Tulsa. Also playing for dancing in the same town that evening was one of the nationally known big bands. These swing musicians, who had played to a very small crowd, were seated in the same restaurant close enough to the Wills band for its members to hear them make fun of Wills's music and the appearance of the Texas Playboys. The big band musicians snickered about the "hillbilly" music and what they termed the "Texas Plowboys." As they left the restaurant, they continued to make snide remarks as they walked past Wills's table—that is, all except one man. After apologizing for the conduct of his fellow band members, he said: "I don't know what you guys have, but you have *something special* to draw the crowds you do. I only wish I knew what it is and that we had some of it."*

As Wills's biographer and one who has studied his music most of my life, I am still like that musician. I am not certain what that "something special" is, that magic which has made Wills's music endure from early in the twentieth century to the new millennium. Four years ago, a group of young musicians—some of the most famous in the world, under the leadership of Asleep At The Wheel—produced an album of Wills's music. That tribute album won two Grammy Awards. In August 1999, Asleep At The Wheel, again with some of the best and most popular artists, released another album in tribute to Wills. This album was nominated for six Grammy Awards and won two at the first Grammy Awards Show in 2000. And during the decade of the 1990s, three network television shows were produced on his life and music. On March 15, 1999, at the Waldorf-Astoria Hotel in New York City, Bob Wills, along with Paul McCartney, Billy Joel, and Bruce Springstein, was inducted into the Rock and Roll Hall of Fame. This essay is an attempt to answer the question suggested by the title of this article.

James Robert Wills was not born a fiddler but was a born fiddler. At his birth on March 6, 1905, the first sound he may have heard was a member of his family playing a tune in celebration. As in so many instances, first impressions are the most enduring. On both sides of his family, young Jim Rob was bombarded with fiddle music. His father, John Wills, and his grandfather, Tom Wills, were excellent old-time fiddlers. On his mother Emmaline's side, the Foleys, Jim Rob's uncles and aunts, were champion fiddlers. In such a family environment, it was by nature and tradition that by the time he was five or six he was fiddling around with the violin. At age eight he played his first dance as a fiddler. The Wills and Foley families played almost exclusively for country dances in East Texas, where Jim Rob was born, and later for ranch dances in West Texas, where he lived from age eight to age twenty-five. Wills played the fiddle for dances from 1915 until his career ended in 1973.

Both of these factors—the fiddle and the dance—played important roles in the magic and endurance of Wills and his music. For at least

*This and subsequent quotations are from Charles R. Townsend, *San Antonio Rose: The Life and Music of Bob Wills* (Urbana: University of Illinois Press, 1976), or from personal interviews conducted by the author.

two centuries, the fiddle had been the most popular instrument in American music—especially as the frontier moved from east to west. The fiddle was the perfect instrument for the trip west. Unlike bulky pianos, organs, and other large instruments, the violins could be tucked away in a box of clothing in covered wagons or even transported in a flour sack tied to a saddle. The fiddler was often one of the most popular persons on the frontier. Americans have a long history of their love affair with the fiddle in folk and popular music and the violin in symphonic music.

With the fiddle, Wills tied his musical wagon to a star. Why was he so successful? Why not another of the hundreds of fiddlers in every area of the United States? Because Wills was no ordinary fiddler, in part because of his natural talent and in part from environment and musical and cultural taste. Initially he was a breakdown fiddler, playing the frontier folk music that he learned from his family. "Breakdowns" included music played for round dancing, waltzes, and folk dances (square dances and the schottische). Jim Bob (as he was known in West Texas) played and recorded breakdown fiddle music all of his life. He never had an equal in playing folk fiddle music. He eventually did more than anyone else to make folk fiddle music, as well as fiddle music in general, popular. It is one of his greatest contributions to American culture. He told me when I was interviewing him for his biography that he wished he had recorded more traditional fiddle music: "I didn't record one-tenth of my own daddy's tunes."

Although it is a fact that Wills was the most influential breakdown fiddler ever, he changed the role of fiddling from just folk music and folk dancing to popular twentieth-century dance music. Had he not accomplished this feat, his ability as a breakdown fiddler would never have been known, and he almost certainly would never have entered a studio to record any kind of music. Just how and why did Wills's transformation of fiddle music occur? Trite as it sounds, Wills decided before he reached age ten that he would play his fiddle differently.

There were two basic influences on the musical development of young Jim Rob Wills. Besides the influence on him of the fiddle music of his family was the music and culture of African Americans—"colored people" or "Negroes," as they were called in Wills's childhood. The section of East Texas where he lived until he was eight has been called the Black Belt, not only because of the fertile black soil, but also because blacks were so numerous there. The farm near Kosse where Wills was born was surrounded by African-American farmers and their families.

Young Wills became a part of two cultures, one white, the other black. He told me that other than his older sister Ruby and younger brother Johnnie Lee, all his childhood playmates were black. Though prejudice and segregation prevailed in that area, the two races were much closer in their daily lives than they are in many places in America today.

Wills and his family knew the parents of the children with whom he and his brother and sister played. They shared in the good times and the bad: the poverty, the isolation, the deprivations, and the lack of medical and dental care. Regardless of color, the people on those poor farms had little opportunity or few aspirations for bettering their lot. Like so many people in the "pre-Depression" era, they took comfort in the fact that almost everyone was equally deprived, equally poor. People such as the Willses and their neighbors hardly knew when the real Depression began. For them, depression was a way of life.

Denied many of the necessities, luxuries, and opportunities that other Americans took for granted, these people, black and white, had one consolation. They found escape in their music. As a historian of American music, I feel qualified to conclude that the greatest contributions in American music have been made by the poor, the often forgotten, the neglected, the used, and the uneducated. Certainly there are exceptions, but the basis of American music is blues and jazz, and blues and jazz originated with people much like the folks whom Wills knew as a child. Some of them were only a generation or two removed from slavery. What would the music of the better educated, more affluent Americans be like had they not built on the foundation of the music that these poor, ignorant, deprived people created?

Wills was multicultural before nomenclators found a term for it. He shared with his African-American friends hard work with little reward, the feeling of being considered second-class citizens, being defenseless when used, and put down and persecuted by those with better education and with larger bank accounts. The Wills family and their African-American neighbors also shared their music. Wills's older sister told me that "Bob was more taken with their music than anyone else." He really did not see it as "our" white fiddle music versus "their" black music. He thought it was all his: both were fun, both were entertaining, both were appealing, both were part of his musical makeup. He combined white fiddle music with black blues and jazz. Although it would be called "Western Swing," "Texas Swing," and "Country Swing," it, to this day, is really just Bob Wills.

There is more to the Bob Wills sound than the marriage of black and white folk music. His early life with his black neighbors had a marked influence on him. He tried to get their blues sound, particularly that of the women, in his fiddle music. He told me, "I slurred my fiddle to play the blues." As a singer, Wills sang novelty and pop songs, but he was at his best as a singer of the blues, which was as natural for him as breathing; he learned the blues with the very people who created it. At least one of the most respected historians on the subject believes that the blues originated in East Texas. Some years after Wills had left East Texas for the western part of the state, he rode horseback fifty miles to see and hear the legendary Bessie Smith.

He learned more than just the blues; he also learned the rhythm, timing, and beat. Ruby Wills Sullivan told me that after the whites and blacks had picked cotton or worked in the fields all day, they would get together on the front porches of their homes or around a wagon loaded with cotton and have jam sessions. When I asked Bob if the blacks played fiddles, he replied, "No, they always had trumpets and guitars. I loved those trumpets and later used them in my band." Ruby said, "When the music got to going good, the little Negro kids got between the guitars on one end and trumpets on the other and jig danced. Papa made me and Bob dance with them." His rhythm section was always one of the strongest parts of his band, and Wills insisted it reflect the lessons that he had learned from the blacks. His ability to create superb rhythm and beat amazed formally trained musicians who joined his band. Ray De Geer, who played with Wills, Harry James, Charlie Barnett, and several symphony orchestras, told me: "Bob couldn't count four beats to a bar. But he could lay down the most perfect dance beat I've ever seen in any musical group." Even Fats Domino told Wills's musicians that he patterned his rhythm section after Wills's band.

Another reason that Wills's music has endured is that he was free and uninhibited in the way he performed. Again, much of this style he got directly from the blacks. For example, he continually talked to his musicians while they played. Two men once listened to a Wills recording; one had long admired Wills's style while the other was listening to him for the first time. When asked how he liked it, the newcomer said: "The music is good, but some damn fool keeps hollering and talking." One afternoon, Bob and I were alone in his sickroom where I conducted many interviews, and he told me why and where he picked up the unique technique of taunting and teasing his musicians. He motioned me to bring my recorder closer to him and his bed. "Please give credit to the Negroes who influenced my music. That's where I got my talkin' I do with my band. I saw them do this when I was a kid." Then he smiled and said, "I know I talk like them. My speech was affected by them, too." Other bandleaders have tried to imitate Wills by hollering at their band members, calling their names or even giving out with Wills's signature "Ahhaaa." In an interview with bandleader Hank Penny, Wills said, "Others try to imitate my hollering and bantering with the band, but it just doesn't fit. They do it to be like me. But I do it only when the music is especially good, in the groove, swinging. It's natural with me, not forced." Some people have thought his antics were for show, but his musicians refute the idea. Once a man "danced by the bandstand and said, 'Holler, Bob.' Bob frowned, turned to the band, and said 'I ain't gonna holler for no son-of-a-bitch.' " Smokey Dacus, his longtime drummer, recalled, "Some of these hollers you would swear never came out of a human. It just came out and moaned and molded into the music." It "was sort of eerie." Wills was expressing his deepest feelings, much like the African-American call and response. Although they were unaware of it, his black neighbors were indoctrinating their white friends' boy in the ways of soul music.

It is imperative to point out that Wills learned blues and jazz not *from* African Americans but *with* them. Benny Goodman, Harry James, and others absorbed their music from afar, from recordings or by watching black bands in Chicago or New York. A black disc jockey said, "You can't have soul unless you have felt the last-hired-first-fired-back-of-the-bus feeling." Wills, like his African-American neighbors, knew poverty, snobbery, and verbal and mental persecution. I mentioned how the swing band musicians made fun of Wills. Even worse, the musicians' union in Tulsa refused to admit him and his band to membership because the union concluded, "You have to be a musician to join. Your band doesn't play what we think of as music."

Between 1913 and 1928, Wills lived in Hall County, southeast of the country around Amarillo, on several cotton farms, finally settling between Little Red River and Big Red River, near Turkey. Poverty plagued the family in West Texas just as it had in East Texas. Farming provided only a bare existence, if that. Only the musical talents of the Willses kept them "out of the poor house," as they said at the time. Jim Bob had by 1920 the focus of his musical career—the fiddle music of his family and the blacks' blues and jazz.

In 1929, about a month before the Big Crash, Wills decided to move to Fort Worth. Never believing that he could make a living in music, he practiced his trade as a barber and played "house dances" to supplement his meager income. He teamed with Herman Arnspiger to form the Wills Fiddle Band. The two-man "band," fiddle and guitar, recorded two selections for the Victor Talking Machine Company: "Wills' Breakdown" (from his family's fiddle repertoire) and "Gulf Coast Blues" (a black-influenced Bessie Smith song). By 1931 his band had begun playing over the Clear-Channel radio station WBAP under the name Light Crust Doughboys. The personnel had doubled with three musicians and a singer: Bob Wills, fiddle; Herman Arnspiger and Durwood Brown, guitars; and Milton Brown, vocalist.

Before Wills arrived in Fort Worth, the state did not have a distinctly "Texas music." After a few months, W. Lee O'Daniel, the president of Burrus Mill and Elevator Company and sponsor of the Light Crust Doughboy radio show, put the Doughboys on the syndicated Texas Quality Network. People in nearly all of Texas and most of Oklahoma heard the new, swinging music that Wills brought to Fort Worth. To this day, when people think of Texas music, they think of fiddle bands playing swinging, happy, upbeat music. The musical group Alabama understood it best and on their 1984 album *Roll On* sang, "If you're going to play in Texas you gotta have a fiddle in the band."

Swinging, happy, upbeat music—this may be the most important reason why Wills's musical magic has endured. But why did it catch on so quickly and have such instant appeal? Wills's music was successful, in part, because it was Depression-born and fit the needs of the people during those hard times. In the fall of 1933, Wills moved from Texas to Oklahoma where he first called his band Bob Wills and His Texas Playboys. Although the Depression generation (1930–1942) was not one of whiners, the people nevertheless did not want to be reminded of their poverty or the rise of dictators and possible war. In short, they wanted music that entertained them and at the same time helped them escape the problems of the real world. Wills's famous steel guitarist, Leon McAuliffe, told me, "We tried to help people escape reality, not to find it." He added: "We never played music that had sad lyrics, except when Bob was between wives, he wrote some sad songs."

Even when Wills's songs had sad lyrics, they were usually played with a lilting, upbeat rhythm. Tommy Duncan, Wills's longtime vocalist, might be singing about "bubbles in my beer" and a wasted life, yet the piano player would be banging out a happy, danceable tune. A sad song under Wills's direction became a satire of the drinker's problem; it was almost impossible for him to be serious about a piece of music. Indeed, the same generation of musicians—Count Basie, Glenn Miller, Jimmy Dorsey, Duke Ellington, Harry James, and many other swing bands—shared his viewpoint. So did the movies, with such themes and formulas as "good over evil," "the goodness of human nature," "crime doesn't pay," and "live happily ever after." Did it work? Yes! It helped America through one of its most difficult periods and produced what Tom Brokaw calls "The Greatest Generation."

In addition to the lack of realism in the lyrics, the style in which the Wills band performed added to the happy spirit of the music, and it was first, last, and always meant for dancing. The Texas Playboys was basically a jazz band. Until the early 1940s, jazz was nearly always dance music, whether it was a black band in New Orleans, the big swing sound of Tommy Dorsey, or the fiddle band with guitars, reeds, and brass of Bob Wills. The fiddle band was always closer to the New Orleans or Dixieland style than that of the big bands. Although Wills's music did not have the same sound as Dixieland, the basic elements were there —the rhythm, the beat, the heat and swing of the blues, the syncopation, and the jazz solos when the players would improvise. The sound differed from Dixieland because of the use of fiddles, guitars, and mandolins.

The Depression generation was the "dancingest" one in American history, and when people spent what little money they had to go to a dance, they did not want to be reminded of hard times. On a network television tribute to Wills on September 29, 1999, country music star Reba McEntire summed up why his music had such appeal: "If you're down, it picks you up. You can't be sad. It makes you happy. When I hear it, I've got to look for some flat ground to dance on." Wills merely practiced what President Franklin D. Roosevelt had advocated early in the Depression—that the right kind of music could help us sing and whistle our way out of the troubled times, or at least to cope better with the problems they brought. In this sense, Bob Wills and His Texas Playboys were more than entertainers; they were therapists. They played a vital role in American life during the Great Depression, and later during World War II.

Another explanation for the endurance of Wills's music was his uninhibited and experimental approach. Never one for rules or "correctness," there were aspects of his style that he would not compromise.

First, the music had to be danceable. It had to include the jazz idioms that made it swing, which made it upbeat and lyrically happy. Second, since hard country music was stylistically and lyrically sad, Wills never liked it or played it. Otherwise, he experimented with most any kind of music: pop, Broadway, folk, race music (the term used to describe African-American music during the era 1920–1948), boogie woogie, big band swing, and western. The lyrics of one of his songs said it best: "You can change the name of an old song, rearrange it, and make it swing." As Ray De Geer put it, "Bob was the first man I ever saw who could make a breakdown swing." He even recorded a dance arrangement of the "William Tell Overture."

Wills experimented with so many musical forms because he wanted to appeal to the broadest possible audience. In short, times were hard. To survive not only musically but also financially, he continually changed the makeup of his band. By 1934 he had two front lines (the section of the band that begins the selection, generally with the melody), one of fiddles, the other of trumpet, saxophone, and trombone. He even added drums, the first ever in a country and western band. With this combination, he could play his trademark swinging fiddle music as well as the black music (with the horns) that he had always loved.

By 1938 the big band swing of Benny Goodman, Paul Whiteman, Harry James, and Count Basie had become the most popular music in the United States. Remember the swing musicians who made fun of Wills and his music? He decided to beat them at their own game. Between 1938 and his April recording session at Dallas in 1940, Wills put together one of the best swing "orchestras" in the nation. It numbered eighteen members, with a fiddle section, guitar section, and reed and brass sections; the latter had appeared in some of America's premiere dance bands. They played either the freer Dixieland jazz or ensemble work (reading from sophisticated arrangements). Wills loved it! "He could drop his fiddle bow," one musician said, "and that band would blow him off the bandstand."

In 1940, Wills—the poor little white boy from the cotton fields of East Texas—took his place as one of the best known and admired band leaders in America. What catapulted Bob Wills and His Texas Playboys from the provincialism of Texas and Oklahoma onto the national scene was a fiddle selection originally written and recorded by Wills as an instrumental. Arthur Satherly at Columbia Records named it "San Antonio Rose." Irving Berlin heard the recording, liked it, and wanted to produce it at his publishing company in Manhattan. Berlin's contract with Wills specified that Bob add lyrics. Wills added the lyrics and asked Eldon Shamblin and Everett Stover to write arrangements of the old fiddle melody—not for the fiddle section, but for the eighteen-piece swing band. "New San Antonio Rose" was strictly a big band recording in the style of Goodman, Miller, or Dorsey. Not a fiddle or stringed instrument was used except for Shamblin's rhythm guitar. The recording swept the nation almost overnight. Big swing bands recorded it in New York and Los Angeles; Tex Ritter, the Sons of the Pioneers, and Gene Autry recorded it in Hollywood; and western bands played it in movies, on the radio, and on bandstands across the nation.

Wills always believed that the most important moment in his career was when Bing Crosby recorded "New San Antonio Rose." The Crosby version, made one year after the Wills recording reached the music stores, sold over 1.5 million copies and won Crosby his second gold record. "New San Antonio Rose" had brought together the best of two musical worlds—the world of big band swing and that of what would be called country and western.

The success of "New San Antonio Rose" brought even more first-rate horn musicians into the band. By 1942, Wills's fiddle and McAuliffe's steel guitar were the only stringed instruments (other than rhythm guitar) in most Wills recordings. His big bands of the 1940–1942 years were his all-time favorites. "This is the band I would have kept forever if I could have," he told me. The band broke up in 1942 when Bob joined the U.S. Army. As soon as he was discharged, he began to build another one, this time with former musicians of the Glenn Miller and Tommy Dorsey orchestras. "The band played some of the most beautiful music I've ever heard," Laura Lee Owens told me. MCA booked the Wills band in the best ballrooms on the West Coast, from San Diego in the south to Portland in the north.

The age of the big bands began to come to an end by 1946, and fortunately for Wills he was forced to return to a band made up almost entirely of strings. Club managers and recording companies wanted more Bob Wills and his fiddle and less Bob Wills and his brass and reeds. He fought the change, resented it, and did not realize that the change would save his music from becoming dated. The use of stringed instruments, of course, was not new to Wills; he began his career with them. But after he gave up his big horn band in 1944, he used more strings than ever before. Instead of using fiddles and horns as front line instruments, he used fiddles (sometimes as many as five) and guitars along with steel guitars and electric mandolins. The music and emphasis never changed at all. Wills merely played the same music that he had always played and used stringed instruments to do what the reeds and brass did in his big horn band. It was swing and even more western.

By 1950 a new age in American music was dawning, and the demands of club owners and recording companies took Wills, kicking and screaming, into that age. He was not only part of the new age, but he also influenced the two musical forms that have dominated American music from the early 1950s down to the beginning of the new millennium—country and western and rock and roll.

As noted earlier, Wills was influenced by the fiddle music of his family and the African-American blues and jazz of his friends. Even before he developed his great string bands of the 1940s and 1950s, the music that he inherited from his family had made a deep impact on "hillbilly music," as country music was derisively called until 1948, when the trade magazines first called it country-western. It would be difficult to overemphasize Wills's influence, which began in the 1930s and has become even more pronounced since that time. After the success of "San Antonio Rose," many country musicians in Nashville, on the West Coast, and in the Dallas-Fort Worth area emulated and idolized him. Because country musicians have incorporated the sounds of Wills and his band members into the mainstream country genre, radio stations and trade publications have always labeled Wills country—a claim he always denied. Indeed, he never had a *country* band; he had a *dance* band. Fortunately for Wills, country claimed him, and the Country Music Association enshrined him in their Country Music Hall of Fame. Ironically, while Wills claimed that he was not country, country music has played the leading role in keeping his sound alive. In September 1999 a young country star who probably was not even born when Wills died on May 13, 1975, said that she loved his music because "it sounds like the music of today. . . . It is timeless."

The other musical genre that has helped to make Wills sound modern or timeless is rock and roll. His fiddles, guitars, and horns appealed to rockers, but it was his use of African-American music that endeared him to rock musicians. Before the term "Country and Western" was used, record companies did not know how to categorize him. Some called him "Hillbilly," but they knew that his recordings did not fit that genre. So in the 1930s, Vocallion Records (Columbia) listed Wills's recordings in the same catalogs with race music. That choice was appropriate because he probably recorded more race music than all the other white bands in the country at the time. Bessie Smith's "Empty Bed Blues,"

"Fan It," and "Oozlin' Daddy Blues," all recorded by Wills, were not polite enough for Glenn Miller or Benny Goodman. Wills could get away with it, however, because people and record companies thought his music was traditional, or, as Columbia Records called it, "Old Time Music." When Wills recorded "Trouble In Mind," "Thirty-First Street Blues," or "She's Killing Me," white audiences who had never heard this kind of music asked him where he had found this "new music."

In the mid-1940s, nearly ten years before Bill Haley's rise to fame, Wills was playing boogie woogie with his string band, anticipating the beat and "guitar licks" of the rockabillies. Musical prejudice was every-where. A historian of country music told me that even if Wills did in-fluence rock, "it's nothing to be proud of." Tommy Allsup said that when he left a western swing band to join Buddy Holly and The Crick-ets, all he did "different was to tune my guitar a little differently."

By 1958 rock and roll had all but wiped out the big bands, pop, country, and Wills's western swing. A reporter interviewed Wills, think-ing that he would make a stinging attack on rock, but Wills surprised the interviewer: "Rock and Roll? Why, man, that's the same kind of music we've been playin' since 1928. . . . it's just basic rhythm and has gone by a lot of different names in my time. It's the same, whether you follow just a drumbeat like in Africa or surround it with a lot of instru-ments. The rhythm's what's important." Now, inducted into the Rock and Roll Hall of Fame under the category "Early Influence," Wills's plaque is near those whom he influenced and those who loved him—Bill Haley, Buddy Holly, Elvis Presley, Paul McCartney, Eric Clapton, and others. Wills had managed to bridge the gap between the race mu-sic of the 1930s and 1940s and the rock and roll of the 1950s and be-yond. He is one of the few persons admitted to both the Country Music Hall of Fame and the Rock and Roll Hall of Fame.

The explanation for Wills's longevity in American music lies in his character, his ability as a bandleader, and putting his soul into music. His character and his ability are intertwined. His excessive drinking, which led to such troubles as his failing to show up for performances, is well known. Those were times of personal and financial problems for both Wills and the band. The brighter side of his character reveals deep concern for the lives of his musicians and their families. When his pi-ano player's wife died, Wills loaned Al Stricklin the money for funeral expenses. When Stricklin tried to pay him back, he said, "You don't owe me anything. Can't a man help his friends?" After more than thirty years, Al cried when he told me this story. Bob's widow, Betty, whom he had married on August 10, 1942, told me how Joe Holly asked for money for medical expenses when his wife needed cancer treatment. Holly had left Bob's band several years earlier; nevertheless, Bob told Betty to go to the bank and borrow several thousand dollars. Holly told me of this incident but never knew that Wills had had to borrow money to help him.

Jimmy Wyble, one of America's greatest guitarists, was quite young when he joined the band in the mid-1940s. Bob not only invited him to spend a couple of days with him and Betty but also gave him $400 to start a savings account. Wyble told my wife and me this story and, in a voice choked with emotion, said, "I love that man so much I can't talk about him. I've never loved any man like I love him." Frankie McWhorter, a Texas Playboy fiddler, recalled that "he was like a father to me. . . . He was my teacher, my financial advisor, and my therapist. If I had my head on wrong, he talked to me and straightened me out. There are times when I wish I had his advice. Bob had his problems, but he made better men out of a lot of us."

Somehow, musicians played better for Wills than for any other leader. Bob White, a fiddler in the band in the early 1950s, told me, "I could never play as well for anyone else as I could for Bob. I can't tell you why." His first female vocalist, Laura Lee Owens, remarked, "I could never sing for anyone like I did for Bob. He lifted me up and inspired me." Eldon Shamblin told me that "Bob Wills was the key to our music. Bob's band, without Bob, was just another band. We could play our hearts out and get by without Bob. But when Bob came on the bandstand, it was a great band." He added that "everything was better; we played better; everybody began to dance. Bob was the key." As for me, when I wrote the notes for Wills's last album, he was in a coma; nevertheless, from that deathbed he inspired me. When I accepted a Grammy Award for those notes, I said, "Bob's musicians used to tell me he made them play over their heads, to play more music than they were otherwise capable of. I thank Bob Wills. He made me write over my head."

There was more to the presence of Wills on the bandstand than the inspiration he gave his musicians. He drew a sound out of a fiddle that no other fiddler had ever done. This, in my opinion, was more important in the magic and appeal of his band than any other single factor. That sound was easy to hear and even easier to feel, but it is difficult to explain. Wills put his entire being into his playing. McAuliffe understood this better than anyone. He had a band of his own for over twenty years and employed fiddlers who, musically speaking, were better trained than Wills. McAuliffe told me that for Wills, "the only word that will fit is *soul* or *feeling*. His fiddle had soul, it had feeling. It communicated with people. He played from sincerity. It had a mournful soul, yet it was really smooth. They all tried to imitate it. But there never was another fiddler like him. They got close to him, because he left so much on record for them to hear." But, McAuliffe added, "They could never really play like him, because they didn't have his soul."

Suggested Readings

Boyd, Jean Ann. *The Jazz of the Southwest: An Oral History of Western Swing.* Austin, 1998.

Sheldon, Ruth. *Hubbin' It: The Life of Bob Wills.* Tulsa, 1938.

Stricklin, Al. *My Years with Bob Wills.* 2d ed. Burnet, TX, 1980.

Townsend, Charles R. *San Antonio Rose: The Life and Music of Bob Wills.* Urbana, IL, 1976.

Suggested CDs

The Essential Bob Wills 1935–1947 (Sony/Columbia); ASIN: B00000288D

Best of Bob Wills (MCA); ASIN: B000002O3P

King of Lonestar Swing (President); ASIN: B000024OMD

13

Emma Tenayuca
Vision and Courage

Julia Kirk Blackwelder

In the first half of the twentieth century, San Antonio, a city with a rich Tejano legacy, hosted numerous industries that employed Mexican Americans at literally pennies per day. The majority of these workers lived on the West Side, a district of dilapidated housing, poor sanitation, and overwhelming poverty and disease. The Great Depression pushed wages to their lowest point and exacerbated the wretched living conditions. For women who worked, conditions on the job were equally oppressive. They toiled as cigar rollers, pecan shellers, and at other menial tasks under wages far below the minimum set by the National Recovery Act. Into this scene stepped Emma Tenayuca. Throughout the 1930s she remained a persistent nemesis to business owners, managers, and city leaders who resisted her efforts at every turn. Even though Tenayuca's politically minded family had endowed her with an ardent sense of social justice, she was neither employed alongside the women she championed nor supported by the institutions that should have been their guardians. Indeed, the Church, the unions, and the Hispanic advocacy group LULAC (League of United Latin American Citizens) often sought to distance themselves from her radical efforts to organize labor, seek relief for unemployment, and obtain citizenship for workers threatened with deportation. Tenayuca enjoyed few immediate gains, but she laid important groundwork for the social and political changes that became her legacy.

Julia Blackwelder is professor of history at Texas A&M University and the author of *Women of the Depression: Caste and Culture in San Antonio, 1929–1939* (1984) and *Now Hiring: The Feminization of Work in the United States, 1900–1995* (1997).

Today we remember Emma Tenayuca as "la Pasionaria," the charismatic young woman who campaigned fervently for improvements in the lives and working conditions of San Antonio's Mexican-American laborers of the 1930s. At the height of her labor activism, law enforcement officers harassed Tenayuca, and the press in the Alamo City vilified her, charging her with "impersonating a worker" and leading "Emma's Reds" into lawlessness and violence. Yet, when she died at the end of the century, leaders from the Anglo and the Mexican-American communities lionized her. Maligned in youth and respected in old age, Tenayuca's rehabilitation bears witness to the historical developments of the post-Depression years. As prosperity drew near and as Mexican Americans gained political influence and economic power in San Antonio after World War II, Tenayuca's vision and courage gradually overshadowed her radicalism in the memories of the residents of San Antonio. Changes in their attitudes about Tenayuca tell us as much about the major social and political changes of the late twentieth century as they do about a dark, sad chapter in the city's past and the gifted woman who sought to lift the veil of despair that had covered the Hispanic community in the 1930s.

Emma Tenayuca, one of eleven children, was born on December 21, 1916, in a South Side neighborhood of modest working-class homes. South San Antonio differed from most of the city in that blue-collar Anglos and Tejanos lived in close proximity to each other. Tenayuca's loyalty to the needs of San Antonio's Mexican-American residents defined who she was, but from childhood she learned to move easily among Anglos. Such a gift would prove essential as she attempted to negotiate on behalf of poor Hispanics in the 1930s.

Tenayuca's mother descended from Spanish settlers in Texas and her father from Indian parents. While Tenayuca reveled in her Indian heritage, she believed that her Indian surname clearly marked her as a victim of racism. As she recalled much later, "I think it was the combination of being a Texan, being a Mexican, and being more Indian than Spanish that propelled me to take action."[1] Her parents and her grandparents took pride in their citizenship as well as in their ethnicity, and they voted conscientiously despite the economic hardship of the poll tax. In the evenings the extended Tenayuca family gathered around the kitchen table or on the front porch to discuss politics. These animated conversations ranged from the implications of President Franklin D. Roosevelt's recovery programs to the abuses and injustices against Tejanos committed by San Antonio officials. The political debates rose to a fevered pitch after Tenayuca's grandfather lost his savings in 1932 in a bank closing.

At the time of Emma Tenayuca's birth, San Antonio was already manifesting the social, political, and economic characteristics that would elicit her fervent commitment to change. San Antonio became Mexican first and only later "Anglo," an irony not lost on the city's dispossessed Mexican-American workers as the press condemned Hispanics as unAmerican newcomers. In addition to the families who had settled in the

Bexar County region while it passed from Spanish hands to Mexican, San Antonio attracted thousands of Mexicans fleeing poverty and political unrest in Mexico in the early twentieth century. San Antonio drew migrants partly because it had never really ceased being a city of Mexicans, but also because it hosted a number of largely seasonal jobs that complemented the migratory agricultural work that employed the neediest workers. While San Antonio offered industrial and service jobs to the residents of the West Side, the city's employers paid some of the lowest wages in the nation. West Side residents dwelt in the worst slums and suffered the highest infant death rates in the nation. Tuberculosis reached epidemic proportions among the Mexican-American residents and hunger stalked the community. San Antonio was a caldron of misery ready to overflow; the political tensions and human suffering of the Depression brought the roiling waters to full boil.

The majority of Tejanos and Mexican immigrants, a population in excess of 80,000, crowded into substandard housing in a four-square-mile section of land between the San Antonio River and the Missouri Pacific Railroad depot to its west. In the winter months, displaced migrant workers flocked into the city, further depressing the low wage scale. Mexican and Mexican-American workers in San Antonio had endured very low wages before the Depression. As the federal government attempted to cope with economic failures in the 1930s through the National Recovery Administration (NRA), it institutionalized a discriminatory scale that paid African-American and Mexican-American workers less than their Anglo counterparts and women less than men. Tejanas suffered the double jeopardy of race and gender, finding themselves at the very bottom of the pay scale, earning less than the poorly paid African-American domestic workers in the city. The concentration of Mexican Americans on the West Side reflected their poverty and the discrimination practiced by the city's Anglo citizens. Residents of the West Side, then, found themselves bound together by proximity, by similar circumstances, and by cultural heritage. In such a setting a charismatic leader might become an overnight sensation commanding the enthusiasm of thousands of followers. Such a person would be found in Emma Tenayuca.

The unique set of circumstances that drew Mexican and Mexican-American workers to San Antonio also encouraged the city's elites, Anglo and Hispanic, to turn their backs on the residents of the overwhelmingly poor West Side. The League of United Latin American Citizens (LULAC) struggled to enlarge the political and economic influence of

San Antonio's citizens of Mexican heritage. In the labor struggles of the 1930s, LULAC sought to protect itself from any flavor of political radicalism and any charges of unpatriotic activities. While the members of LULAC cooperated with the Mexican consul in San Antonio in defending local residents from unlawful deportations, the organization distanced itself from the economic protests of West Side residents. Most clergy in San Antonio's Catholic churches likewise distanced themselves from radical causes. The city's major newspapers, the San Antonio *Light* and the *Express,* generally backed the agendas of the Chamber of Commerce and of the ultraconservative mayor, C. K. Quinn, and his administration.

Business owners and managers from the West Side employed every measure to keep wages below the minimum standards of the NRA. Moderately minded businessmen and civic reformers focused on the danger to public health posed by substandard housing and sanitation on the West Side rather than on the plight of the area's residents. The San Antonio Trades Council, the local umbrella organization for affiliates of the American Federation of Labor (AFL), initially supported only the protests of those Mexican-American workers who had integrated themselves into the skilled crafts represented by the AFL. The majority of Mexican and Mexican-American craft workers in San Antonio were women whom the AFL perceived as unorganizable or as unfair competition with male craft workers. San Antonio in the 1920s and 1930s hosted the least organized working class of any major city in the United States, and the AFL fought through the Depression to maintain its limited influence on the city's blue-collar workers.

Through the labor troubles of the Depression the Trades Council openly condemned Tenayuca's efforts to organize the West Side. During the 1933 Finck Cigar Company strike, the *Weekly Dispatch*, the Trades Council organ, reported that "so far as organized labor is concerned, the strikers refused to accept any of the overtures to unionize."[2] In this instance and all those that followed, the *Dispatch* joined Anglo community leaders in lumping U.S.-born Mexican Americans, naturalized Mexican Americans, and Mexican citizens into the single category of "Mexicans"—people of suspicious allegiance and identity. The Trades Council plainly saw Mexican-American labor as undermining the welfare of San Antonio's Anglo craft workers and condemned the Hispanic community for embracing their heritage, blaming their culture rather than employers for the deplorable working conditions. After a mass meeting of Mexican-American workers in February 1934 the *Dispatch* reported that "the question of their nationality, and that of politics and religion, have been methods that have kept Mexicans from gaining for themselves a fair share of the profits that issue from their labors."[3]

In the face of unsympathetic employers, indifferent New Deal administrators, circumspect middle-class Mexican Americans, neglectful Anglo labor leaders, and hostile city officials, the residents of West San Antonio would have to find their own voice and raise up their own leadership. Emma Tenayuca proved equal to this task and this is the legacy that she bequeathed to San Antonio's Mexican-American workers, even though most of the protests she led ultimately failed to bring immediate material rewards to the poor.

Tenayuca's leadership gifts emerged forcefully in adolescence. She excelled at school, not only in traditional subjects but also in oratory. She could mesmerize fellow students with her words, but talent could not overcome all prejudice and she felt the clear stings of racial discrimination at school. Feelings of ostracism fueled her determination to reshape the world around her. The strong Catholic faith and solidarity of the Tenayuca family as well as the political radicalism of the kitchen table instilled a deep sense of duty in the young girl. At the knee of her grandfather, Francisco Zepeda, Emma learned to cherish a vision of a better future for the poor and powerless, a world proffered by socialism. Her radicalism was both homegrown and as basic to her as the family she cherished. As her leadership blossomed, Tenayuca moved beyond socialism to communism. Despite her "incendiary" speaking style, Tenayuca's radicalism was unequivocally nonviolent, and the acts of violence that surrounded her work were both not of her making and deeply troubling to her.

Tenayuca first came face-to-face with the opportunity to make a difference in 1933. While still a high-school student and months short of her seventeenth birthday, her sympathies with Tejana working women drew her into the struggle of local cigar workers against the low pay and strict controls of the Finck Cigar Company. Finck had opened in San Antonio, far from the nation's tobacco fields, because the city's Tejana workforce met the exacting criteria of a manufacturer seeking highly skilled labor at rock-bottom prices. Finck had laid off hundreds of workers in 1931 in response to the lagging sales of the Great Depression, but the firm still employed more than 300 women at the time of the 1933 strike, making Finck one of the city's larger private employers.

Tejana and Mexicana workers walked off the job in August 1933 to protest unhealthful working conditions and low pay. Police rushed the picket line and arrested a number of the demonstrators, almost all of them women. Tenayuca soon joined the drive and added her name to the list of strikers hauled off to jail by police. Her decision to place herself in a visible position in the Finck strike and other major protests subjected her to frequent police detention.

Tenayuca's arrest also set the stage for press and police condemnation of Tenayuca as an "outside agitator" by the press and police. While Tenayuca clearly was not an outsider in working-class San Antonio, she also plainly was not an industrial worker, and local officials focused on her status as a nonemployed citizen in their efforts to sabotage her leadership. She became Chief of Police Owen W. Kilday's nemesis. During the 1938 pecan shellers' strike, Kilday openly announced his intent to arrest Tenayuca at the slightest provocation. Tenayuca generally spent little or no time in jail, facing fines as her stiffest penalties, but her serial arrests kept her name before the public and helped to build her status as a troublemaker, on the one hand, and the savior of West Side workers, on the other.

While the demonstrators were determined to persist in the 1933 Finck strike, the cigar makers faced a dilemma that would be met again and again by Mexican-American workers in Bexar County during the 1930s. Finck had ceased to be a highly profitable firm, a reality that discouraged company improvements and encouraged the owners to cut pay rates. Workers taking to the picket lines in 1933 were unaware of Finck's negotiations with a larger firm that had offered to buy the company and replace the cigar makers with rolling machines. The cigar makers did know that Finck workers earned between $2 and $7 per week in violation of the NRA's specified minimum of $12.

Days into the strike the Finck Company hoisted the "Blue Eagle" banner that signified an employer's compliance with wages and standards set by the NRA. Clearly offering far below the NRA minimum, Finck claimed that the NRA had granted a special dispensation to the beleaguered company. The strike and Finck's brazen defiance made news headlines around the country and attracted interest at AFL national headquarters. Representatives of the International Cigar Makers Union (ICU) came to San Antonio at this time in an effort to draw the workers into their organization, but gender as well as ethnicity and West Side community bonds encouraged the striking workers to shun the national organization. Emma Tenayuca, talented, charismatic, and dedicated, entered the door to labor leadership that remained closed to the ICU for many months to come. She spoke with the skilled and unskilled workers of the West Side on a regular basis. Soon, most cigar makers knew Emma Tenayuca and trusted her to speak up for their interests.

The Finck Cigar Company strike of 1933 collapsed rapidly, partly through repeated police interference. The strike failed not only because the struggling company had little to gain in negotiating with workers, but also because the cigar workers lacked a coherent plan and the financial resources that a labor union could provide. The walkout had brought Emma Tenayuca to the fore as a spokesperson for her community, and her initial arrest led her to turn to labor organizing as a serious pursuit, thus setting the course for her leadership in the years that followed. After her high-school graduation in 1934, Tenayuca worked night and day to organize West Side industrial workers, persevering until violence at the end of the decade effectively ended her abilities to lead.

Through the 1930s, Tenayuca focused on a core of employment concerns: worker organization, relief for unemployed workers, and citizenship rights. As a child, Tenayuca had frequently accompanied her grandfather to San Antonio's Plaza del Zacate, a gathering place for discussions of Tejano politics. On one occasion, Emma and her grandfather joined a rally on behalf of a family of agricultural workers who had been run off at gunpoint from the farm where they worked. The rally generated a march on the Mexican consulate in San Antonio to demand that charges be brought against the landowner who had displaced the family. Information soon surfaced that they were Texas-born Americans, not immigrants whose plight might best be taken up by Mexican officials. The irony was not lost on young Emma Tenayuca, who learned early that state and federal officials rarely came to the defense of Tejano rights.

In San Antonio in the mid-1930s, Tenayuca confronted hostile local officials, especially in Mayor Quinn and Chief of Police Kilday, but also in lesser officeholders and bureaucrats. The mayor and the chief of police worked hand in hand to suppress peaceful as well as violent protest. For Tejanos, the pair posed a unique threat as the city moved to deport outspoken Mexican Americans, not pausing to separate American citizens from aliens. The threat of deportation, despite its illegality in the case of citizens, hung like a broadax over the West Side. Citizenship rights in this menacing climate intertwined with West Side residents' need for relief for the unemployed and living wages for jobholders. From 1934 onward, Tenayuca led efforts to address these issues through the West Side Unemployed Council and its successor, the Workers'

Alliance (WA). During 1935 the West Side Relief Council under Tena-yuca's leadership mounted mass demonstrations in protest against the termination of most of the city's relief support for West Side families and the adoption of employment rules governing Works Progress Administration (WPA) jobs that closed most of these opportunities to Tejanos.

When Finck cigar workers again struck the company in 1934, Tenayuca provided encouragement and support without undercutting the leadership generated among the cigar rollers. The strike centered on the issues that provoked the 1933 walkout. Specifically, the 1934 protest demanded an end to fetid workroom conditions and to the company policy of withholding payments for uniforms and towels used at work from employees' pay. The 1934 strike led to the formation of the AFL's Cigar Workers International Union Local No. 346 as the union had learned to work with, rather than against, the leaders chosen by the strikers. Through the 1934 strike, Tenayuca supported and encouraged the workers without interfering with the leadership generated among them, a movement led by Sra. W. H. Refugio Ernst, Hilaria Castro, and María Louisa Gonzales. The work stoppage culminated in a federal investigation of wages and working conditions at Finck. The Regional Labor Board found fault with the company, condemned its abusive labor practices, and ordered the reinstatement of the women who had been fired for forming the union.

The Tejana workers' acceptance of AFL leadership had brought a powerful ally to their side. The Trades Council, which had routinely condemned Tejano and Mexican workers as stubborn Mexican patriots, now came to their defense. After the strike ended, the *Weekly Dispatch* suddenly found sympathy with pecan shellers and castigated the "exploitation of Mexican labor in this city by a class of manufacturers that are inhumane enough to profit from the misery and poverty of a race that populates fair San Antonio, and instead of being nursed as a liquid asset through the purchasing power of a decent wage, they are held in involuntary bondage."[4]

The 1934 strike had shown workers how to mobilize and how to gain the sympathies of outsiders, but it had won no financial improvements for the cigar makers. In 1935, Finck workers struck once more. Organized labor in San Antonio openly supported the workers, attacking the repressive tactics of law enforcement officers, the Chamber of Commerce, and the Finck Company. The *Dispatch* castigated Finck for its "inhuman and slavish conditions" and for abandoning its promise to maintain minimum pay under the NRA.[5] The labor voice attacked the

Chamber for pressing the federal government to grant Finck an exemption from the NRA code.

The difficulty of closing down production at Finck proved a stumbling block for the workers. At the outset of the 1935 incident the police had harassed peaceful strikers, attempting to drive them into the factory and back to work. When the women resisted, several were injured. Tenayuca worked unsuccessfully to dissuade dozens of cigar rollers from crossing the Finck picket lines as scab workers. A melee of hair pulling and dress tearing between strikers and scabs led to numerous arrests of AFL members, including the movement's leader, Sra. Ernst. Still, one week later, Justice of the Peace John Onion dismissed all charges against the women. A negotiator from the Department of Labor worked to bring Finck to accept some of the workers' familiar demands: an end to the practice of charging for towel rentals and for health examinations, and a modification of the company policy of extending credit to employees at an interest rate of 8 percent per week.

When the AFL-affiliated Finck cigar workers struck again in 1935, the *Weekly Dispatch* unequivocally supported their demands and urged Anglo union members not to forsake their Mexican-American co-workers. Nevertheless, the newspaper continued to see Mexican heritage as a liability. The *Dispatch* reported that "the inferior [*sic*] complex of the Mexican people, so much emphasized and desired in those who live upon the exploitation of these workers, will evidently be broken through this strike."[6]

During the two major labor protest movements that followed the Finck strike—strikes of the garment workers and of pecan shellers—the orientation of the *Dispatch* continued to depend upon the AFL's stake in representing workers. The *Dispatch* took up the banner of outrage on behalf of the unskilled pecan shellers whom the craft-defined AFL would not organize. Still, the union's sympathies with garment workers' protests clearly followed racial lines as the Trades Council portrayed Mexican and Mexican-American workers as strikebreakers.

Tenayuca's demonstrated ability to bridge the gap between West Side Hispanic workers and the Anglo officials of national labor unions facilitated the formation of International Ladies' Garment Workers Union (ILGWU) locals in San Antonio in 1934 and 1935. Tenayuca was there to help when the Dorothy Frock Company garment workers struck in 1936, when the Shirlee Frock Company employees walked out in 1937, and when Texas Infant Dress Company sewers pushed for higher wages in 1938. Rebecca Taylor, a San Antonio resident employed by the national office of the ILGWU, always regarded Tenayuca as a rival even though Tenayuca did not attempt to draw workers into the WA at the expense of the AFL or its newly formed San Antonio affiliate chapter of the ILGWU.

While Tenayuca had worked hard to convey West Side fears and concerns to the representatives of organized labor, Anglos seemed never to entirely overcome their resentment of the community's fierce loyalty to "la Pasionaria." Without question, both the AFL and the Congress of Industrial Workers (CIO), but especially the CIO, sought to distance itself from charges of political radicalism. The CIO included both Communists and Socialists in the 1930s, and it sought to purge these radicals in an effort to establish its claims to represent the true interests of patriotic American workers. The CIO purges led to some Red baiting within the organization itself, and ethnic radical leaders such as Emma Tenayuca became logical targets. Despite her homegrown leadership claims and her efforts to nourish labor unions in San Antonio, Tenayuca eventually found herself labeled by the Trades Council as a dangerous outsider. Although Anglos and middle-class Mexican Americans shunned her, most working-class Tejanos remained her loyal followers through 1938 when Tenayuca reached the pinnacle of her influence in the pecan shellers strike. These were also the years of her most radical politics.

In looking back at the hostility that Mexican-American workers faced from the Anglo press, from the AFL, from civil authorities, and sometimes from the Catholic Church, the narrowness and implications of Tenayuca's political choices emerge forcefully. Thousands of Mexican Americans in San Antonio were unemployed or only partially employed. Thousands more worked literally for pennies per day. The more fortunate among the unemployed gained short-term federal relief jobs. None of these workers had organizational representation to put their plight before public officials, sympathetic citizens, or public or private employers. The clear path for Tenayuca was to organize workers into new labor unions or unemployed workers' associations.

The Workers' Alliance emerged in the 1930s to foster the interests of relief workers and the unemployed. The organization grew out of demands voiced at the 1935 Washington, DC, gathering of Socialist Party members. Like the CIO, the WA decried racial and gender segregation in the workplace. It differed from labor unions in seeking compensation for the unemployed and partially employed that would match the earnings of union workers with similar occupational skills. It differed from labor unions as well in advocating legislative solutions to workers' problems and in seeking a radical redirection of public revenues and of corporate earnings. Unlike socialism itself, the WA did not seek restrictions of the activities of private enterprise but advocated heavy taxation to fund benefits for the unemployed.

In 1936 the WA staged its largest and most dramatic demonstration, marching on the New Jersey legislature to demand a variety of tax measures to fund direct payments to the unemployed. After WA spokespersons had been permitted to present their demands to the State Assembly, the body adjourned with only sarcastic attention to the WA agenda. As the New Jersey legislators left the room, WA members quietly occupied their seats, taking over the hall and holding a rump legislative session. The WA continued its encampment in one or the other of the State Assembly's houses for nine days, vacating after adopting a series of mock tax measures and a resolution condemning the elected state officials as the tools of industry and commerce.

As was the case in San Antonio, the WA won no victories in terms of financial benefits for its members, but it was one of the few groups that provided a sense of purpose and self-worth to the unemployed. Through her ties to the Socialist Party, Tenayuca followed the development of the WA and soon joined the movement. Unlike the Bonus Marchers who had descended on the nation's capital early in the Depression, and unlike the agricultural cooperatives that withheld goods from market, the WA sought long-term protections for the unemployed from all sectors of the economy. For workers on San Antonio's West Side, who had consistently suffered seasonal unemployment and had long subsisted on the nation's lowest wages, occasional private charity or temporary public relief seemed weak medicine for their ills. The WA thus appealed strongly to Tenayuca and her followers. The Communist Party also held a strong attraction for Tenayuca, and she joined the party in 1937, following her husband, Homer Brooks, and she even ran for office within the party. Tenayuca did not conceal her communism, but her passion was the working poor of San Antonio. She refused to compromise their cause by hoisting the Red flag above the daily campaign to organize and assist the unemployed and underemployed. When the Soviet Union accepted the Nonaggression Pact with Nazi Germany in 1939, Tenayuca left the party.

In February 1937, Tenayuca led a group of some seventy-five angry West Side relief clients, carrying the WA banner before them, to the offices of Mayor Quinn. With Tenayuca as the spokeswoman, the group protested the inadequate services provided by the WPA surplus commodities center in the Hispanic community and demanded that Quinn act to correct the situation. The mayor reportedly ordered an immediate increase in staffing at the WPA office from which food was distributed to the unemployed. Three days later, Tenayuca was back in Quinn's office to protest the arrest of one of her group. She claimed in addition that police had arrested several unemployed persons and had turned them over to immigration authorities who beat them.

The WA victories against San Antonio civil officers were few and far between, but Tenayuca's popularity with the Mexican-American working class continued to grow. She had gained a position on the national WA Executive Council and had fostered ten San Antonio WA chapters over which she presided. On May Day 1937 thousands of West Side residents attended a mass rally that Tenayuca had called in San Pedro Park to protest the city's denial of a parade permit for the Workers' Alliance, the arrest of Tenayuca, and the ejection of 200 WA-led relief clients from a City Hall sit-in a few days earlier.

Pecan shellers held the dubious distinction of taking home the least pay of any major occupational group in San Antonio. Pecan work was seasonal, lasting for a few months after each year's harvest, and was carried out on contract at home or at piece rates in the 120-some shelling plants in the city. Commercial hand-shelling took place in cramped quarters where workers sat side-by-side on long benches pulled up to tables in small sheds. In the early 1930s workers earned 6 cents per pound for delivering unbroken pecan halves, less when the halves were broken in the shelling. Because of their extremely poor earnings and their frequent unemployment, the WA held particular appeal to pecan shellers who had come to know Tenayuca through her WA organizing and leadership.

By 1938, Tenayuca's membership in the Communist Party was an openly known fact that had antagonized the Catholic Church and LULAC. She had also entered a brief marriage to Homer Brooks, who had earlier stood as the Communist Party candidate for governor in Texas. Her radical associations had begun to isolate Tenayuca from her early supporters and those who had inspired her in her childhood. Some members of her own family had begun to question her judgment, but Tenayuca persisted and pecan shellers followed.

Earlier pecan strikes in which Tenayuca had not participated directly had collapsed, and the AFL had been partly to blame. Despite its craft orientation, the AFL had tried to organize shellers in the early 1930s. A rival unaffiliated local union, the Pecan Shelling Workers Union

(PSWU), had formed in 1934 and initiated a walkout following a pay cut. As in the case of the cigar workers, the local police pledged assistance in escorting strikebreakers into the sheds so that a total work stoppage could not be effected. The refusal of the AFL and its skeleton shellers' union to endorse the strike further exacerbated the difficulties of the PSWU, but roughly one-quarter of the 8,000 workers had left their posts within two weeks, and a police presence failed to keep the plants in operation. Despite the widespread character of the strike, the shellers won no victories in their efforts, and the impoverished workers returned to their jobs because they had no financial resources with which to continue their efforts. A similar walkout in 1935 failed to mobilize workers citywide and resulted in temporary disruption at only a few sheds.

Wages and labor conditions in pecan shelling failed to improve between 1935 and 1938, and shellers were ready to refuse work. In the meantime an important new player had appeared on the scene. The CIO had been formed earlier and had achieved a major victory in the 1937 General Motors Sitdown Strike, in which the affiliated United Automobile Workers had shut down production at General Motors and brought the CIO to prominence. The General Motors Strike began at the end of December 1936, and by late summer 1937 the CIO announced that its membership had topped 3 million. The CIO differed from the AFL in concentrating on industrially based appeals rather than the occupationally based or craft definition that the AFL employed. Where the AFL was exclusive, the CIO was inclusive, and these open policies included an avowed opposition to racial and gender discrimination that the AFL and its locals had practiced. CIO organizers came to San Antonio in the spring of 1937 and attempted to offset opposition from the Trades Council and the AFL by announcing their intent to appeal only to pecan shellers and to operatives in commercial laundries.

Because of the unskilled nature of both industries, neither group of workers had been consistently courted by the AFL. With the CIO in the national spotlight and CIO recruiters making progress in San Antonio, the AFL announced a massive drive to bring in shellers and laundry workers, but it failed to attract a West Side following. Mexican Americans had little incentive to join with local organizations that had labeled Mexican immigration as the source of San Antonio's low wages and high unemployment, going so far as to "estimate that the Mexican alien is greatly responsible for most of San Antonio's minor crimes."[7] By 1938 the CIO had succeeded in bringing numerous shellers into a

fledgling union that laid the groundwork for a major strike against pecan producers. On February 1, 1938, 5–6,000 thousand shellers walked
out, and the CIO dues-paying membership soon rose to 3,000. CIO
resources proved a considerable asset as the organization moved swiftly
to set up soup kitchens for the striking shellers. Pecan workers welcomed the CIO, but they continued to embrace the local leaders whom
they trusted.

At the time of the walkout, the strikers turned for guidance to the
woman who had so often spoken and demonstrated on behalf of them
and their families, Emma Tenayuca. *La Prensa*, San Antonio's Spanish-
language newspaper, identified WA chief Emma Tenayuca and Minnie
Randón and Leandro Avila, respectively secretary and president of the
International Pecan Shellers Union, as the major leaders of the workers.
Police Chief Kilday, keeping with the public philosophy of labeling
Tenayuca as an outside meddler, ordered her arrest because "Reds" would
not be permitted to participate in the strike. Tenayuca stood with the
pickets on February 1 and met with the usual police harassment. Although authorities detained them only briefly, police rounded up
Tenayuca, Randón, and Avila, all of whom had left the strike lines to
organize other work sites, and trucked them off to jail.

Within days of the strike's onset, estimates of participation had risen
to 8,000, and pickets reported that they were being gassed by police
despite the peaceful nature of the demonstrations. Local prosecutors
countercharged that the pickets had perjured themselves in testimony,
and the city enjoined the Health Department to close down strike-
relief kitchens wherever code violations could be cited. When officers
arrested two young nonstriking women in front of their home, their
mother ran from the house in protest and the police arrested her as
well. Another woman testified that she had also been arrested near a
picket line although she had not been demonstrating, and that the police cursed her and tore her clothing. Charges of Communist infiltra-
tion and domination of the strike abounded. The San Antonio Ministers'
Association called for justice and offered to negotiate between workers
and owners, but the clergy demanded that "all communistic, fascist or
any un-American elements not be parties of the settlement."[8]

Early in March shellers gained support from an unexpected quarter
when San Antonio Congressman Maury Maverick telegraphed from
Washington to endorse the action. Nevertheless, Anglo officials and
businessmen, including the Anglo press, continued their harassment of
the workers. Three pickets, whose pay ranged from pennies to $2.50

per week before the strike, were each fined $10 for carrying placards without a permit. Two teenaged girls who were picketing were arrested on charges of juvenile delinquency and held in the city jail pending their appearance in court. As the police, elected officials, and the Anglo press continued to Red bait strike leaders, some workers moved to turn away from radical leadership or from the participation of CIO representatives from outside Texas. The *San Antonio Light* reported that the president of the shellers' union had been attacked, and that the perpetrators had been Communists intent on bringing violence to the demonstrations. The repeated charges of Communist subversion within the labor movement and appeals from the CIO to keep her name out of the headlines convinced Tenayuca to step back from the front lines of the strike. CIO organizer Donald Henderson had also been painted Red by the press and public officials. The CIO made the decision to recall Henderson, who left the city on February 23, and replace him with another organizer. While she continued privately to encourage the workers, Tenayuca avoided the picket lines and public gatherings. With Henderson out of the city and Tenayuca working behind the scenes, the strikers began to turn around public opinion and to bring the pecan producers closer to the bargaining table.

Both the attacks on demonstrators and the prosecutions of strikers had generated national sympathy for the pecan shellers. Members of the Women's League for Peace and Freedom repeatedly urged Mayor Quinn to end the persecution, and the American Civil Liberties Union represented the shellers at court. By March 10, the first of the larger employers agreed to arbitration of the workers' demands, and the strikers could taste victory. On March 19 some 15,000 strike sympathizers attended a union dance and fundraising at Military Plaza in honor of a group of strikers who recently had been released from jail. By the middle of April industry-wide negotiations had begun. The fledgling CIO unions succeeded in winning their major demand, a restoration of pay rates to 7 and 6 cents per pound, respectively, for pecan halves and pieces.

The sheds reopened and the shelling of the season's crop continued, but the victory was shortlived. The nation's first industrial minimum wage of 25 cents per hour had been adopted and would soon take effect. In response to the legislation, pecan producers circumvented Congress's intent by closing down the shelling plants, selling the pecans to families and twenty individuals who took them home to shell and then sold them back to producers. One producer signed a union contract guaranteeing the minimum wage, but others did not comply.

Henderson had returned to San Antonio in the fall of 1938 and promised local workers that the CIO would strike to ban the home shelling of pecans, but the union failed to win producer agreements. In 1940, San Antonio passed an ordinance forbidding the home shelling and reselling of nuts, but those intent on evading the law simply sold their produce to residents beyond the city limits. In time, most producers replaced hand labor with machine shelling, thus eliminating thousands of poorly paying jobs.

The producers' capitulation to arbitration was not only a fleeting moment of success for workers, but it also freed police to concentrate on political ends other than breaking the strike. Tenayuca had continued to operate a small school for workers at Alliance headquarters. On April 15 the police arrested seven students, alleging that they were Communists, and seized boxes of literature from the WA office. On the following day the press reported that five of the young people arrested would be deported by federal immigration authorities. WA fortunes had taken a decided turn for the worse.

Tenayuca endeavored to keep the radical cause alive as the shellers' cases were settled, but the majority of her followers had been concerned about concrete issues and immediate needs. Sustaining active commitment to long-term political change proved exceedingly difficult. Tenayuca hoped that a massive rally set for the American Legion Municipal Auditorium early in 1939 would rekindle the enthusiasm engendered by her earlier demonstrations. This time, she advertised openly that communism would be freely discussed at the meeting. Outraged American Legion members demanded that Maverick, who had left Congress and become San Antonio's mayor, revoke the city permit issued for the gathering, which had been openly billed as a Communist rally. Maverick, who had come to City Hall on a liberal platform, stood up for the constitutional rights of assembly and free speech. On the night of the meeting a bare 150 brave souls showed up for the rally as an angry mob surrounded the Municipal Auditorium in protest. The antirally demonstrators broke windows and forced their way into the building as the terrified audience fled in the opposite direction. With little interference the mob vandalized the building, ripping up seats and tearing down draperies. Tenayuca's leadership came to an abrupt and painful end, although no one had been injured in the melee. The mayor was hanged in effigy and political analysts later claimed that Maverick's support of "Emma's Reds" brought his defeat in the next city election.

Following the Municipal Auditorium debacle, twenty-three-year-old Tenayuca, deeply discouraged and suffering the lingering effects of tuberculosis, retired from public life. Her marriage had ended, and she turned her attention to the Tenayuca family. She stayed in San Antonio through World War II, leaving for California in 1948. Subsequently she returned to San Antonio, enrolled in college, and earned a teaching degree. She completed a Master's degree at St. Mary's University and taught in the public schools until she retired in 1982.

If her legacy were judged in terms of material gains for her community, Emma Tenayuca would have had little to claim in the way of solid achievements, but such criteria miss the point of her youthful activism. Her fiery inspiration motivated unemployed and downtrodden workers to demand that public officials and employers recognize their rights to a dignified life. Tenayuca was the single figure in San Antonio in the 1930s who could mobilize the West Side, and her advocacy for the unemployed forced city officials to act. Her repeated arrests embodied a self-sacrificing spirit and solidified loyalty and determination among beleaguered workers. Tenayuca's guidance of workers ultimately assisted both the AFL and CIO in organizing Mexicanas and Tejanas. The radical alternatives that Tenayuca presented also elevated and enlarged the political and social influence of more conservative Hispanic institutions, including West Side churches and LULAC. Facing a perceived but imaginary threat of radical subversion in the city, Anglo public figures found comfort in reaching out to more moderate Hispanic forces. Both Tenayuca's radicalism and her magnetic appeal carried the story of West Side misery beyond San Antonio and outside of Texas. As the end of the 1930s approached, federal investigators condemned both the dreadful living conditions on the West Side and the exploitation of the community's labor force. New Deal dollars trickled in to improve the West Side and wartime spending began to lift San Antonio's Mexican Americans from the sad distinction of being the nation's poorest population.

During the years of her second tenure in San Antonio, 1962 until her death in 1999, Emma Tenayuca assiduously avoided the limelight as the city elected its first Mexican-American mayor and the Chicano movement delivered political strength and economic improvements to Tejanos. While she had retired from public life, Tenayuca's past leadership had broken a pattern of powerlessness on the West Side and showed the path for Tejanos and Tejanas to follow. As Mexican Americans repeatedly broke down barriers of discrimination, the lasting legacy of Emma Tenayuca came clearly into focus.

Notes

1. Quoted in Roberto Calderón and Emilio Zamora, "Manuele Solis Sager and Emma Tenayuca," in Teresa Córdova et al., eds., *Chicana Voices: Intersections of Class, Race, and Gender*, 2d ed. (Colorado Springs, CO, 1990), 40.
2. *Weekly Dispatch* (San Antonio), August 24, 1933.
3. Ibid., February 2, 1934.
4. Ibid., July 20, 1934
5. Ibid., March 22, 1934.
6. Ibid., March 29, 1935.
7. Ibid., October 9, 1936.
8. *San Antonio Light*, February 3, 1938.

Suggested Readings

Blackwelder, Julia Kirk. *Women of the Depression: Caste and Culture in San Antonio, 1929–1939*. College Station, TX, 1984.

Cordova, Teresa, et al., eds., *Chicana Voices: Intersections of Class, Race, and Gender*, 2d ed. Colorado Springs, CO, 1990.

Croxdale, Richard, and Melissa Hield. *Women in the Texas Workforce: Yesterday and Today*. Austin, 1979.

Higginbotham, Elizabeth, et al. *Women and Work: Exploring Race, Ethnicity, and Class*. Thousand Oaks, CA, 1997.

Vargas, Zaragosa. "Tejana Radical: Emma Tenayuca and the San Antonio Labor Movement during the Great Depression." *Pacific Historical Review* 66, no. 4 (1997): 553–80.

14

Hermine Tobolowsky
Mother of Texas's
Equal Legal Rights Amendment

Tai Kreidler

During the post-World War II years, Texas, like the rest of the country, changed rapidly. Changing social conditions required new laws in order to create an equal legal ground for minorities and women, and Hermine Tobolowsky fought for women's rights long before that issue moved to the front of the social agenda. Her struggle, which began in the 1940s, did not end until the state legislature in 1972 crowned her efforts with the Equal Legal Rights Amendment. Like Emma Tenayuca, Tobolowsky hailed from a family who cultivated her maverick ways. Encouraged to become an attorney, she completed law school where she learned to steel herself against harassment by both her classmates and her professors. The hostile environment proved to be a good training ground. When Tobolowsky began to press the state legislature for action that would expand women's rights, lawmakers greeted her with open ridicule and contempt. She persisted, however, and eventually developed a powerful network of supporters that proved capable of unseating her elected opponents. Moreover, under her leadership the strategy for gaining women's rights changed from promoting piecemeal legislation to advocating a comprehensive constitutional amendment. While her efforts have largely gone unheralded, Tobolowsky nevertheless played a pivotal role in achieving legal equality for Texas women.

Tai Kreidler is the archivist of the Southwest Collection at Texas Tech University and the executive director of the West Texas Historical Association.

In July 1995, Hermine Tobolowsky, mother of the Texas Equal Legal Rights Amendment and one of the major supporters of the national movement, died quietly. Her death ended a fifty-two-year legal career and a very public life that brought her to the forefront of the equal rights crusade for women. Tobolowsky came onto the scene at a time before the issue for women's equal rights had yet to emerge. Betty Friedan, author of the influential *Feminine Mystique*, the outspoken Gloria Steinem, and others were not yet major players on the national stage when Tobolowsky first joined the fight for equal rights. Working within the system and gathering the support of both men and women, she convinced Texans that treating 50 percent of the populace as second-class citizens limited the opportunities for women and hamstrung the economic and political potential of all Texans. Angered by the short-sighted "he-man" traditionalism wherein "Texas was fine for men and horses, but hell on dogs and women," Tobolowsky committed herself to legislation that once and for all gave the state's women equal legal status. In 1972 her efforts were crowned by the passage of the Equal Legal Rights Amendment that eliminated the second-class status that had long been imposed upon Texas women.

Hermine Tobolowsky was born in 1921 in San Antonio to Maurice and Nora Brown Dalkowitz. Her father came to America from Lithuania in 1901, joining family members who had already established themselves in the mercantile trades. Hermine's mother grew up in Belton and met Maurice while working in the same store. Hermine was the product of a family who cultivated diversity and encouraged women to be outspoken and self-reliant. Coming from a close-knit family with strong parental role models, Hermine grew up confident and reached out to make her mark in the world. Her father had the most significant influence upon her. From the beginning, Maurice Dalkowitz recognized his daughter's intelligence and encouraged her to be independent in thought, morally strong, and self-confident. He told her that if she did not take charge of her life, someone else would.

For her own protection, Maurice Dalkowitz thought that his daughter should be an attorney. From his example, Hermine understood the importance of remaining true to her principles, even if it meant taking an unpopular or unconventional stand. Once, her father had posted bond for a banker who had been accused of embezzlement. When citizens pressured him about his support for the accused, he stood his ground. Later, when the banker was found innocent, Dalkowitz's strength of character was redeemed.

With an attitude developed by that kind of background, Hermine took on the world. Mature beyond her years, she became confident in what she knew and had no reservations about voicing her ideas. She had cultivated this side of her personality even as a child. From an early age she loved interacting with the diverse household in which she grew up. Full of uncles, aunts, family friends, and neighbors, her childhood home gave her the opportunity to socialize with adults. As a result, she was more confident and self-assured than her childhood friends.

Hermine proved to be an irrepressible student. Excelling in public school, she attended Incarnate Word College in San Antonio from 1938–39. After one year, she transferred to the University of San Antonio (now Trinity University), majoring in history and political science. She ranked near the top of her class, but she soon realized that in spite of her academic achievements and intellect, her career opportunities would be limited by her gender. Remembering her father's advice, she turned to the study of law. In 1940 she entered law school at the University of Texas with eleven other women.

In the 1940s the social climate against female lawyers was oppressive. Few women attended law school, and those who did usually never finished. Male students and faculty targeted female students with insults, social ostracism, and discriminatory acts. Hermine underwent similar treatment. Soon after her arrival one of the law school deans asked her to pick a husband from a list he had compiled, thus saving the state the expense of educating a female attorney. Also, second- and third-year law students tried to feed false study information to her and to other first-year female students. Moreover, one particularly belligerent law professor regularly singled out Hermine for verbal harassment in the classroom.

The young woman, however, was determined to succeed. After her first year she ranked in the top 10 percent of her class. By her second year she joined the *Texas Law Review*, and by her third year she became its editor, published several articles in the *Law Review*, and worked as a research assistant for several professors. Although she had faced her share of discrimination, she preferred to talk about the many students and faculty who had been supportive. But the key to her success was her own tenacity. She never let any person, or institution, tell her what she could or could not do. Mentally tough and determined, she never passed up a challenge. And, once committed, she never failed to achieve a goal.

After graduation from law school in 1943, Hermine faced the daunting task of establishing a legal career in a business dominated by men. Although some companies did hire women, most used them as support staff, allowing only men to publicly represent the firm. But Hermine refused job offers that might minimize her role and contributions. She eventually joined the San Antonio law firm of Lang, Byrd, Cross, and Ladon, but only after a spirited recruitment wherein she had turned down the job at least twice. She stayed with the firm for four years before setting up her own practice.

In 1951, Hermine met and married Hyman Tobolowsky of Dallas, who worked for E. M. Kahn and Company Department Store. Introduced by her family, Hermine and Hyman found in each other a common interest in the world of ideas and intellectual discussion. Soon after the wedding she left San Antonio and opened a law practice at her new home in Dallas. As she herself recounted, this was one of the turning points in her life. Not only did she change jobs and move to another city, but the former Miss Dalkowitz also found in her new husband an unrelenting supporter, friend, and adviser who would help her in the biggest challenge of her life—the passage of the Texas Equal Legal Rights Amendment.

Hermine Tobolowsky had begun her quest to change the Texas legal landscape while in law school. There she learned about the underlying legal basis for state laws that placed considerable hardship upon women. They stemmed from British Common Law and the assumptions in Spanish Law that surrendered all decision-making responsibilities to men. Among the forty-four statutes that discriminated against women she was particularly incensed at the laws preventing married women from managing their own property and entering into business partnerships. In Texas a married woman was not considered a responsible party with whom contracts could be made. Rather, the law regarded the husband as the only legally responsible agent in a marriage. Married women had no legal status and therefore were excluded from entering into legal contracts and agreements. Unmarried women experienced the same difficulty because their legal status could change when they married. Essentially, Texas law treated women as second-class citizens. Tobolowsky read numerous cases that reinforced the point. In one situation, a woman who had been abandoned by her husband built a successful business. Later, her husband returned and took control of the property even though he had done nothing to foster its growth.

Tobolowsky learned that Texas women were hamstrung in other ways. A woman who wanted to sue for damages could not do so if her husband refused. Also, labor laws prevented women from securing overtime benefits. Neither were women considered legal guardians of their own children, thereby complicating medical care and custodial issues. Moreover, a woman could be charged with murder if she killed her husband's lover, but if a man killed his wife's lover, the act was considered justifiable homicide. Deeply troubled over her fellow women's inability to take charge of their own legal and financial destiny, Tobolowsky resolved to change matters.

The Texas Federation of Business and Professional Women's Club (BPW) was indispensable to Tobolowsky's fight for legal change. Though not a woman who usually joined clubs, Tobolowsky became interested in the BPW because of its program to eliminate sex discrimination. Already promoting the interests of business and professional women on the job, the BPW had started a campaign in the 1940s to pass legislation permitting women to serve on juries. In the 1950s it took an interest in supporting the national Equal Rights Amendment that had been initially proposed in 1922. And, in 1957, the BPW considered formulating a state amendment and a slate of bills that would change the discriminatory legal climate. With 8,400 members and 185 clubs statewide, the Texas Federation had the potential for being a powerful legislative lobbying group and could be used to educate voters and legislators about pending bills.

After moving to Dallas, Tobolowsky became increasingly active in the BPW. She took a special interest in legislative action and soon became the chairperson of the legislative committee. In 1957 she represented the Dallas BPW in Austin when two bills it supported came up for a hearing before the Senate State Affairs Committee. One bill would permit married women to control separate property; the other would allow married women to convey real property without a husband's approval. Tobolowsky prepared herself in the nuances of the law and compiled anecdotal information regarding actual hardships. When the time came to present her case, she provided the committee with a succinct brief on the matter. Rather than asking questions about her findings and points of law, the committee attacked Tobolowsky personally and ridiculed women in general. Leading the charge was Senator Wardlow Lane from Center, in deep East Texas. At one point during her testimony, he told Tobolowsky: "these bills may be alright for you . . . for you have nothing better to do than run around to clubs and find out about these things, but what about the stupid little women with twelve kids that I represent?"* Another senator offered to give her a cigar since she wanted to be a man. Their disdain perhaps stemmed from the lawmakers' belief that this women's movement that confronted them would quickly evaporate, much like a thundershower during a West Texas summer. Lieutenant Governor Ben Ramsey was said to have declared:

---

*This and subsequent quotations are from interviews with Marcus Dalkowitz, San Antonio, Texas, May 1999, Southwest Collection, Texas Tech University.

"They're not speaking for the women of Texas. I think if they submit it to a vote, the people'll take care of it and kill it dead." Texas had always been a conservative state, and every indication showed that its government would continue to be unsympathetic to social change. Therefore, experienced politicians such as Lt. Governor Ramsey and Senator Lane were contemptuous of Tobolowsky and the BPW.

In contrast, Tobolowsky had gone to Austin certain that she could open the eyes of lawmakers. She had naively believed that legislators would support her bill once they were shown the legal inequities. Though stunned by the hostility exhibited by the members of the committee, Tobolowsky was not easily intimidated. She lectured them on the principles of responsive and effective government and chided them for their disservice to both men and women as representatives.

Her "good government" lecture did much to win her the admiration and support of legislators and citizens. Although the "facts" were lost on the committee, other senators and representatives understood her position and could see change coming to Texas. Tobolowsky represented the cutting edge of a society increasingly more receptive to individual rights and social issues. The wave of civil rights was already building, and within a few years the 1960s and the activism of that era would become a compelling agent for change. Women's rights and the struggle for equality under the law would become an important issue of the times. Forming at least one-half of the Texas electorate, women began in the late 1950s to fight for equal access to rights and privileges as citizens.

From her first encounter with the legislature, Tobolowsky developed the arguments and tactics she would use throughout her equal rights campaign. Her level-headed demeanor and her insistence that legal change would benefit both men and women won over many legislators. She argued that the current level of gender discrimination in Texas law was an unfair burden upon both sexes. As for irreconcilable opponents such as Senator Lane and Lt. Governor Ramsey, Tobolowsky avoided personal attacks. Instead, she worked to inform constituents about their activities, saying: "Citizenship carries with it duties and privileges. The only way to pass legislation is to unseat those who are against it." She thought that the truth would compel voters to flush the obstructionists from office.

Although the 1957 legislative session ended unsuccessfully, it nevertheless held important consequences for the future. First, Tobolowsky changed her strategy. Instead of sponsoring individual bills, she pushed for a comprehensive constitutional amendment that would negate most of the discriminatory statutes. She realized that passing individual bills would be too difficult and take too much time. Second, Tobolowsky personally resolved to change the law. Essentially told by the legislators that her presence and opinions were not welcomed, she responded to the challenge in typical style. She committed herself and all of her resources to fight for equal rights and the right of all citizens for responsive government.

By 1958 the BPW argued for the passage of an Equal Legal Rights Amendment (ELR) to the Texas Constitution. The measure simply stated that "Equality Under the Law Shall Not be Denied or Abridged Because of Sex." Working with sympathetic legislators, Tobolowsky and the BPW introduced proposed amendments in both the House and Senate. Having stumped the state in speaking engagements and having distributed thousands of brochures and pamphlets, Tobolowsky and the BPW felt confident about their chances for success. During the 1959 legislative session, the bill was assigned to the Senate Constitutional Amendments Committee. Even after a successful public hearing and a review by the State Attorney General, the amendment died in committee. Meanwhile, the measure did not fare much better in the House. Representatives failed to vote on the measure before the end of the session.

Tobolowsky and the BPW became familiar with the stalling tactics used by their opponents in the Texas Legislature. In sessions from 1957 to 1969, ELR opponents buried the bill in committee and subcommittee numerous times, referred the measure to the Attorney General for an opinion, changed the amendment's original intent, and sponsored concurrent discriminatory bills. Even "friendly" legislators often failed to live up to their promises. Pressured by colleagues or motivated by other factors, many lawmakers paid lip service to Tobolowsky and the BPW but were absent during important votes. Some used the well-known "restroom" excuse that would have amused Tobolowsky if it had not had such a deadly effect upon the BPW legislative program. Other men strayed openly, promising support but not delivering. As a result, Tobolowsky and the BPW spent a lot of time in Austin attending sessions, visiting with wavering lawmakers, and convincing less sympathetic ones to support the ELR. Frequently, legislators with more nerve than common sense did not show up for appointments with her. In typical Tobolowsky style she would simply say, "I sure wish you would have seen me today because next year you won't be here."

In 1961 delay tactics once again blocked votes on the ELR in both the House and Senate. In spite of the setback, Tobolowsky and the BPW sensed increasing public awareness and empathy for equal rights. As a result, lawmakers began to sponsor bills that either changed or eliminated specific discriminatory statutes. In addition, legislative opponents were increasing their personal attacks against her. Such meanspiritedness only convinced Tobolowsky that the ELR campaign was gaining ground.

As her cause gained momentum, Tobolowsky developed a powerful network of supporters as well as sources of information. Using the long reach of the BPW, her husband's connections in the Retail Merchants Association, her core of legislative supporters in both the House and Senate, and lobbyist friends, she was privy to back-room deals, political maneuverings, and vacillating lawmakers who had pledged to support her bills. Through it all she followed a simple rule: "To always do what you say you'll do so people can depend upon your word."

Some women, however, became worried about her forthright tactics. Not a timid soul, Tobolowsky reminded them that she was not in a popularity contest—she was seeking the passage of laws ending sex discrimination. In the heat of debate and argument, opponents tried many times to make her angry or move her to tears. One legislator accused her of public drunkenness and the use of profanity; another called her a prostitute; and one senator asked her if she were having trouble at home with her husband. Instead, Tobolowsky kept a level head, stood her ground, and counterattacked with her quick wit and verbal barbs. Adversaries were frustrated that they could not provoke her. On the contrary, instead of embarrassing her, they became the object of laughter and ridicule by other politicians and journalists. Reporters enjoyed following Tobolowsky when she was in Austin. There was always something to write about.

Tobolowsky and the BPW hoped to make the 1963 session the watershed year for the passage of the amendment. Much of their high expectations was based upon success at the 1962 polls. With women's groups such as the Women's Rights Society effectively mobilized, opposition legislators had been fighting for reelection. Senator Lane, who had made the biting reference about the "stupid little women," was defeated in his bid for another term. Meanwhile, others scrambled for reelection against a surprisingly effective statewide campaign orchestrated by the Dallas BPW.

As a result, the Senate in 1963 made short work of the bill, and on March 5 voted 26 to 5 to approve the ELR. Meanwhile, the House bill died. Representative Bill Heatly from Paducah sponsored the amendment. As chairman of the House Appropriations Committee he had the clout to successfully steer it through the House. Instead, it ran into substantial opposition. First, the amendment was not introduced immediately; then, the measure was buried in the Constitutional Amendment Committee. Heatly did nothing to compel committee action, and neither did committee chairman James Cotton, a well-known opponent of the ELR. Tobolowsky took responsibility for fatally assigning the sponsorship to Heatly, but she blamed him for killing the amendment. She had trusted the proverbial fox to guard the henhouse and confessed later that she did not know much about him.

In addition to Heatly, the BPW blamed House Speaker Byron Tunnell for his failure in getting the bill out of committee in time. Although Tunnell eventually forced Cotton to hold committee meetings, it was too late. As a result, the BPW targeted Tunnell for defeat at the next election. In addition, the BPW redoubled its efforts to garner unwavering legislative support for the ELR. Having learned a bitter lesson with Tunnell and Heatly, the BPW asked for written pledges from its legislative supporters, thus giving a reliable indication of its House and Senate strength. More important, the written pledges then could be used against lawmakers who failed to honor their commitments. The pledges would document any breach of good faith.

Despite their determined course of action, Tobolowsky and the BPW saw opponents use a variety of methods to block passage of the ELR Amendment. In 1965, Senator Dorsey Hardeman (San Angelo) effectively dry-docked the ELR Amendment by adding a provision "for the protection of women" that actually undermined the equal rights intent of the bill. Supporters of the ELR tried unsuccessfully to table the "Hardeman changes," but a close Senate vote approved them. Supporters of the amendment were then faced with a number of unsavory options: either they could remove the changes that required a two-thirds Senate vote, or they could simply let the amendment die. The bill was eventually tabled. Meanwhile, in the House the BPW came tantalizingly close to passing the amendment, but it eventually failed by one vote.

Throughout the long struggle, Tobolowsky and the BPW operated without the open support from organizations that many thought should be receptive to the passage of the ELR Amendment. The Texas Bar Association declined to back it; early in the 1965 session it had voiced reservations about passing such a measure. Joyce Cox of Houston, president of the association, and Joe McKnight, a member of the bar and a Southern Methodist University law professor, said that the amendment would cause confusion and destroy the community property system in Texas. They were certain that if the amendment passed, the state would be victimized by years of litigation and court action. Rather than advance the cause of equal rights, they feared that the amendment would delay it. The refusal of the Bar Association to support the ELR Amendment worked to undermine public credibility of Tobolowsky and the BPW as well as their assertion that women were indeed suffering under the Texas legal system.

During the 1965 legislative session, Tobolowsky and the BPW decided to support individual bills that would change the legal situation. Although they were unsuccessful in passing the ELR, she and the BPW secured the legislative approval of a number of new laws protecting women's rights. These bills provided for changes in Texas statutes such as: 1) both parents could serve as guardians of a child's estate; 2) married women could sign bail bonds; 3) either spouse could claim jury service exemption when both were called to serve on the same panel; 4) a wife could render her own separate property for tax purposes; 5) either spouse could secure a divorce on the basis of adultery; 6) married women could make partnership contracts; and 7) marriage could not dissolve a pre-existing partnership agreement. Although these proposals did not equate to the comprehensive change provided for in the proposed ELR Amendment, the new laws finally symbolized an important step toward correcting the awkward and crippling legal situation for women. In addition, in April 1965 the Bar Association and the BPW joined forces in "studying, drafting, and sponsoring" specific legislation that would "eliminate or correct" discriminatory laws. The Bar Association and the BPW ran out of time in 1965 but renewed their efforts during the 1967 session through the "Bar Bill" that continued to address community property inequities.

Meanwhile, in 1967 and 1969, legislative opponents continued to fight a rear-guard action and effectively blocked another attempt to pass the ELR Amendment. Similar to previous scenarios, the Senate reported favorably on the bill, but House opponents obstructed its passage. Tobolowsky argued that the legislators' fear of women prompted them to oppose the ELR. They were afraid to give women property control. Others, she assumed, perhaps thought that women were inferior and were not capable of handling property responsibilities. The belief that

Texas women needed the protection of men was pervasive among the opposition and underscored arguments against the ELR Amendment. As a student of human nature, Tobolowsky also understood that opposition stemmed from the irrational fear of the unknown. Anxiety over change manifested itself in ludicrous arguments against the amendment. Claims circulated that the ELR would sanction same-sex marriages and encourage the proliferation of unisex restrooms. Critics tried to smear the ELR campaign with the "liberal Communist conspiracy" label.

On April 27, 1971, the Texas governor at last signed into law the Equal Legal Rights Amendment. The Senate passed the amendment without much delay. The House, which had been derailing the measure during the last few sessions, finally organized sufficient support to pass it. Quite simply, opposition lawmakers had tired of the struggle. Their ranks having been thinned by the BPW's election campaigning, they finally passed the amendment rather than subject themselves to further electoral abuse. Besides, they believed that the Texas electorate would defeat the bill when it was set before the people.

Tobolowsky and the BPW had finally brought the amendment to a popular vote. They could not claim victory, however, until that last hurdle was cleared. Seizing every opportunity, they traveled throughout the state and spoke to every club, association, and organization that would listen. They printed pamphlets and placed advertisements in newspapers and on radio and television at a cost to the organizations of roughly $100,000. Because they did not have enough money, Tobolowsky personally guaranteed fee payment for the television spots and paid for her own travel expenses. She also organized every county, regardless of whether it had a BPW club, and funneled news releases, fact sheets, and pamphlets to outlying areas. She advised supporters to emphasize the universality of the ELR irrespective of "race, creed, religion and national origin"; it was "a matter of simple justice." She even wrote canned speeches that were distributed by way of a speakers' bureau, each one tailored to a specific audience. Tobolowsky poured herself into the ratification campaign to the point that she nearly gave up her law practice. She was on the road constantly; and even when she was in Dallas, everything she did supported the fight for passage.

Then, on November 7, 1972, the citizens of Texas overwhelmingly approved Proposition Seven with a vote of 2,156,536 to 548,422. It was a victory margin of nearly 4 to 1, one of the largest in the state's constitutional history. As a consequence the ELR became part of the

Texas Constitution and, in a watershed event, eliminated most of the discriminatory aspects of Texas law and assured all its citizens of legal equality.

Tobolowsky and the BPW succeeded where few observers thought they might. Not only had they fought to change the Texas Constitution and legal statutes, but they also had to change the way people thought about themselves as both men and women. She compelled them to consider the larger possibilities of what both genders could achieve given the limitless horizons in a state that had always prided itself as a land of opportunity and a frontier for new beginnings. Somewhere, Texans had lost sight of those possibilities, thereby restricting opportunity to females who had long shaped that state's history either as pioneers, farmers, ranchers, doctors, businesswomen, or even railroad tycoons. Tobolowsky and her colleagues understood that they were not only fighting for equal rights, but they were also fighting to reestablish a Texas that provided equal opportunity for all.

Tobolowsky was always modest about her achievements and credited the movement's success to the BPW and to the hardworking legislators who shared their vision. She even credited her 1957 legislative opponents who insulted her and derailed her first bills for sowing the seeds of a personal resolve that led to success in 1972. But, on balance, immense credit must be given to Tobolowsky, who was unafraid, willing to stand alone, and eager to sound the call for change. Once certain that she was right, Tobolowsky gave her heart, soul, and money to the cause. On several occasions her personal safety was even in jeopardy because of bomb threats and shotgun blasts. Most significant, she sacrificed her most precious possession—time that could have been spent with her beloved husband, Hyman, who died in 1968, long before the fight was over. However great her sacrifice, Tobolowsky firmly believed in her obligation as a citizen to demand good government. She used every office and resource to alleviate the pain and suffering brought about by iniquitous laws, and she believed in her family, friends, country, and most of all her state—Texas.

Suggested Readings

Crawford, Ann Fears. *Women in Texas: Their Lives, Their Experiences, Their Accomplishments.* Burnet, TX, 1982.
Downs, Fane, and Nancy Baker Jones, eds. *Women and Texas History: Selected Essays.* Austin, 1993.

Humphrey, Janet G., ed. *A Texas Suffragist: Diaries and Writings of Jane Y. McCallum.* Austin, 1988.

Lazarou, Kathleen Elizabeth. *Concealed under Petticoats: Married Women's Property and the Law of Texas, 1840–1913.* New York, 1986.

McAdams, Ina May Ogletree. *Texas Women of Distinction; A Biographical History.* Austin, 1962.

Ornish, Natalie. *Pioneer Jewish Texans.* Dallas, 1989.

Seligman, Claudia Dee. *Texas Women: Legends in Their Own Time.* Dallas, 1989.

Winegarten, Ruthe. *Governor Ann Richards and Other Texas Women: From Indians to Astronauts.* Austin, 1993.

Winegarten, Ruthe, and Judith N. McArthur, eds. *Citizens at Last: The Woman Suffrage Movement in Texas.* Austin, 1987.

Wintz, Cary. "Women in Texas," in *The Texas Heritage.* Ben Procter and Archie P. McDonald, eds. 3d ed. Wheeling, IL, 1998.

15

Gary Gaines
Under Autumn Skies

Ty Cashion

Texas high-school football grew into one of the state's identifying social institutions during the twentieth century. For coaches such as Gary Gaines, football has provided much more than a livelihood; it has been a way of life. Gaines grew up on the football fields of West Texas and turned his love for the game into a career that has spanned three decades and has led to coaching stops at nine different towns. At the high-school level between 1971 and 1999 he worked with state champions as well as teams that struggled to produce a win. Gaines believed that his real accomplishment at both ends, however, could be measured only in the success that he enjoyed as a mentor to his players. In 1989, while coaching at Odessa's Permian High School, his faith in that tenet was put to the test. The high-school football culture of which he was so prominently a part became the subject of a critical national bestseller. Yet, in contrast to the harsh light that it cast on Odessa and the misplaced priorities of Texas high-school football fans, the author accorded Gaines a grudging respect for his professionalism and stewardship of youth. Gary Gaines is still active, having recently been named head coach at Abilene Christian University.

Ty Cashion is assistant professor of history at Sam Houston State University and the author of *Pigskin Pulpit: A Social History of Texas High-School Football Coaches* (1998).

Gary Gaines could not remember the exact moment when he decided to become a football coach. But, then again, he could not remember a time when the path to that profession did not seem clearly marked. His father's brother, Richard, had blazed the trail for him at Haskell, just north of Abilene, where he was a popular assistant coach. "Every time I saw my uncle, he was at the center of all the action, and I wanted to be just like him,"[1] remarked Gary. Like other Texas schoolboys of the 1950s and early 1960s, he dreamed of running for touchdowns and being the star of the team, but just as often he saw himself as the man on the sidelines who directed the action on the field. Gaines's earliest memories involved Friday night—"football night"—and long road trips across barren stretches of West Texas, where the road out of

Crane, his home town, took him to such places as McCamey, Denver City, and Pecos. "Wherever the Golden Cranes were playing, that's where we went," he recalled. Once or twice per season, however, the road out of town led to Haskell, where he could stand on the sidelines with his uncle. There he felt the turf under his feet; breathed the stale air of sweat, blood, and dirt; searched the determined looks on young faces; and heard up close the hard licks of crashing bodies. "I knew then what I wanted to do with my life," said Gaines, "and I never wavered. Even through high school and college I knew that I was going to be a coach, and I never considered doing anything else."

When Gary was eleven years old, the tragic and untimely death of his uncle reinforced that resolve. Just twenty-eight himself, Richard had developed brain cancer. In 1960 such a diagnosis was a death sentence. Gary had always seen him surrounded by adoring young people, and even grown men enjoyed his company. Every time he saw Richard on the job, it seemed as if the entire town came out to watch. And when his team won—and most often it did—Gary could not imagine him wanting to trade places with anyone else on Earth.

When the cancer struck, it was as though a pall had descended over Haskell. The town that had seemed so festive to Gary went into mourning for his uncle, even while he was still alive. The school district at that time did not carry health insurance for its teachers, so boosters and friends paid all of Richard's hospital bills. They also made sure that his wife, Martha, never had to prepare a meal while he was convalescing at home. For as long as he could, Richard stuck to his usual routine. He continued to attend practices, even if only to sit on an upturned bucket at the edge of the field, holding his head in his hands.

Football for men such as Richard and Gary Gaines has been much more than a livelihood—it has been their way of life. For many other Texans, too, the sport has cut a wide swath through the cultural fabric. From modest beginnings, high-school football in the Lone Star State grew into one of its identifying social institutions. The agricultural society that first embraced the sport saw football seasons unfold at a time when the autumn harvest had been brought in, leaving farmers with some idle time and a little extra money in their pockets. Moreover, great distances and bad roads between towns made football even more appealing to people stuck at home and starved for entertainment. And for Texans who fancied themselves raw and rowdy products of the frontier, this rough-and-tumble sport allowed them to project onto the gridiron all of the exaggerations that they had come to see in themselves.

Interest in high-school football first soared in the 1910s and 1920s after progressives organized the University Interscholastic League. The UIL set standards at a time when schools were consolidating and looking for competitive outlets. In 1920 it joined together every part of the state by hosting a championship game that has continued uninterrupted to the present day. Coaches themselves organized a clinic in 1933 that introduced sophistication and scientific methods to the game. It also attracted college coaches, who jumped at the chance to share their ideas and cooperate with the men who supplied them with talent. After struggling through decades of depression and war, high-school football reached its zenith by the 1950s and enjoyed something of a golden age that lasted until the mid- to late 1960s, before other activities began competing for the interests of young people.

Gary Gaines, who was born in 1949, grew up during that time, an era that was marked by conformity. "I never questioned the way it was," he said. "Crane was an oil company town, and being a company person meant something to those people, and I grew up feeling that sense of loyalty to who you worked for and what you did for a living." While his mother remained at home, Gary's father labored in the oil fields for Gulf Petroleum. Together the couple encouraged their son in every activity that he pursued—which usually included the sport of the season. "When we got home from school, there wasn't a lot to do, other than play ball or do homework. There wasn't much on television either, and video games hadn't even been invented."

The Gaineses were also active members of the Church of Christ, and although their involvement left Gary with a deep sense of spirituality, he also realized the heavy burden of living up to expectations. The church of his youth was strict in its demands—much more so, he estimated, than the church today. "There were so many 'don'ts'—you know, going to dances is a pretty good deal for kiddoes, but the church wouldn't allow it—so some kids fell by the wayside because of the strict stance that the church took on some things." Still, he said, "that's just the way it was." At the same time, Gaines found the fellowship supportive, and through the challenging times of high school and college his church kept him from straying too far from center. Indeed, his faith continues to illuminate his thoughts and actions.

Still, it was football that captured young Gaines's heart and occupied his time, and no one outside of his home taught him more about values than his coach, Dan Anderegg. "He was old school," Gaines recalled. "He was stern, he demanded a lot of his players, and he worked them hard." Anderegg, like most coaches of his day, motivated more by the "stick" than by the "carrot." Occasionally, he would ruffle the feelings of a player, but his lone assistant, Jack Gothard, would always be there to "pick up the pieces. Coach Anderegg would challenge your manhood, and you had to respond the best you could."

Anderegg was from another era, the product of the Great Depression and World War II. He hailed from the Hill Country, near the community of Doss, where his family ran a seventeen-thousand-acre ranch. Yet despite the surface appearance of prosperity, the future coach was a far cry from a country squire. His father put him and his little brother to work seven days per week stringing fence and grubbing up cedars before they were even old enough for kindergarten. "We worked like dogs," Anderegg insisted, "and we grew up fast." The old coach, typical of his generation, would no doubt seem unduly severe to the players whom Gaines has coached. But in Anderegg's own time, a coach's methods went unchallenged; players did not question him, and parents supported him almost unconditionally.

As tough as Anderegg was, Gaines was quick to point out that he demanded as much from himself as he expected from his players. Moreover, the old coach knew every kid in school and most of their parents. And he was consummately organized. In a day when most coaches kept their players on the practice field until the sun went down, Anderegg drilled his boys through crisp, well-planned workouts that typically lasted only two hours, and he did it with only one assistant. Such attention to detail extended beyond the football field as well. A math teacher, he also was reputed to be a taskmaster in the classroom. Anderegg, who earned the universal respect of his fellow teachers, would arrive at school long before the first bell to meet with students. "He had no pass-no play before it was ever dreamed up," Gaines added.

> As I look back on it, his [Anderegg's] strength in terms of motivation was to lay a challenge out before the team. And that's still a powerful motivator—kids still respond to that. But kids today want to know "why," and you have to tell them. I always tell our guys that I might not always be nice, but that doesn't mean I don't love them. "I'm going to raise my voice to you, and I'm going to expect a lot out of you, but don't take it personal. I'm not going to criticize you as a person; it's going to be your performance." And I think they buy into that. If you let them know you care about them beyond the football field, they'll play for you.

Of himself as a player, Gaines admitted: "I'm glad I had a suit when I had it, because when you compare me to the kids today who are so much bigger, faster, and stronger, I was pretty average." His modesty, however, belied the fact that by 1966 the rangy senior had grown into a six-foot, 170-pound halfback. He also had three hashmarks on his varsity letter jacket, one for each year in which he played a leading role in contributing to the Golden Cranes' success.

Even though Gaines played on some good football teams, his greatest disappointment was never having been able to compete in a postseason game. Until the early 1980s, when runners-up entered the playoffs, only one team represented each district. In 1964 and 1965, Crane had been ranked in the state's top ten, finishing with records of 8-2 and 9-1, respectively. In both years, however, district rival Alpine grounded the Golden Cranes in bitter contests that ended by razor-thin margins of 3 to 0 and 10 to 7.

It was that 10 to 7 loss during Gaines's junior year that has remained one of the most vivid recollections of his high-school days and one that later would prove an object lesson to him as a coach. "The thing that haunts me about that one is that we had a halfback pass called down inside the 'red zone' late in the game, and we'd practiced it all week and felt like it was going to work. So, we ran the play, and when the quarterback handed me the ball, I rolled around the right end and threw the ball into coverage, and it fell incomplete. When you see it on the film . . . I could have run it in. I made a poor decision, and it probably cost us the football game." No one could have been any more crestfallen than Dan Anderegg, but even though he let Gaines know that the run was there, he did not belittle him and never mentioned it again. For Gaines, it was a good, if bitter, lesson.

Many Texans who played high-school football have looked back on their gridiron days as the high watermark of their youth. Until sometime around World War II, the typical future awaiting young men graduating from high school was a job outdoors, whether it was in agriculture, road building, oil-field work, or some other labor-intensive industry. Before the GI Bill, college was beyond the reach of the average Texan. The rigors of playing football, then, provided a good training ground for most young men. And, in light of the monotony and anonymity of workaday life, memories of their playing days would grow even fonder.

Gary Gaines had made up his mind long before graduating that he wanted to go on to college. Still, he had a taste of what it was like to toil outdoors. "It made me appreciate my education, let me tell you," he asserted. Until the summer before his senior year, his age limited him to working for the school custodians cutting grass, repairing bleacher seats, and doing other maintenance chores. As soon as he became old enough, he found a summer job on a construction crew that was building a gasoline compressor station twenty miles outside of Crane. "The thing I remember most, besides it being so hot and those old sand hills, was that there was a bad accident that happened one day." An electrician who had climbed up a metal pole fell backward when his belt slipped, and he plummeted to the ground. "The only thing that saved his life was that he hit an eight-foot chain-link fence on the way down, and it flipped him over; otherwise he would have landed head first. . . . Being twenty miles from the hospital, it took a long time for them to get an ambulance there."

"We were always taught to believe that West Texans were a little tougher than most folks," he confided. "I don't know if that's true anymore, but we surely believed it at the time." That attitude helped Gaines through four years of college football at Angelo State University. It was a time when Grant Teaff, who later enjoyed a long and successful tenure at Baylor, was hired to rebuild the Rams' flagging program. "My junior year, he weeded out a lot of people. The first spring we barely finished with enough players to have a spring game. We had to recruit somebody out of the P.E. [Physical Education] Department just to put on a suit and have enough bodies out there to play the game."

Teaff, said Gaines, did turn the program around—in large measure "because he surrounded himself with good people." Paul Horne, Gaines's position coach, was one of those men. If Anderegg had impressed upon Gaines the mechanics of the profession, it was Horne who was most responsible for helping him find a sharper focus for his career. "He helped me get my head screwed on right as far as what I wanted to do with my life and what kind of coach I wanted to be." After such a strict upbringing, Gaines found a freedom at Angelo State that he had never known. "Not that I was a terrible person," he said, "but I wasn't going to church very regularly and had gotten to where I was enjoying the college life more than I should have." Coach Horne "had a lot to do with me thinking about the future and how the present would affect me later on."

Graduation and "real life" always approach faster than students expect them to, and Horne knew that Gaines's future was about to take some important turns. The most life-affecting change came during the summer before his senior year, when he married his college sweetheart, Sharon. Ironically, her father, who had taken a job with El Paso Natural Gas, had moved his family to Crane when the pair were sophomores at Angelo State. They did not meet, however, until they were both home during a Christmas break. As it turned out, he smiled, "we did, and we fell in love and got married." After graduating in May 1971, Gaines became an assistant coach at the small trans-Pecos town of Fort Stockton. For the first time he had a little money in his pocket and the freedom to call some shots on a football field. "We had a young staff and all of us thought we knew more than we really did," he laughed, "but I was gung-ho and couldn't have been any happier if I was at the University of Texas."

Fort Stockton was the first stop in a career that would take Gary and Sharon to eight other West Texas communities. Along the way they would add to the family a son, Bradley, and a daughter, Nicole. In 1972 the couple went to Monahans, where they spent four years. Then, Gaines landed his first head coaching job at Petersburg, in the Panhandle. From there they went to Denver City, Odessa, Lubbock, Amarillo, Abilene, and San Angelo. On a recent trip to his childhood home of Crane, Gaines reflected on having lived his entire life in West Texas: "I just kept looking out the window and saw how barren and desolate it was and thought, 'Man, how did I spend fifty years in this place?' But then I thought that it really is a unique land, and everywhere we've lived the people have been good." Talking about how all the moves affected his wife, Gaines conceded that Sharon did not have much of a choice. "She's cried everywhere we've left, and she's been happy everywhere we've ever been. She's been a great coach's wife."

For every man in the profession who makes his home in one spot, many others find themselves riding what they call the "coaching carousel." Typically, it is the nature of the job. Coaches find offers from bigger schools of better pay and greater challenges too tempting to pass up. And, just as easily, losing seasons can leave entire coaching staffs with no choice but to pack up and start calling on colleagues who might have a spot open. "There's always some sadness in your heart when you leave a place, because you hate to leave your kids [that is, the players]. You can feel like you're leaving them high and dry."

Moving from Abilene to San Angelo in 1996 might have been the hardest, even though Gary and Sharon had always dreamed of returning to the Concho Valley: "That was our college home, and it's the place where we wanted to come if the opportunity ever presented itself." Still, it meant leaving a program that was building on two seasons where he won only five games. "The San Angelo job came open during the summer," Gaines continued, "and I didn't even get a chance to say anything to the players." Torn between what he wanted and what he felt obligated to do left him with one of the toughest decisions of his career.

Fortunately, all but one of Gaines's moves was made easier by knowing that his vacancy allowed an assistant coach to move up in the profession's pecking order. "That's always left me with a good feeling," he said. "Somebody must have been proud of the job we had done, and it gave those guys a chance to become a head coach." At Abilene, his assistant coach, Steve Warren, was able to step in at the moment when Abilene was poised to turn the corner and return to its old winning ways. In 1999, Warren led the Eagles into the playoffs, and they went farther than any Abilene team since their halcyon days of the late 1950s.

For Gaines, the carousel turned early. After the end of his first semester, in 1971, Jerry Gibson retired as Fort Stockton's head coach to open an insurance agency. A respected colleague, Jerry Larned of Monahans, heard about Gaines's predicament and invited him to join his staff. "Jerry had a good program in place, and we had good kids. . . . He was really an intense man and demanded a lot out of his coaches and his players," remarked Gaines. "That was where I first figured out what it meant to put in long hours to work and prepare and give your players every edge that you possibly could by doing your homework." According to Gaines, it paid off. He got to be part of two district champions in his four years there. "It was exciting to see how a town gets behind a team. There's just nothing like high-school playoffs to unite a community."

The greatest lesson that Gaines learned from Larned, however, had little to do with football. Coaches can be persistent, even obstinate men who, like Jacob, would dare to wrestle God Himself if He challenged them one on one. Dealing with a problem without a physical solution, then, might leave them feeling especially frustrated and helpless. Yet, while Gaines was at Monahans, Larned and his wife coped with such a situation every day. "Jerry and Beth had a son by the name of Todd who was born with cystic fibrosis, and he died while we were coaching together. He was nine years old." The way that the couple carried their burden impressed upon Gaines the lessons of dignity and grace. "They were tough people, and they handled it better than anybody I could imagine."

Young Todd's routine was oxygen tents and trips to the medical center in Houston, but his life revolved around the Monahans Lobos. "Todd was such a fighter. He knew every player and tried to make it to every game. He was always an inspiration to me and to the team and everybody who was associated with Jerry and Beth." The Larneds attended the Methodist Church, Gaines continued, "and the preacher there, a guy named Harrington, went up to the hospital to see Todd right before he passed away, and he asked Todd if he knew where he was going. And Todd said, 'I'm going to Heaven.' He knew he was going to die. . . . That kind of thing sure puts your mortality into perspective and makes you think about why you're doing what you're doing. Coaching is nice, it's fun, and it's a great profession, but we're here for something far more important than winning and losing."

After leaving Monahans for a two-year stint at Petersburg, where he headed the program, Gaines arrived in 1978 to take over a struggling team at Denver City, a place that enjoyed the memory of some good years. At the beginning of every season the fans there measured their prospects against the squad that won the 2-A crown in 1960. Gaines had played against those teams when he was in high school himself and remembered being impressed by Denver City's traditions and the crowds who turned out to support the kids. He relished the challenge that lay before him. "We made some inroads that first year. Went four and six; our freshmen went undefeated. . . . Looked like things were going up."

But then coach John Wilkins asked Gaines to join his staff in Odessa at Permian High School. After three years as top man, Gaines did not at first consider such a career move to be wise. On the other hand, Odessa was the Mecca of high-school football. "I knew that if I were ever going to be a really good coach, that this would give me a chance to learn some football. I'd always respected that program and felt like it was a good opportunity."

In the 1970s, Texans had begun to talk about Permian in the same breath with schools such as Waco, Amarillo, Abilene, and a handful of others whose trophy cases full of tarnished brass bowls and weathered footballs attested to a one-time dominance of the game. The Permian Panthers had clawed their way to the pinnacle of this tradition-rich state with disciplined players exhorted to victory by a band, cheerleaders, and a community following that would make many colleges envious. "Mojo," an incantation of Permian High spirit whose origins no one quite seems to know, became the manifestation of the Panthers' mystique. The tingling chant MO!-JO! arising from the throats of ten thousand or more black-and-white clad fans had most opposing teams ready to fold before the first ball was ever snapped.

The more Gaines considered Wilkins's proposition, the more appealing it seemed. "After he offered us the job, Sharon and I went down

there and told them we'd think about it." At length, the couple decided
that Gary would decline the post, but Wilkins did not take "no" for an
answer so easily. "He told me, 'Look, Gary, that [coaching] clinic is
coming up at San Angelo in a couple of weeks, so don't shut the door all
the way until we can visit about it some more.' "

When that weekend rolled around, Sharon thought it would be a
good time to visit her mother in Midland. "Without consulting my
wife, I told John I'd take the job," Gaines winced. Unable to reach her,
he went ahead and contacted a real estate agency in Denver City and
told them to put their house up for sale. "Before I could get word to
Sharon, she goes back to Denver City, and the first thing she sees is the
'For Sale' sign. She wasn't very happy with me," the coach deadpanned,
"but by the time we got the boxes unpacked, she was talking to me
again."

The experience at Permian was everything that Gaines had hoped
for, and more. In his first year the Panthers lost only two games, but
one of them cost the team a trip to the playoffs; it would be a couple
more years until runners-up were able to compete in the postseason.
"That wasn't a very good year for them, but we came back in 1980 and
beat Port Arthur Jefferson for the state championship."

Looking back on that season, Gaines remarked, "What made the
biggest impression on me was how fortunate you've got to be to win it
all. You have to stay healthy and have some luck from time to time."
Going into the final regular season game, Permian had to beat or tie
their bitter crosstown rival, Odessa High, just to make the playoffs.
After falling behind, the Panthers were indeed lucky to come away with
a 14-to-14 deadlock. "Then we go into bi-district and play Sherman in
a 'mud bowl' at Abilene and ended up tying that game zero-to-zero."
Advancing to the next round on a statistical advantage (there was no
"sudden death" then), they finally got on a roll, crushing their next
three opponents by a combined score of 85 to 3. A solid Highland Park
squad was among those teams, which had called on then-Dallas Cowboys quarterback Roger Staubach to deliver their pep rally speech. "We
were the underdog in just about every game we played," admitted Gaines,
"but that bunch of kids just thought they were supposed to win."

And this time it was "the kids" who took their coaches to school.
"That happens all the time," Gaines reflected, "those lessons don't just
flow one way." More than anyone else that year, it was Jerry Hicks, a
five-foot-seven, 138-pound quarterback who was the teacher. "He inspired me," said the coach.

He was a "gamer"; he could get it in the end zone. Jerry was such a competitive kid—a great athlete and a good field general. It was so awe-inspiring just to watch him and watch the way the team looked up to him. But if you looked at him you wouldn't have picked him out of a crowd to be a 5-A quarterback, especially on a state championship team.

Jerry proved to me that you can't measure the size of a kid's heart. Even as you were watching him with your own eyes, you'd be saying, "There's no way a kid could be capable of doing what he just did." Whether it was scrambling to make a key first down or throwing a play-action pass for a touchdown. . . . I mean, he just made big play after big play. Even on those sweeps, he'd pitch the ball out and then throw that 138-pound body into those linebackers like he thought he was supposed to do it—chopped 'em down like cordwood.

Gaines also learned a lot from Wilkins. After two seasons at Odessa, Gaines went on to Amarillo's Tascosa High School, once again as head coach, and then back to Monahans, where he directed the Lobos to two district championships in three years. After the 1985 season, Wilkins became athletic director and once again asked Gaines if he were interested in joining him—this time as head coach of the Permian Panthers. Gaines's various jobs had given him a renewed sense of what the game was all about and what his own role was. Coaching under Gibson, Larned, and Wilkins as well as heading up programs of his own made Gaines realize that "being a head coach is an awesome responsibility. You've got to love it, and you've got to work hard, but most of all you have to be yourself. If you try to act like somebody else or adopt somebody else's style, you'll come off looking like a phony. Developing that trust among your staff and your players is where it all begins."

And because football is a game where success depends on physical effort, one of the greatest tasks is player motivation, a responsibility that falls squarely on the shoulders of the head coach. "I've always tried to do it with a lot of energy and enthusiasm and put some excitement into the game. Hopefully, it's been fun for the kids, and they've enjoyed playing. Of course, *there ain't nothing more fun than winning!*"

Further, Gaines has observed that "different teams and different individuals are motivated in different ways. Some groups who have a lot of experience may not need the same kind of motivation that a young team might need. And again, you've got to motivate every *individual* differently, and for that, you've got to make sure that your position coaches develop good relationships with their players." For motivating the team collectively, "we'd pull out all the stops. Anytime I hear a good story or anecdote, I'll write it down, and chances are when the right situation comes up I might be able to use it."

Still, he emphasized, "You can never forget that you're dealing with kids. Kids are sensitive, and you're going to hurt their feelings from time to time. You just can't ever get to the point where you feel so big that you can't tell them that you crossed the line and you're sorry." Once, at Permian High, Gaines had chewed out a backup player who had blown an assignment. "I thought he wasn't hustling. I lost my temper and berated him. Just wouldn't let go of it. Bawled him out real good right there in front of his teammates. I knew I had gone overboard, and for the rest of practice I just felt like a dog. When it was over, I called him aside and told him I was wrong—not in getting on him, but for getting on him as long as I did and for embarrassing him. We shook hands, and I gave him a hug, and, luckily, there weren't any hard feelings."

Thin skin and sensitivity, however, are not luxuries that the man at the top can afford. Gaines, too, has pulled into the driveway to see "For Sale" signs punched into the yard, but they did not get there because opportunity beckoned; rather, they seemed to materialize on nights after close losses. When Gaines got the call from Wilkins, Permian's principal and Odessa's school district superintendent told him what their expectations were. "Of course, they were all high," laughed the coach. "And they weren't going to tell me anything I didn't already know. Sharon and I knew there was some pressure associated with the position, and ultimately you were going to have to produce at a high level or you wouldn't last long."

There seemed to be a contradiction between words and action. On the one hand, Gaines talked a lot about kids, but on the other hand, his job was to win the game. However, he said:

> I don't see a problem there, juggling those things. Ultimately, if you mistreat kids you're not going to last long anyway. If you have a program that parents want their kids to be a part of, then that's what you're shooting for. We just worked the snot out of them and continued the same basic program that they'd had for many, many years. As a coach, you just have to know that there's a hard and fast line between abusing a kid and developing a good work ethic. Kids won't play for you if you're not honest with them. A lot of it has to do with "attitude" and your approach. And typically, when you have an unusual group of kids like we had in '80 or '89, then you're going to have a chance to win it all.

Then in 1990 came *Friday Night Lights*, a book that Gaines thought made a mockery of his high ideals, the school's widely envied program, and even the town that supported it. The author, *Philadelphia Inquirer* editor Buzz Bissinger, had called Gaines and asked if he could come to Odessa and live among the team and staff for a season. In the foreword that he would eventually write, Bissinger said that he wanted "to discover the essence of high school football. . . . A variety of names came up, but all roads led to West Texas, to a town called Odessa."[2]

At first, Gaines refused Bissinger's request. Coincidentally, the coach had just finished reading John Feinstein's *A Season on the Brink*, an unflattering biography of Indiana basketball coach Bobby Knight, and that had given him pause. But Bissinger was persistent and traveled to Odessa to make his case. He appealed to Gaines, telling him that he wanted to write a Texas version of the 1987 movie *Hoosiers*, the transcendent story of a small town's glorious march to an Indiana high-school basketball crown. So Gaines relented, and after a meeting with Wilkins and the school district's superintendent, the author got the green light.

For four months during the 1988 season, Odessa opened its doors to Bissinger. With notepad and tape recorder in hand, he attended staff meetings, observed workouts, and watched the coaches grade films. He ate with team members and coaches at their homes, prayed with them, celebrated with them, and commiserated with them, but, ultimately, in their view, he betrayed them. What emerged in the bestseller was a dark and derisive portrait of a semirural backwash with its priorities woefully out of balance. Bissinger called Odessa "an armpit" of a place, a description that was "actually a few rungs up from its usual anatomical comparison with a rectum."[3] His characters seemed always to be either victims or predators; his situations seemed always to contrast the laudable and condemnable. Any place that Bissinger might have seen as gray, complained townspeople, he painted black every time.

All Bissinger needed to make his caustic tale complete was an abusive drillmaster like *Varsity Blues*'s Bud Kilmer, the fictional coach in the popular 1999 movie that *Friday Night Lights* inspired, but such a man did not exist in Odessa. There, the coaching staff made sure that their players kept in perspective their brief moment in the spotlight. The coaches praised but did not coddle; they criticized but did not condemn; they prodded but did not push. Yet rather than praise the Permian staff, Bissinger sarcastically compared the Permian coaches to Jaime Escalante, the inner city Los Angeles teacher whom Hollywood portrayed in the 1988 movie, *Stand and Deliver*. Bissinger concluded that in Odessa such methods were wasted on the football field rather than invested in the classroom.

Still, it was plain that Bissinger had developed a grudging respect for Gaines. He had to concede that the coach reacted admirably when the Panthers faced their two biggest rivals. Rather than appeal to the baser emotions of his players, Gaines pulled out some stories he had been saving. Before facing crosstown foe Odessa High, for example, he related the saga of two opposing Civil War scouts. When blue-collar Permian boys played the starch-shirted boys from Midland Lee, he told them about Olympic swimmer Steve Genter, who "split his stitches" competing at Munich with a collapsed lung. His players, like Genter, "had come too far to let it all go." And at halftime in another game, Gaines had to confront a running back who had just fumbled away two scoring opportunities. Taking him into "the little coaches' room," Bissinger wrote, Gaines "threw him a football." Perhaps the coach was thinking about how Dan Anderegg had reacted when Gaines misread that crucial play so long ago. This time, however, there was still half a game left in which to salvage a win. Looking at the player, all he said was, "Hold on to it."[4]

The Panthers that year reached the state semifinals before losing to a troubled Dallas Carter team that would go all the way, only to be stripped of its state title after it was revealed that the players' grades had been doctored to keep them eligible. The Dallas program would endure even greater ignominy the next year when some stars on the team took part in a crime spree involving a series of armed robberies. The episode provided an epilogue for Bissinger's book. Texans, in the author's estimation, had fashioned high-school football into some kind of golden calf.

Another season, however, would pass before *Friday Night Lights* hit the bookstores. In the meantime, Gaines would lead the Permian Panthers to the 1989 Class 5-A state championship. The big win propelled him to the top of his profession. The game, set for noon at Texas Stadium, was televised and pitted the Panthers against Houston Aldine. "I remember it was tremendously cold that day. At the hotel, when we woke up, there was ice on the inside of the window. When we got to the stadium, it was nine degrees on the floor of that field. But by the time the game was over, middle afternoon, it had 'warmed up' to near freezing."

The 28-to-14 victory capped a season in which the talented Permian squad had been ranked first in the state from start to finish. According to Gaines, it was the fulfillment of a contract with tradition.

> Every year the upperclassmen knew that people were going to remember that particular Permian team by that group of seniors, and they responded more often than not. That '89 bunch was one that just thought they were sup-

posed to win. . . . These kids grow up hoping to be a part of that program, believing in MOJO, and those that end up making it are usually pretty good football players. . . . You've got to understand, too, that the basic offense and defense that they've run out there for the last twenty years has changed very little, and most of them started running it in the seventh grade. . . . By the time they become seniors they're ready to play some football, but they also feel like the monkey's on their back, and they don't want to be the team to let that tradition down. The way those seniors responded every year to it being "their time in the barrel" was always impressive to me.

In the next spring, people in Odessa were still basking in the glow of that state championship when *Friday Night Lights* debuted. They were shocked. Many of the people who had cooperated willingly with Bissinger voiced their resentment and feelings of betrayal. The *Odessa American*, the local newspaper, was besieged by vitriolic letter writers, and, when HarperCollins Publishers tried to arrange a book signing in Odessa, the event had to be canceled because of death threats against the author.

Gaines himself never read the book. Just before it hit the stores, Bissinger called to say that he was sending him and Sharon an advance copy, still maintaining that it would be the positive portrayal that he had promised all along. By then, Gaines had taken a job at Texas Tech and had his hands full. "After he called, I didn't think anything else about it. Then, my wife calls one day. She had gotten the book and read it cover to cover, and she was just in tears and ended up throwing it away. The kids looked at it, I think, but I didn't ever see it. Besides, Sharon told me what all was written. A month or so later he [Bissinger] called and left a message for me to call him back, but I never did. Wouldn't have served any useful purpose. By that point in time the deed was done."

The positive reception for *Friday Night Lights* elsewhere laid bare some long-simmering animosities toward high-school football by critics of the game and underscored the bitterness that had accompanied a recent "no pass-no play" rule. Proponents of the legislation had laid much of the blame for the failures of education on a society that placed too much emphasis on the sport at the expense of academic achievement. The Bissinger book, it appeared, provided the proof.

Former L. D. Bell coach Tim Edwards, who had defended his institution on television's "Nightline," reflected on changes in society and the tenuous position of high-school football. Pointing to such developments as the massive stadiums that communities have built and the regionwide broadcasts of championship games, he commented: "[High school football] is not nearly as important as it once was, but it's bigger now in some ways than it's ever been. . . . When we've reached a point where 'Johnny can't read,' but he can play football in some of the stadiums that you see in these 5-A school districts, then you've invited a backlash."

To a society that has come to value conflict resolution over competition, perhaps football seems to have fallen out of step with the times. Where coaches see a sport that promotes good character and cultivates a sense of fair play, critics see a spectacle of unhealthy competition that breeds violence and brutality. But where coaches have been accused of "winning at all costs," Gaines believes that the dual lens should be checked more closely. Often, he said, it is the coach who stands between his players and boosters who would do anything to win. "As long as I've been in this profession, I haven't seen too many coaches who were that way, and they didn't last long."

In a recent historiography, "Why Sports Matter," novelist Wilfred Sheed wrote: "It's hard to say exactly when the new era began, but at some point . . . sports went from being officially a bad thing to being a very good thing."[5] Judging by the response to books such as *Friday Night Lights* and the way coaches were pilloried over no pass-no play, then perhaps society has come full circle. Yet, spend some time with any coach, said Gaines, and you will most likely find a man who is passing on the same lessons that he learned from men such as Dan Anderegg and Paul Horne. "Those kinds of lessons are timeless. They stick with kids, they carry over, and I think they are just as relevant today as they were when I was playing."

After leaving Texas Tech for a stint at San Angelo's Central High School, Gaines is back in the college ranks, this time as head coach at Abilene Christian University. The move has given him the opportunity to guide a program under the auspices of the Church of Christ. In twenty-nine autumns and counting, the old coach has seen more than most of his peers—from small high schools to the NCAA; from near-winless seasons to an undefeated state championship; from relative obscurity to the national limelight. Through it all, Gaines has led a life that has counted. It is the hope of any coach to win, but the good ones do not look only at the scoreboard to count their victories.

Notes

1. This and subsequent quotations are from interviews in the author's possession, unless otherwise noted.

2. H. G. Bissinger, *Friday Night Lights: A Town, a Team, and a Dream* (New York, 1990), xi.

3. Ibid., 31–32.

4. Ibid., 125.

5. Wilfred Sheed, "Why Sports Matter," *Wilsonian Quarterly* 19 (Winter 1995): 11.

Suggested Readings

Bissinger, H. G. *Friday Night Lights: A Town, a Team, and a Dream*. New York, 1990.

Cashion, Ty. *Pigskin Pulpit: A Social History of Texas High-School Football Coaches*. Austin, 1998.

McMurray, Bill. *Texas High-School Football*. South Bend, IN, 1985.

Miracle, Andrew W., Jr., and C. Roger Rees. *Lessons of the Locker Room*. New York, 1994.

Ratliff, Harold. *Autumn's Mightiest Legions: History of Texas Schoolboy Football*. Waco, TX, 1963.

Reid, Jan. *Vain Glory*. Fredericksburg, TX, 1986.

Stowers, Carlton. *Friday Night Heroes: A Look at Texas High-School Football*. Austin, 1983.

Suggested Films

Dazed and Confused (1993). Directed by Richard Linklater. Set in Huntsville, Texas, in the 1970s, this film depicts the clash of values between traditional ways and an emerging youth culture. The high-school football coach is caricatured as an out-of-step relic.

The Last Picture Show (1971). Directed by Peter Bogdanovich. This strong story reflects the post-frontier disillusionments with life in West Texas. High-school football is portrayed as one element in the effete small-town culture.

Varsity Blues (1999). Directed by Brian Robbins. In a story of "good versus evil," high-school players rebel against their coach, who is at the center of everything wrong with this Texas community's priorities.